A Concise Introduction to Logic

A Concise Introduction to Logic

CRAIG DELANCEY

OPEN SUNY TEXTBOOKS

ISBN: 978-1-942341-42-0 ebook
978-1-942341-43-7 print

This publication was made possible by a SUNY Innovative Instruction Technology Grant (IITG). IITG is a competitive grants program open to SUNY faculty and support staff across all disciplines. IITG encourages development of innovations that meet the Power of SUNY's transformative vision.

Published by Open SUNY Textbooks

Milne Library
State University of New York at Geneseo
Geneseo, NY 14454

For my mother

Contents

About the Textbook ix

Reviewer's Notes x
Adam Kovach

0. Introduction 1

Part I: Propositional Logic

1. Developing a Precise Language 9
2. "If...then...." and "It is not the case that...." 21
3. Good Arguments 38
4. Proofs 59
5. "And" 70
6. Conditional Derivations 89
7. "Or" 100
8. Reductio ad Absurdum 113
9. "... if and only if ...", Using Theorems 124
10. Summary of Propositional Logic 140

Part II: First Order Logic

11. Names and predicates 147
12. "All" and "some" 157
13. Reasoning with quantifiers 173
14. Universal derivation 184
15. Relations, functions, identity, and multiple quantifiers 200
16. Summary of first order logic 216

Part III: A Look Forward

17. Some advanced topics in logic   225

Bibliography   261

About the Author   263

About Open SUNY Textbooks   264

Changelog   265
Craig DeLancey

About the Textbook

A Concise Introduction to Logic is an introduction to formal logic suitable for undergraduates taking a general education course in logic or critical thinking, and is accessible and useful to any interested in gaining a basic understanding of logic. This text takes the unique approach of teaching logic through intellectual history; the author uses examples from important and celebrated arguments in philosophy to illustrate logical principles. The text also includes a basic introduction to findings of advanced logic. As indicators of where the student could go next with logic, the book closes with an overview of advanced topics, such as the axiomatic method, set theory, Peano arithmetic, and modal logic. Throughout, the text uses brief, concise chapters that readers will find easy to read and to review.

Reviewer's Notes

ADAM KOVACH

True to its name, *A Concise Introduction to Logic*, by Craig DeLancey, surveys propositional logic and predicate logic and goes on to introduce selected advanced topics, in little over 200 pages. The book provides an integrated presentation of basic syntactic and semantic concepts and methods of logic. Part I starts with the concept of a formal language. The concept of valid inference, truth tables and proofs are introduced immediately after the first two propositional connectives. Connectives and inference rules are introduced in alternation, to develop a complete simple natural deduction system for propositional logic. Part II, adds the apparatus of quantification and proof rules for a complete predicate logic. The text covers the logic of relations, sentences with multiple quantifiers and Russell's theory of definite descriptions. The presentation of concepts and principles is orderly, clear and thought provoking. Many topics are introduced with examples of philosophical arguments drawn from classic sources, adding depth of knowledge to an introductory course. The first two parts end with systematic overviews. The focus is on formal deductive logic throughout. Informal fallacies and traditional syllogistic logic are not covered. Advanced topics covered in the final part of the text include an axiomatic approach to logic, mathematical induction, a deduction theorem for propositional logic, and brief introductions to set theory, modal logic and number theory.

The reviewer, Adam Kovach, is Associate Professor of Philosophy at Marymount University in Arlington, VA, where he teaches courses in many subjects including logic.

0. Introduction

0.1 Why study logic?

Logic is one of the most important topics you will ever study.

"How could you say such a thing?" you might well protest. And yet, consider: logic teaches us many things, and one of these is how to recognize good and bad arguments. Not just arguments about logic—*any* argument.

Nearly every undertaking in life will ultimately require that you evaluate an argument, perhaps several. You are confronted with a question: Should I buy this car or that car? Should I go to this college or that college? Did that scientific experiment show what the scientist claims it did? Should I vote for the candidate who promises to lower taxes, or for the one who says she might raise them? And so on. Our lives are a long parade of choices. When we try to answer such questions, in order to make the best choices, we often have only one tool: an argument. We listen to the reasons for and against various options, and must choose between them. And so, the ability to evaluate arguments is an ability that is very useful in everything that you will do—in your work, your personal life, your deepest reflections.

If you are a student, note that nearly every discipline, be it a science, one of the humanities, or a study like business, relies upon arguments. Evaluating arguments is the most fundamental skill common to math, physics, psychology, literary studies, and any other intellectual endeavor. Logic alone tells you how to evaluate the arguments of any discipline.

The alternative to developing these logical skills is to be always at the mercy of bad reasoning and, as a result, you will make bad choices. Worse, you will always be manipulated by deceivers. Speaking in Canandaigua, New York, on August 3, 1857, the escaped slave and abolitionist leader Frederick Douglass observed that:

> Power concedes nothing without a demand. It never did and it never will. Find out just what any people will quietly submit to and you have found out the exact measure of injustice and wrong which will be imposed upon

them, and these will continue till they are resisted with either words or blows, or with both. The limits of tyrants are prescribed by the endurance of those whom they oppress.[1]

We can add to Frederick Douglass's words that: find out just how much a person can be deceived, and that is just how far she will be deceived. The limits of tyrants are also prescribed by the reasoning abilities of those they aim to oppress. And what logic teaches you is how to demand and recognize good reasoning, and so how to avoid deceit. You are only as free as your powers of reasoning enable.

0.2 What is logic?

Some philosophers have argued that one cannot define "logic". Instead, one can only show logic, by doing it and teaching others how to do it. I am inclined to agree. But it is easy to describe the benefits of logic. For example, in this book, you will learn how to:

- Identify when an argument is good, and when it is bad;
- Construct good arguments;
- Evaluate reasons, and know when they should, and should not, be convincing;
- Describe things with a precision that avoids misunderstanding;
- Get a sense of how one can construct the foundations of arithmetic;
- Begin to describe the meaning of "possibility" and "necessity".

That is by no means a complete list of the many useful things that logic can provide. Some of us believe that logic and mathematics are ultimately the same thing, two endeavors with the same underlying structure distinguished only by different starting assumptions. On such a view, we can also think of logic as the study of the ultimate foundations of mathematics. (This is a reasonable characterization of logic, but those afraid of mathematics need not fear: logic must become quite advanced before its relation to mathematics becomes evident.)

Ultimately, the only way to reveal the beauty and utility of logic is to get busy and do some logic. In this book, we will approach the study of logic by building several precise logical languages and seeing how we can best reason with these. The first of these languages is called "the propositional logic".

0.3 A note to students

Logic is a skill. The only way to get good at understanding logic and at using logic is to practice. It is easy to watch someone explain a principle of logic, and easier yet to watch someone do a proof. But you must understand a principle well enough to be able to apply it to new cases, and you must be able to do new proofs on your own. Practice alone enables this.

The good news is that logic is easy. The very goal of logic is to take baby steps, small and simple and obvious, and after we do this for a long while we find ourselves in a surprising and unexpected new place. Each step on the way will be easy to take. Logic is a long distance walk, not a sprint. Study each small step we take, be sure you know how to apply the related skills, practice them, and then move on. Anyone who follows this advice can master logic.

0.4 A note to instructors

This book incorporates a number of features that come from many years of experience teaching both introductory and advanced logic.

First, the book moves directly to symbolic logic. I don't believe that informal logic is worth the effort that it requires. Informal logic largely consists of memorization (memorizing seemingly disconnected rules, memorizing fallacies, and so on). Not only is this sure to be the kind of thing that students will promptly forget, but it completely obscures the simple beauty of why the various rules work, and why the fallacies are examples of bad reasoning. A student who learns symbolic logic, however, is learning a skill. Skills are retained longer; they encourage higher forms of reasoning; and they have far more power than a memorized list of facts. Once one can recognize what makes an argument good, one can recognize the fallacies, regardless of whether one has memorized their names.

Second, this book focuses on some of the deeper features of logic, right at the beginning. The notions of semantics and syntax are introduced in the first chapter. Ideas like *theorem*, and a *model*, are discussed early on. My experience has shown that students can grasp these concepts, and they ultimately pay off well by greatly expanding their own understanding.

Third, this book uses examples, and constructs problems, from our intellectual history in order to illustrate key principles of logic. The author is a philosopher, and understands logic to be both the method of philosophy and also one of the four fundamental sub-disciplines of philosophy. But more importantly, these examples can do two things. They make it clear that arguments matter. Weighty concerns are discussed in these arguments, and whether we accept their conclusions will have significant effects on our society. Seeing this helps one to see the importance of logic. These examples can also make this book suitable for a logic course that aims to fulfill a requirement for an introduction to the history of thought, an overview of Western civilization, or the knowledge foundations of a related discipline.

Fourth, I follow a no-shortcuts principle. Most logic textbooks introduce a host of shortcuts. They drop outer parentheses, they teach methods for shrinking truth tables, and so on. These moves often confuse students, and for no good reason: they have no conceptual value. I suspect they only exist to spare the impatience of instructors, who would like to write expressions and truth tables more quickly. In this book, except in the last chapter that looks to advanced logic, we will not introduce exceptions to our syntax, nor will we spend time on abridged methods. The only exception is writing "*T*" for *true* and "*F*" for *false* in truth tables.

Fifth, this book includes a final chapter introducing some advanced topics in logic. The purpose of this chapter is to provide students with some understanding of the exciting things that they can study if they continue with logic. In my experience, students imagine that advanced logic will be just more proofs in first order logic. Giving them a taste of what can come next is valuable. My hope is that this chapter will motivate students to want to study more logic, and also that it can serve as a bridge between their studies in basic logic and the study of advanced logic.

Finally, about typesetting: quotation is an important logical principle, and so I adopted the precise but comparatively rare practice of putting punctuation outside of quotes. This way, what appears in the quotations is alone what is being defined or otherwise mentioned. I use italics only to indicate the meaning of a concept, or to distinguish symbolic terms of the object language from functions of the object language. Bold is used to set aside elements of our metalanguage or object language.

0.5 Contact

The author would appreciate any comments, advice, or discoveries of errata. He can be contacted at: craig.delancey@oswego.edu

0.6 Acknowledgements

The typesetting of proofs used the lplfitch LaTex package developed by John Etchemendy, Dave Barker-Plummer, and Richard Zach.

Thanks to two reviewers for the Open SUNY Textbook program; and to Allison Brown and the other people who help make the Open SUNY Textbook program work; and to Carol Kunzer, Karen Gelles, and Carrie Fishner for copy editing the text. Thanks to Derek Bullard for catching some errata.

---

[1] From Blassingame (1985: 204), in a speech titled "The Significance of Emancipation in the West Indies."

PART I: PROPOSITIONAL LOGIC

1. Developing a Precise Language

1.1 Starting with sentences

We begin the study of logic by building a precise logical language. This will allow us to do at least two things: first, to say some things more precisely than we otherwise would be able to do; second, to study reasoning. We will use a natural language—English—as our guide, but our logical language will be far simpler, far weaker, but more rigorous than English.

We must decide where to start. We could pick just about any part of English to try to emulate: names, adjectives, prepositions, general nouns, and so on. But it is traditional, and as we will see, quite handy, to begin with whole sentences. For this reason, the first language we will develop is called "the propositional logic". It is also sometimes called "the sentential logic" or even "the sentential calculus". These all mean the same thing: the logic of sentences. In this propositional logic, the smallest independent parts of the language are sentences (throughout this book, I will assume that sentences and propositions are the same thing in our logic, and I will use the terms "sentence" and "proposition" interchangeably).

There are of course many kinds of sentences. To take examples from our natural language, these include:

What time is it?

Open the window.

Damn you!

I promise to pay you back.

It rained in Central Park on June 26, 2015.

We could multiply such examples. Sentences in English can be used to ask questions, give commands, curse or insult, form contracts, and express emotions. But, the last example above is of special interest because it aims to describe the world. Such sentences, which are sometimes called "declarative sentences", will be our model sentences for our logical language. We know a declarative sentence when we encounter it because it can be either true or false.

1.2 Precision in sentences

We want our logic of declarative sentences to be precise. But what does this mean? We can help clarify how we might pursue this by looking at sentences in a natural language that are perplexing, apparently because they are not precise. Here are three.

Tom is kind of tall.

When Karen had a baby, her mother gave her a pen.

This sentence is false.

We have already observed that an important feature of our declarative sentences is that they can be true or false. We call this the "truth value" of the sentence. These three sentences are perplexing because their truth values are unclear. The first sentence is vague, it is not clear under what conditions it would be true, and under what conditions it would be false. If Tom is six feet tall, is he kind of tall? There is no clear answer. The second sentence is ambiguous. If "pen" means writing implement, and Karen's mother bought a playpen for the baby, then the sentence is false. But until we know what "pen" means in this sentence, we cannot tell if the sentence is true.

The third sentence is strange. Many logicians have spent many years studying this sentence, which is traditionally called "the Liar". It is related to an old paradox about a Cretan who said, "All Cretans are liars". The strange thing about the Liar is that its truth value seems to explode. If it is true, then it is false. If it is false, then it is true. Some philosophers think this sentence is, therefore, neither true nor false; some philosophers think it is both true and false. In either case, it is confusing. How could a sentence that looks like a declarative sentence have both or no truth value?

Since ancient times, philosophers have believed that we will deceive ourselves, and come to believe untruths, if we do not accept a principle sometimes called "bivalence", or a related principle called "the principle of non-contradiction". Bivalence is the view that there are only two truth values (true and false) and that they exclude each other. The principle of non-contradiction states that you have made a mistake if you both assert and deny a claim. One or the other of these principles seems to be violated by the Liar.

We can take these observations for our guide: we want our language to have no vagueness and no ambiguity. In our propositional logic, this means we want it to be the case that each sentence is either true or false. It will not be kind of true, or partially true, or true from one perspective and not true from another. We also want to avoid things like the Liar. We do not need to agree on whether the Liar is both true and false, or neither true nor false. Either would be unfortunate. So, we will specify that our sentences have neither vice.

We can formulate our own revised version of the principle of bivalence, which states that:

> Principle of Bivalence: Each sentence of our language must be either true or false, not both, not neither.

This requirement may sound trivial, but in fact it constrains what we do from now on in interesting and even surprising ways. Even as we build more complex logical languages later, this principle will be fundamental.

Some readers may be thinking: what if I reject bivalence, or the principle of non-contradiction? There is a long line of philosophers who would like to argue with you, and propose that either move would be a mistake, and perhaps even incoherent. Set those arguments aside. If you have doubts about bivalence, or the principle of non-contradiction, stick with logic. That is because we could develop a logic in which there were more than two truth values. Logics have been created and studied in which we allow for three truth values, or continuous truth values, or stranger possibilities. The issue for us is that we must start somewhere, and the principle of bivalence is an intuitive way and—it would seem—the simplest way to start with respect to truth values. Learn basic logic first, and then you can explore these alternatives.

This points us to an important feature, and perhaps a mystery, of logic. In part, what a logical language shows us is the consequences of our assumptions. That might sound trivial, but, in fact, it is anything but. From very simple assumptions, we will discover new, and ultimately shocking, facts. So, if someone wants to study a logical language where we reject the principle of bivalence, they can do so. The difference between what they are doing, and what we will do in the following chapters, is that they will discover the consequences of rejecting the principle of bivalence, whereas we will discover the consequences of adhering to it. In either case, it would be wise to learn traditional logic first, before attempting to study or develop an alternative logic.

We should note at this point that we are not going to try to explain what "true" and "false" mean, other than saying that "false" means *not true*. When we add something to our language without explaining its meaning, we call it a "primitive". Philosophers have done much to try to understand what truth is, but it remains quite difficult to define truth in any way that is not controversial. Fortunately, taking *true* as a primitive will not get us into trouble, and it appears unlikely to make logic mysterious. We all have some grasp of what "true" means, and this grasp will be sufficient for our development of the propositional logic.

1.3 Atomic sentences

Our language will be concerned with declarative sentences, sentences that are either true or false, never both, and never neither. Here are some example sentences.

2+2=4.

Malcolm Little is tall.

If Lincoln wins the election, then Lincoln will be President.

The Earth is not the center of the universe.

These are all declarative sentences. These all appear to satisfy our principle of bivalence. But they differ in important ways. The first two sentences do not have sentences as parts. For example, try to break up the first sentence. "2+2" is a function. "4" is a name. "=4" is a meaningless fragment, as is "2+". Only the whole expression, "2+2=4", is a sentence with a truth value. The second sentence is similar in this regard. "Malcolm Little" is a name. "is tall" is an adjective phrase (we will discover later that logicians call this a "predicate"). "Malcolm Little is" or "is tall" are fragments, they have no truth value.[2] Only "Malcolm Little is tall" is a complete sentence.

The first two example sentences above are of a kind we call "atomic sentences". The word "atom" comes from the ancient Greek word "atomos", meaning *cannot be cut*. When the ancient Greeks reasoned about matter, for example, some of them believed that if you took some substance, say a rock, and cut it into pieces, then cut the pieces into pieces, and so on, eventually you would get to something that could not be cut. This would be the smallest possible thing. (The fact that we now talk of having "split the atom" just goes to show that we changed the meaning of the word "atom". We came to use it as a name for a particular kind of thing, which then turned out to have parts, such as electrons, protons, and neutrons.) In logic, the idea of an atomic sentence is of a sentence that can have no parts that are sentences.

In reasoning about these atomic sentences, we could continue to use English. But for reasons that become clear as we proceed, there are many advantages to coming up with our own way of writing our sentences. It is traditional in logic to use upper case letters from P on (P, Q, R, S....) to stand for atomic sentences. Thus, instead of writing

> Malcolm Little is tall.

We could write

> P

If we want to know how to translate P to English, we can provide a translation key. Similarly, instead of writing

> Malcolm Little is a great orator.

We could write

> Q

And so on. Of course, written in this way, all we can see about such a sentence is that it is a sentence, and that perhaps P and Q are different sentences. But for now, these will be sufficient.

Note that not all sentences are atomic. The third sentence in our four examples above contains parts that are sentences. It contains the atomic sentence, "Lincoln wins the election" and also the atomic sentence, "Lincoln will be President". We could represent this whole sentence with a single letter. That is, we could let

If Lincoln wins the election, Lincoln will be president.

be represented in our logical language by

S

However, this would have the disadvantage that it would hide some of the sentences that are inside this sentence, and also it would hide their relationship. Our language would tell us more if we could capture the relation between the parts of this sentence, instead of hiding them. We will do this in chapter 2.

1.4 Syntax and semantics

An important and useful principle for understanding a language is the difference between syntax and semantics. "Syntax" refers to the "shape" of an expression in our language. It does not concern itself with what the elements of the language mean, but just specifies how they can be written out.

We can make a similar distinction (though not exactly the same) in a natural language. This expression in English has an uncertain meaning, but it has the right "shape" to be a sentence:

Colorless green ideas sleep furiously.

In other words, in English, this sentence is syntactically correct, although it may express some kind of meaning error.

An expression made with the parts of our language must have correct syntax in order for it to be a sentence. Sometimes, we also call an expression with the right syntactic form a "well-formed formula".

We contrast syntax with semantics. "Semantics" refers to the meaning of an expression of our language. Semantics depends upon the relation of that element of the language to something else. For example, the truth value of the sentence,

"The Earth has one moon" depends not upon the English language, but upon something exterior to the language. Since the self-standing elements of our propositional logic are sentences, and the most important property of these is their truth value, the only semantic feature of sentences that will concern us in our propositional logic is their truth value.

Whenever we introduce a new element into the propositional logic, we will specify its syntax and its semantics. In the propositional logic, the syntax is generally trivial, but the semantics is less so. We have so far introduced atomic sentences. The syntax for an atomic sentence is trivial. If P is an atomic sentence, then it is syntactically correct to write down

P

By saying that this is syntactically correct, we are not saying that P is true. Rather, we are saying that P is a sentence.

If semantics in the propositional logic concerns only truth value, then we know that there are only two possible semantic values for P; it can be either true or false. We have a way of writing this that will later prove helpful. It is called a "truth table". For an atomic sentence, the truth table is trivial, but when we look at other kinds of sentences their truth tables will be more complex.

The idea of a truth table is to describe the conditions in which a sentence is true or false. We do this by identifying all the atomic sentences that compose that sentence. Then, on the left side, we stipulate all the possible truth values of these atomic sentences and write these out. On the right side, we then identify under what conditions the sentence (that is composed of the other atomic sentences) is true or false.

The idea is that the sentence on the right is dependent on the sentence(s) on the left. So the truth table is filled in like this:

Atomic sentence(s) that compose the dependent sentence on the right	Dependent sentence composed of the atomic sentences on the left
All possible combinations of truth values of the composing atomic sentences	Resulting truth values for each possible combination of truth values of the composing atomic sentences

We stipulate all the possible truth values on the bottom left because the propositional logic alone will not determine whether an atomic sentence is true or false; thus, we will simply have to consider both possibilities. Note that there are many ways that an atomic sentence can be true, and there are many ways that it can be false. For example, the sentence, "Tom is American" might be true if Tom was born in New York, in Texas, in Ohio, and so on. The sentence might be false because Tom was born to Italian parents in Italy, to French parents in France, and so on. So, we group all these cases together into two kinds of cases.

These are two rows of the truth table for an atomic sentence. Each row of the truth table represents a kind of way that the world could be. So here is the left side of a truth table with only a single atomic sentence, P. We will write "*T*" for *true* and "*F*" for *false*.

P	
T	
F	

There are only two relevant kinds of ways that the world can be, when we are considering the semantics of an atomic sentence. The world can be one of the many conditions such that P is true, or it can be one of the many conditions such that P is false.

To complete the truth table, we place the dependent sentence on the top right side, and describe its truth value in relation to the truth value of its parts. We want to identify the semantics of P, which has only one part, P. The truth table thus has the final form:

P	P
T	*T*
F	*F*

This truth table tells us the meaning of P, as far as our propositional logic can tell us about it. Thus, it gives us the complete semantics for P. (As we will see later, truth tables have three uses: to provide the semantics for a kind of sentence; to determine under what conditions a complex sentence is true or false; and to determine if an argument is good. Here we are describing only this first use.)

In this truth table, the first row combined together all the kinds of ways the world could be in which P is true. In the second column we see that for all of these kinds of ways the world could be in which P is true, unsurprisingly, P is true. The second row combines together all the kinds of ways the world could be in which P is false. In those, P is false. As we noted above, in the case of an atomic sentence, the truth table is trivial. Nonetheless, the basic concept is very useful, as we will begin to see in the next chapter.

One last tool will be helpful to us. Strictly speaking, what we have done above is give the syntax and semantics for a particular atomic sentence, P. We need a way to make general claims about all the sentences of our language, and then give the syntax and semantics for any atomic sentences. We do this using variables, and here we will use Greek letters for those variables, such as Φ and Ψ. Things said using these variables is called our "metalanguage", which means literally the *after language*, but which we take to mean, *our language about our language.* The particular propositional logic that we create is called our "object language". P and Q are sentences of our object language. Φ and Ψ are elements of our metalanguage. To specify now the syntax of atomic sentences (that is, of all atomic sentences) we can say: If Φ is an atomic sentence, then

Φ

is a sentence. This tells us that simply writing Φ down (whatever atomic sentence it may be), as we have just done, is to write down something that is syntactically correct.

To specify now the semantics of atomic sentences (that is, of all atomic sentences) we can say: If Φ is an atomic sentence, then the semantics of Φ is given by

Φ	Φ
T	T
F	F

Note an important and subtle point. The atomic sentences of our propositional logic will be what we call "contingent" sentences. A contingent sentence can be either true or false. We will see later that some complex sentences of our propositional logic must be true, and some complex sentences of our propositional logic must be false. But for the propositional logic, every atomic sentence is (as far as we can tell using the propositional logic alone) contingent. This observation matters because it greatly helps to clarify where logic begins, and where the methods of another discipline ends. For example, suppose we have an atomic sentence like:

Force is equal to mass times acceleration.

Igneous rocks formed under pressure.

Germany inflated its currency in 1923 in order to reduce its reparations debt.

Logic cannot tell us whether these are true or false. We will turn to physicists, and use their methods, to evaluate the first claim. We will turn to geologists, and use their methods, to evaluate the second claim. We will turn to historians, and use their methods, to evaluate the third claim. But the logician can tell the physicist, geologist, and historian what follows from their claims.

1.5 Problems

1. Vagueness arises when the conditions under which a sentence might be true are "fuzzy". That is, in some cases, we cannot identify if the sentence is true or false. If we say, "Tom is tall", this sentence is certainly true if Tom is the tallest person in the world, but it is not clear whether it is true if Tom is 185 centimeters tall. Identify or create five declarative sentences in English that are vague.

2. Ambiguity usually arises when a word or phrase has several distinct possible interpretations. In our example above, the word "pen" could mean either a writing implement or a structure to hold a child. A sentence that includes "pen" could be ambiguous, in which case it might be true for one interpretation and false for another. Identify or create five declarative sentences in English that are ambiguous. (This will probably require you to identify a homonym, a word that has more than one meaning but sounds or is written the same. If you are stumped, consider slang: many slang terms are ambiguous because they redefine existing words. For example, in the 1980s, in some communities and contexts, to say something was "bad"

meant that it was good; this obviously can create ambiguous sentences.)

3. Often we can make a vague sentence precise by defining a specific interpretation of the meaning of an adjective, term, or other element of the language. For example, we could make the sentence "Tom is tall" precise by specifying one person referred to by "Tom", and also by defining "...is tall" as true of anyone 180 centimeters tall or taller. For each of the five vague sentences that you identified or created for problem 1, describe how the interpretation of certain elements of the sentence could make the sentence no longer vague.

4. Often we can make an ambiguous sentence precise by specifying which of the possible meanings we intend to use. We could make the sentence, "Tom is by the pen" unambiguous by specifying which Tom we mean, and also defining "pen" to mean an infant play pen. For each of the five ambiguous sentences that you identified or created for problem 2, identify and describe how the interpretation of certain elements of the sentence could make the sentence no longer ambiguous.

5. Come up with five examples of your own of English sentences that are not declarative sentences. (Examples can include commands, exclamations, and promises.)

6. Here are some sentences from literary works and other famous texts. Describe as best you can what the role of the sentence is. For example, the sentence might be a declarative sentence, which aims to describe things; or a question, which aims to solicit information; or a command, which is used to make someone do something; and so on. It is not essential that you have a name for the kind of sentence, but rather can you describe what a speaker would typically intend for such a sentence to do?

   a. "Though I should die with thee, yet will I not deny thee." (From the King James Bible)
   b. "Get thee to a nunnery." (William Shakespeare, *Hamlet*.)
   c. "That on the first day of January, in the year of our Lord one thousand eight hundred and sixty-three, all persons held as slaves within any State or designated part of a State, the people whereof shall then be in rebellion against the United States, shall be then, thenceforward, and

forever free." (From "The Emancipation Proclamation".)

d. "Sing, goddess, of the anger of Achilles son of Peleus, that brought countless ills upon the Achaeans." (Homer, *The Illiad*.)

e. "Since the heavens grant that you recognize me, hold your tongue, and do not say a word about who I am to any one else in the house, for if you do, and if heaven grants me to take the lives of these suitors, I will not spare you, though you are my own nurse, when I am killing the other women." (Homer, *The Odyssey*.)

f. "Tyger, tyger, burning bright,
In the forests of the night,
What immortal hand or eye,
could frame thy fearful symmetry?" (William Blake, *The Tyger*.)

g. "As wicked dew as e'er my mother brush'd
With raven's feather from unwholesome fen
Drop on you both! A south-west blow on ye
And blister you all o'er!" (William Shakespeare, *The Tempest*.)

h. "For he to-day that sheds his blood with me
Shall be my brother." (William Shakespeare, *Henry V*.)

i. "Astonishing, Pip!" (Charles Dickens, *Great Expectations*.)

j. "Congress shall make no law respecting an establishment of religion, or prohibiting the free exercise thereof; or abridging the freedom of speech, or of the press; or the right of the people peaceably to assemble, and to petition the government for a redress of grievances." (The Constitution of the United States.)

---

[2] There is a complex issue here that we will discuss later. But, in brief: "is" is ambiguous; it has several meanings. "Malcolm Little is" is a sentence if it is meant to assert the existence of Malcolm Little. The "is" that appears in the sentence, "Malcolm Little is tall", however, is what we call the "'is' of predication". In that sentence, "is" is used to assert that a property is had by Malcolm Little (the property of being tall); and here "is tall" is what we are calling a "predicate". So, the "is" of predication has no clear meaning when appearing without the rest of the predicate; it does not assert existence.

2. "If...then...." and "It is not the case that...."

2.1 The Conditional

As we noted in chapter 1, there are sentences of a natural language, like English, that are not atomic sentences. Our examples included

> If Lincoln wins the election, then Lincoln will be President.

> The Earth is not the center of the universe.

We could treat these like atomic sentences, but then we would lose a great deal of important information. For example, the first sentence tells us something about the relationship between the atomic sentences "Lincoln wins the election" and "Lincoln will be President". And the second sentence above will, one supposes, have an interesting relationship to the sentence, "The Earth is the center of the universe". To make these relations explicit, we will have to understand what "if...then..." and "not" mean. Thus, it would be useful if our logical language was able to express these kinds of sentences in a way that made these elements explicit. Let us start with the first one.

The sentence, "If Lincoln wins the election, then Lincoln will be President" contains two atomic sentences, "Lincoln wins the election" and "Lincoln will be President". We could thus represent this sentence by letting

> Lincoln wins the election

be represented in our logical language by

> P

And by letting

> Lincoln will be president

be represented by

Q

Then, the whole expression could be represented by writing

If P then Q

It will be useful, however, to replace the English phrase "if...then..." by a single symbol in our language. The most commonly used such symbol is "→". Thus, we would write

P → Q

One last thing needs to be observed, however. We might want to combine this complex sentence with other sentences. In that case, we need a way to identify that this is a single sentence when it is combined with other sentences. There are several ways to do this, but the most familiar (although not the most elegant) is to use parentheses. Thus, we will write our expression

(P → Q)

This kind of sentence is called a "conditional". It is also sometimes called a "material conditional". The first constituent sentence (the one before the arrow, which in this example is "P") is called the "antecedent". The second sentence (the one after the arrow, which in this example is "Q") is called the "consequent".

We know how to write the conditional, but what does it mean? As before, we will take the meaning to be given by the truth conditions—that is, a description of when the sentence is either true or false. We do this with a truth table. But now, our sentence has two parts that are atomic sentences, P and Q. Note that either atomic sentence could be true or false. That means, we have to consider four possible kinds of situations. We must consider when P is true and when it is false, but then we need to consider those two kinds of situations twice: once for when Q is true and once for when Q is false. Thus, the left hand side of our truth table will look like this:

P	Q	
T	T	
T	F	
F	T	
F	F	

There are four kinds of ways the world could be that we must consider.

Note that, since there are two possible truth values (true and false), whenever we consider another atomic sentence, there are twice as many ways the world could be that we should consider. Thus, for n atomic sentences, our truth table must have 2^n rows. In the case of a conditional formed out of two atomic sentences, like our example of $(P \rightarrow Q)$, our truth table will have 2^2 rows, which is 4 rows. We see this is the case above.

Now, we must decide upon what the conditional means. To some degree this is up to us. What matters is that once we define the semantics of the conditional, we stick to our definition. But we want to capture as much of the meaning of the English "if...then..." as we can, while remaining absolutely precise in our language.

Let us consider each kind of way the world could be. For the first row of the truth table, we have that P is true and Q is true. Suppose the world is such that Lincoln wins the election, and also Lincoln will be President. Then, would I have spoken truly if I said, "If Lincoln wins the election, then Lincoln will be President"? Most people agree that I would have. Similarly, suppose that Lincoln wins the election, but Lincoln will not be President. Would the sentence "If Lincoln wins the election, then Lincoln will be President" still be true? Most agree that it would be false now. So the first rows of our truth table are uncontroversial.

P	Q	$(P \rightarrow Q)$
T	T	T
T	F	F
F	T	
F	F	

Some students, however, find it hard to determine what truth values should go in the next two rows. Note now that our principle of bivalence requires us to fill in these rows. We cannot leave them blank. If we did, we would be saying that sometimes a conditional can have no truth value; that is, we would be saying that sometimes, some sentences have no truth value. But our principle of bivalence requires that—in all kinds of situations—every sentence is either true or false, never both, never neither. So, if we are going to respect the principle of bivalence, then we have to put either *T* or *F* in for each of the last two rows.

It is helpful at this point to change our example. Let us consider two different examples to illustrate how best to fill out the remainder of the truth table for the conditional.

First, suppose I say the following to you: "If you give me $50, then I will buy you a ticket to the concert tonight." Let

> You give me $50

be represented in our logic by

> R

and let

> I will buy you a ticket to the concert tonight.

be represented by

> S

Our sentence then is

> $(R \rightarrow S)$

And its truth table—as far as we understand right now—is:

R	S	$(R \rightarrow S)$
T	T	*T*
T	*F*	*F*
F	*T*	
F	*F*	

That is, if you give me the money and I buy you the ticket, my claim that "If you give me $50, then I will buy you a ticket to the concert tonight" is true. And, if you give me the money and I don't buy you the ticket, I lied, and my claim is false. But now, suppose you do not give me $50, but I buy you a ticket for the concert as a gift. Was my claim false? No. I simply bought you the ticket as a gift, but, presumably would have bought it if you gave me the money, also. Similarly, if you don't give me money, and I do not buy you a ticket, that seems perfectly consistent with my claim.

So, the best way to fill out the truth table is as follows.

R	S	(R→S)
T	T	T
T	F	F
F	T	T
F	F	T

Second, consider another sentence, which has the advantage that it is very clear with respect to these last two rows. Assume that *a* is a particular natural number, only you and I don't know what number it is (the natural numbers are the whole positive numbers: 1, 2, 3, 4...). Consider now the following sentence.

> If *a* is evenly divisible by 4, then *a* is evenly divisible by 2.

(By "evenly divisible," I mean divisible without remainder.) The first thing to ask yourself is: is this sentence true? I hope we can all agree that it is—even though we do not know what *a* is. Let

> *a* is evenly divisible by 4

be represented in our logic by

> U

and let

> *a* is evenly divisible by 2

be represented by

V

Our sentence then is

$(U \rightarrow V)$

And its truth table—as far as we understand right now—is:

U	V	$(U \rightarrow V)$
T	T	T
T	F	F
F	T	
F	F	

Now consider a case in which *a* is 6. This is like the third row of the truth table. It is not the case that 6 is evenly divisible by 4, but it is the case that 6 is evenly divisible by 2. And consider the case in which *a* is 7. This is like the fourth row of the truth table; 7 would be evenly divisible by neither 4 nor 2. But we agreed that the conditional is true—regardless of the value of *a*! So, the truth table must be:[3]

U	V	$(U \rightarrow V)$
T	T	T
T	F	F
F	T	T
F	F	T

Following this pattern, we should also fill out our table about the election with:

P	Q	$(P \rightarrow Q)$
T	T	T
T	F	F
F	T	T
F	F	T

If you are dissatisfied by this, it might be helpful to think of these last two rows as vacuous cases. A conditional tells us about what happens if the antecedent is true. But when the antecedent is false, we simply default to true.

We are now ready to offer, in a more formal way, the syntax and semantics for the conditional.

The syntax of the conditional is that, if Φ and Ψ are sentences, then

$(\Phi \rightarrow \Psi)$

is a sentence.

The semantics of the conditional are given by a truth table. For any sentences Φ and Ψ:

Φ	Ψ	$(\Phi \rightarrow \Psi)$
T	T	T
T	F	F
F	T	T
F	F	T

Remember that this truth table is now a definition. It defines the meaning of "$\rightarrow$". We are agreeing to use the symbol "$\rightarrow$" to mean this from here on out.

The elements of the propositional logic, like "$\rightarrow$", that we add to our language in order to form more complex sentences, are called "truth functional connectives". I hope it is clear why: the meaning of this symbol is given in a truth function. (If you are unfamiliar or uncertain about the idea of a function, think of a function as like a machine that takes in one or more inputs, and always then gives exactly one output. For the conditional, the inputs are two truth values; and the output is one truth value. For example, put TF into the truth function called "$\rightarrow$", and you get out F.)

2.2 Alternative phrasings in English for the conditional. Only if.

English includes many alternative phrasings that appear to be equivalent to the conditional. Furthermore, in English and other natural languages, the order of the conditional will sometimes be reversed. We can capture the general sense of these cases by recognizing that each of the following phrasings would be translated as $(P \to Q)$. (In these examples, we mix English and our propositional logic, in order to illustrate the variations succinctly.)

If P, then Q.

Q, if P.

On the condition that P, Q.

Q, on the condition that P.

Given that P, Q.

Q, given that P.

Provided that P, Q.

Q, provided that P.

When P, then Q.

Q, when P.

P implies Q.

Q is implied by P.

P is sufficient for Q.

Q is necessary for P.

An oddity of English is that the word "only" changes the meaning of "if". You can see this if you consider the following two sentences.

Fifi is a cat, if Fifi is a mammal.

Fifi is a cat only if Fifi is a mammal.

Suppose we know Fifi is an organism, but, we don't know what kind of organism Fifi is. Fifi could be a dog, a cat, a gray whale, a ladybug, a sponge. It seems clear that the first sentence is not necessarily true. If Fifi is a gray whale, for example, then it is true that Fifi is a mammal, but false that Fifi is a cat; and so, the first sentence would be false. But the second sentence looks like it must be true (given what you and I know about cats and mammals).

We should thus be careful to recognize that "only if" does not mean the same thing as "if". (If it did, these two sentences would have the same truth value in all situations.) In fact, it seems that "only if" can best be expressed by a conditional where the "only if" appears before the consequent (remember, the consequent is the second part of the conditional—the part that the arrows points at). Thus, sentences of this form:

P only if Q.

Only if Q, P.

are best expressed by the formula

$(P \rightarrow Q)$

2.3 Test your understanding of the conditional

People sometimes find conditionals confusing. In part, this seems to be because some people confuse them with another kind of truth-functional connective, which we will learn about later, called the "biconditional". Also, sometimes "if...then..." is used in English in a different way (see section 17.7 if you are curious about alternative possible meanings). But from now on, we will understand the conditional as described above. To test whether you have properly grasped the conditional, consider the following puzzle.[4]

We have a set of four cards in figure 2.1. Each card has the following property: it has a shape on one side, and a letter on the other side. We shuffle and mix the cards, flipping some over while we shuffle. Then, we lay out the four cards:

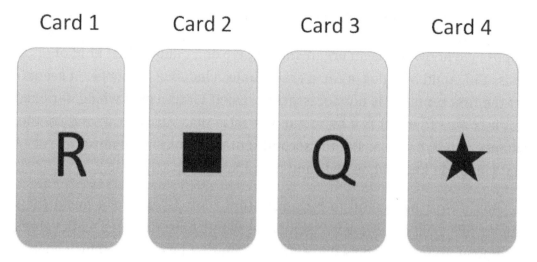

Figure 2.1

Given our constraint that each card has a letter on one side and a shape on the other, we know that card 1 has a shape on the unseen side; card 2 has a letter on the unseen side; and so on.

Consider now the following claim:

> For each of these four cards, if the card has a Q on the letter side of the card, then it has a square on the shape side of the card.

Here is our puzzle: what is the minimum number of cards that we must turn over to test whether this claim is true of all four cards; and which cards are they that we must turn over? Of course we could turn them all over, but the puzzle asks you to identify all and only the cards that will test the claim.

Stop reading now, and see if you can decide on the answer. Be warned, people generally perform poorly on this puzzle. Think about it for a while. The answer is given below in problem 1.

2.4 Alternative symbolizations for the conditional

Some logic books, and some logicians, use alternative symbolizations for the various truth-functional connectives. The meanings (that is, the truth tables) are always the same, but the symbol used may be different. For this reason, we will take the time in this text to briefly recognize alternative symbolizations.

The conditional is sometimes represented with the following symbol: "⊃". Thus, in such a case, (P→Q) would be written

(P⊃Q)

2.5 Negation

In chapter 1, we considered as an example the sentence,

The Earth is not the center of the universe.

At first glance, such a sentence might appear to be fundamentally unlike a conditional. It does not contain two sentences, but only one. There is a "not" in the sentence, but it is not connecting two sentences. However, we can still think of this sentence as being constructed with a truth functional connective, if we are willing to accept that this sentence is equivalent to the following sentence.

It is not the case that the Earth is the center of the universe.

If this sentence is equivalent to the one above, then we can treat "It is not the case" as a truth functional connective. It is traditional to replace this cumbersome English phrase with a single symbol, "¬". Then, mixing our propositional logic with English, we would have

¬The Earth is the center of the universe.

And if we let **W** be a sentence in our language that has the meaning *The Earth is the center of the universe*, we would write

¬**W**

This connective is called "negation". Its syntax is: if Φ is a sentence, then

$$\neg\Phi$$

is a sentence. We call such a sentence a "negation sentence".

The semantics of a negation sentence is also obvious, and is given by the following truth table.

Φ	¬Φ
T	F
F	T

To deny a true sentence is to speak a falsehood. To deny a false sentence is to say something true.

Our syntax always is recursive. This means that syntactic rules can be applied repeatedly, to the product of the rule. In other words, our syntax tells us that if P is a sentence, then ¬P is a sentence. But now note that the same rule applies again: if ¬P is a sentence, then ¬¬P is a sentence. And so on. Similarly, if P and Q are sentences, the syntax for the conditional tells us that $(P \rightarrow Q)$ is a sentence. But then so is $\neg(P \rightarrow Q)$, and so is $(\neg(P \rightarrow Q) \rightarrow (P \rightarrow Q))$. And so on. If we have just a single atomic sentence, our recursive syntax will allow us to form infinitely many different sentences with negation and the conditional.

2.6 Alternative symbolizations for negation

Some texts may use "~" for negation. Thus, ¬P would be expressed with

$$\sim P$$

2.7 Problems

1. The answer to our card game was: you need only turn over cards 3 and 4. This might seem confusing to many people at first. But remember the

meaning of the conditional: it can only be false if the first part is true and the second part is false. The sentence we want to test is "For each of these four cards, if the card has a Q on the letter side of the card, then it has a square on the shape side of the card". Let Q stand for "the card has a Q on the letter side of the card." Let S stand for "the card has a square on the shape side of the card." Then we could make a truth table to express the meaning of the claim being tested:

Q	S	$(Q \rightarrow S)$
T	T	T
T	F	F
F	T	T
F	F	T

Look back at the cards. The first card has an R on the letter side. So, sentence Q is false. But then we are in a situation like the last two rows of the truth table, and the conditional cannot be false. We do not need to check that card. The second card has a square on it. That means S is true for that card. But then we are in a situation represented by either the first or third row of the truth table. Again, the claim that $(Q \rightarrow S)$ cannot be false in either case with respect to that card, so there is no point in checking that card. The third card shows a Q. It corresponds to a situation that is like either the first or second row of the truth table. We cannot tell then whether $(Q \rightarrow S)$ is true or false of that card, without turning the card over. Similarly, the last card shows a situation where S is false, so we are in a kind of situation represented by either the second or last row of the truth table. We must turn the card over to determine if $(Q \rightarrow S)$ is true or false of that card.

Try this puzzle again. Consider the following claim about those same four cards: If there is a star on the shape side of the card, then there is an R on the letter side of the card. What is the minimum number of cards that you must turn over to check this claim? What cards are they?

2. Consider the following four cards in figure 2.2. Each card has a letter on one side, and a shape on the other side.

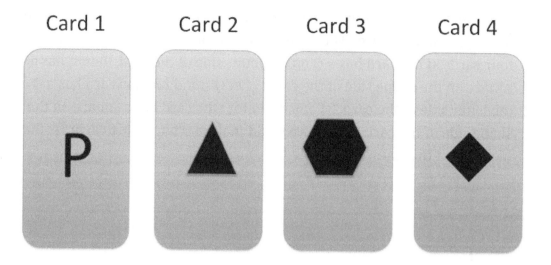

| Card 1 | Card 2 | Card 3 | Card 4 |

Figure 2.2

For each of the following claims, in order to determine if the claim is true of all four cards, describe (1) The minimum number of cards you must turn over to check the claim, and (2) what those cards are.

    a. There is not a Q on the letter side of the card.
    b. There is not an octagon on the shape side of the card.
    c. If there is a triangle on the shape side of the card, then there is a P on the letter side of the card.
    d. There is an R on the letter side of the card only if there is a diamond on the shape side of the card.
    e. There is a hexagon on the shape side of the card, on the condition that there is a P on the letter side of the card.
    f. There is a diamond on the shape side of the card only if there is a P on the letter side of the card.

3. Which of the following have correct syntax? Which have incorrect syntax?

    a. $P \rightarrow Q$
    b. $\neg(P \rightarrow Q)$
    c. $(\neg P \rightarrow Q)$
    d. $(P\neg \rightarrow Q)$
    e. $(P \rightarrow \neg Q)$

f. ¬¬P

g. ¬P¬

h. (¬P¬Q)

i. (¬P → ¬Q)

j. (¬P → ¬Q)¬

4. Use the following translation key to translate the following sentences into a propositional logic.

Translation Key	
Logic	English
P	Abe is able.
Q	Abe is honest.

    a. If Abe is honest, Abe is able.

    b. Abe is honest only if Abe is able.

    c. Abe is able, if Abe is honest.

    d. Only if Able is able, is Abe honest.

    e. Abe is not able.

    f. It's not the case that Abe isn't able.

    g. Abe is not able only if Abe is not honest.

    h. Abe is able, provided that Abe is not honest.

    i. If Abe is not able then Abe is not honest.

    j. It is not the case that, if Abe is able, then Abe is honest.

5. Make up your own translation key to translate the following sentences into a propositional logic. Then, use your key to translate the sentences into the propositional logic. Your translation key should contain only atomic sentences. These should be all and only the atomic sentences needed to translate the following sentences of English. Don't let it bother you that some of the sentences must be false.

    a. Josie is a cat.

    b. Josie is a mammal.

    c. Josie is not a mammal.

    d. If Josie is not a cat, then Josie is not a mammal.

    e. Josie is a fish.

    f. Provided that Josie is a mammal, Josie is not a fish.

g. Josie is a cat only if Josie is a mammal.

h. Josie is a fish only if Josie is not a mammal.

i. It's not the case that Josie is not a mammal.

j. Josie is not a cat, if Josie is a fish.

6. This problem will make use of the principle that our syntax is recursive. Translating these sentences is more challenging. Make up your own translation key to translate the following sentences into a propositional logic. Your translation key should contain only atomic sentences; these should be all and only the atomic sentences needed to translate the following sentences of English.

a. It is not the case that Tom won't pass the exam.

b. If Tom studies, Tom will pass the exam.

c. It is not the case that if Tom studies, then Tom will pass the exam.

d. If Tom does not study, then Tom will not pass the exam.

e. If Tom studies, Tom will pass the exam—provided that he wakes in time.

f. If Tom passes the exam, then if Steve studies, Steve will pass the exam.

g. It is not the case that if Tom passes the exam, then if Steve studies, Steve will pass the exam.

h. If Tom does not pass the exam, then if Steve studies, Steve will pass the exam.

i. If Tom does not pass the exam, then it is not the case that if Steve studies, Steve will pass the exam.

j. If Tom does not pass the exam, then if Steve does not study, Steve won't pass the exam.

7. Make up your own translation key in order to translate the following sentences into English. Write out the English equivalents in English sentences that seem (as much as is possible) natural.

a. (R→S)

b. ¬¬R

c. (S→R)

d. ¬(S→R)

e. (¬S→¬¬R)

f. ¬¬(R→S)

g. (¬R→S)

$$(P \rightarrow (S \rightarrow T))$$

h. $(R \to \neg S)$

i. $(\neg R \to \neg S)$

j. $\neg(\neg R \to \neg S)$

---

[3] One thing is a little funny about this second example with unknown number *a*. We will not be able to find a number that is evenly divisible by 4 and not evenly divisible by 2, so the world will never be like the second row of this truth table describes. Two things need to be said about this. First, this oddity arises because of mathematical facts, not facts of our propositional logic—that is, we need to know what "divisible" means, what "4" and "2" mean, and so on, in order to understand the sentence. So, when we see that the second row is not possible, we are basing that on our knowledge of mathematics, not on our knowledge of propositional logic. Second, some conditionals can be false. In defining the conditional, we need to consider all possible conditionals; so, we must define the conditional for any case where the antecedent is true and the consequent is false, even if that cannot happen for this specific example.

[4] See Wason (1966).

3. Good Arguments

3.1 A historical example

An important example of excellent reasoning can be found in the case of the medical advances of the Nineteenth Century physician, Ignaz Semmelweis. Semmelweis was an obstetrician at the Vienna General Hospital. Built on the foundation of a poor house, and opened in 1784, the General Hospital is still operating today. Semmelweis, during his tenure as assistant to the head of one of two maternity clinics, noticed something very disturbing. The hospital had two clinics, separated only by a shared anteroom, known as the First and the Second Clinics. The mortality rate for mothers delivering babies in the First Clinic, however, was nearly three times as bad as the mortality for mothers in the Second Clinic (9.9 % average versus 3.4% average). The same was true for the babies born in the clinics: the mortality rate in the First Clinic was 6.1% versus 2.1% at the Second Clinic.[5] In nearly all these cases, the deaths were caused by what appeared to be the same illness, commonly called "childbed fever". Worse, these numbers actually understated the mortality rate of the First Clinic, because sometimes very ill patients were transferred to the general treatment portion of the hospital, and when they died, their death was counted as part of the mortality rate of the general hospital, not of the First Clinic.

Semmelweis set about trying to determine why the First Clinic had the higher mortality rate. He considered a number of hypotheses, many of which were suggested by or believed by other doctors.

One hypothesis was that cosmic-atmospheric-terrestrial influences caused childbed fever. The idea here was that some kind of feature of the atmosphere would cause the disease. But, Semmelweis observed, the First and Second Clinics were very close to each other, had similar ventilation, and shared a common anteroom. So, they had similar atmospheric conditions. He reasoned: If childbed fever is caused by cosmic-atmospheric-terrestrial influences, then the mortality rate would be similar in the First and Second Clinics. But the mortality rate was not similar in the First and Second Clinics. So, the childbed fever was not caused by cosmic-atmospheric-terrestrial influences.

Another hypothesis was that overcrowding caused the childbed fever. But, if overcrowding caused the childbed fever, then the more crowded of the two clinics should have the higher mortality rate. But, the Second Clinic was more crowded (in part because, aware of its lower mortality rate, mothers fought desperately to be put there instead of in the First Clinic). It did not have a higher mortality rate. So, the childbed fever was not caused by overcrowding.

Another hypothesis was that fear caused the childbed fever. In the Second Clinic, the priest delivering last rites could walk directly to a dying patient's room. For reasons of the layout of the rooms, the priest delivering last rites in the First Clinic walked by all the rooms, ringing a bell announcing his approach. This frightened patients; they could not tell if the priest was coming for them. Semmelweis arranged a different route for the priest and asked him to silence his bell. He reasoned: if the higher rate of childbed fever was caused by fear of death resulting from the priest's approach, then the rate of childbed fever should decline if people could not tell when the priest was coming to the Clinic. But it was not the case that the rate of childbed fever declined when people could not tell if the priest was coming to the First Clinic. So, the higher rate of childbed fever in the First Clinic was not caused by fear of death resulting from the priest's approach.

In the First Clinic, male doctors were trained; this was not true in the Second Clinic. These male doctors performed autopsies across the hall from the clinic, before delivering babies. Semmelweis knew of a doctor who cut himself while performing an autopsy, and who then died a terrible death not unlike that of the mothers who died of childbed fever. Semmelweis formed a hypothesis. The childbed fever was caused by something on the hands of the doctors, something that they picked up from corpses during autopsies, but that infected the women and infants. He reasoned that: if the fever was caused by cadaveric matter on the hands of the doctors, then the mortality rate would drop when doctors washed their hands with chlorinated water before delivering babies. He forced the doctors to do this. The result was that the mortality rate dropped to a rate below that even of the Second Clinic.

Semmelweis concluded that the best explanation of the higher mortality rate was this "cadaveric matter" on the hands of doctors. He was the first person to see that washing of hands with sterilizing cleaners would save thousands of lives. It is hard to overstate how important this contribution is to human well being. Semmelweis's fine reasoning deserves our endless respect and gratitude.

But how can we be sure his reasoning was good? Semmelweis was essentially considering a series of arguments. Let us turn to the question: how shall we evaluate arguments?

3.2 Arguments

Our logical language now allows us to say conditional and negation statements. That may not seem like much, but our language is now complex enough for us to develop the idea of using our logic not just to describe things, but also to reason about those things.

We will think of reasoning as providing an argument. Here, we use the word "argument" not in the sense of two or more people criticizing each other, but rather in the sense we mean when we say, "Pythagoras's argument". In such a case, someone is using language to try to convince us that something is true. Our goal is to make this notion very precise, and then identify what makes an argument good.

We need to begin by making the notion of an argument precise. Our logical language so far contains only sentences. An argument will, therefore, consist of sentences. In a natural language, we use the term "argument" in a strong way, which includes the suggestion that the argument should be good. However, we want to separate the notion of a good argument from the notion of an argument, so we can identify what makes an argument good, and what makes an argument bad. To do this, we will start with a minimal notion of what an argument is. Here is the simplest, most minimal notion:

> Argument: an ordered list of sentences; we call one of these sentences the "conclusion", and we call the other sentences "premises".

This is obviously very weak. (There is a famous Monty Python skit where one of the comedians ridicules the very idea that such a thing could be called an argument.) But for our purposes, this is a useful notion because it is very clearly defined, and we can now ask, what makes an argument good?

The everyday notion of an argument is that it is used to convince us to believe something. The thing that we are being encouraged to believe is the conclusion.

Following our definition of "argument", the reasons that the person gives will be what we are calling "premises". But *belief* is a psychological notion. We instead are interested only in truth. So, we can reformulate this intuitive notion of what an argument should do, and think of an argument as being used to show that something is true. The premises of the argument are meant to show us that the conclusion is true.

What then should be this relation between the premises and the conclusion? Intuitive notions include that the premises should support the conclusion, or corroborate the conclusion, or make the conclusion true. But "support" and "corroborate" sound rather weak, and "make" is not very clear. What we can use in their place is a stronger standard: let us say as a first approximation that if the premises are true, the conclusion is true.

But even this seems weak, on reflection. For, the conclusion could be true by accident, for reasons unrelated to our premises. Remember that we define the conditional as true if the antecedent and consequent are true. But this could happen by accident. For example, suppose I say, "If Tom wears blue then he will get an A on the exam". Suppose also that Tom both wears blue and Tom gets an A on the exam. This makes the conditional true, but (we hope) the color of his clothes really had nothing to do with his performance on the exam. Just so, we want our definition of "good argument" to be such that it cannot be an accident that the premises and conclusion are both true.

A better and stronger standard would be that, necessarily, given true premises, the conclusion is true.

This points us to our definition of a good argument. It is traditional to call a good argument "valid."

> Valid argument: an argument for which, necessarily, if the premises are true, then the conclusion is true.

This is the single most important principle in this book. Memorize it.

A bad argument is an argument that is not valid. Our name for this will be an "invalid argument".

Sometimes, a dictionary or other book will define or describe a "valid argument" as an argument that follows the rules of logic. This is a hopeless way to define "valid", because it is circular in a pernicious way: we are going to create the rules of our logic in order to ensure that they construct valid arguments. We cannot make rules of logical reasoning until we know what we want those rules to do, and what we want them to do is to create valid arguments. So "valid" must be defined before we can make our reasoning system.

Experience shows that if a student is to err in understanding this definition of "valid argument", he or she will typically make the error of assuming that a valid argument has all true premises. This is not required. There are valid arguments with false premises and a false conclusion. Here's one:

> If Miami is the capital of Kansas, then Miami is in Canada. Miami is the capital of Kansas. Therefore, Miami is in Canada.

This argument has at least one false premise: Miami is not the capital of Kansas. And the conclusion is false: Miami is not in Canada. But the argument is valid: if the premises were both true, the conclusion would have to be true. (If that bothers you, hold on a while and we will convince you that this argument is valid because of its form alone. Also, keep in mind always that "if...then..." is interpreted as meaning the conditional.)

Similarly, there are invalid arguments with true premises, and with a true conclusion. Here's one:

> If Miami is the capital of Ontario, then Miami is in Canada. Miami is not the capital of Ontario. Therefore, Miami is not in Canada.

(If you find it confusing that this argument is invalid, look at it again after you finish reading this chapter.)

Validity is about the relationship between the sentences in the argument. It is not a claim that those sentences are true.

Another variation of this confusion seems to arise when we forgot to think carefully about the conditional. The definition of valid is not "All the premises are true, so the conclusion is true." If you don't see the difference, consider the following two sentences. "If your house is on fire, then you should call the fire department." In this sentence, there is no claim that your house is on fire. It is rather advice about what you should do if your house is on fire. In the same way, the definition of valid argument does not tell you that the premises are true. It tells you what follows if they are true. Contrast now, "Your house is on fire, so you should call the fire department". This sentence delivers very bad news. It is not a conditional at all. What it really means is, "Your house is on fire and you should call the fire department". Our definition of valid is not, "All the premises are true and the conclusion is true".

Finally, another common mistake is to confuse *true* and *valid*. In the sense that we are using these terms in this book, only sentences can be true or false, and only arguments can be valid and invalid. When discussing and using our logical language, it is nonsense to say, "a true argument", and it is nonsense to say, "a valid sentence".

Someone new to logic might wonder, why would we want a definition of "good argument" that does not guarantee that our conclusion is true? The answer is that logic is an enormously powerful tool for checking arguments, and we want to be able to identify what the good arguments are, independently of the particular premises that we use in the argument. For example, there are infinitely many particular arguments that have the same form as the valid argument given above. There are infinitely many particular arguments that have the same form as the invalid argument given above. Logic lets us embrace all the former arguments at once, and reject all those bad ones at once.

Furthermore, our propositional logic will not be able to tell us whether an atomic sentence is true. If our argument is about rocks, we must ask the geologist if the premises are true. If our argument is about history, we must ask the historian if the premises are true. If our argument is about music, we must ask the music theorist if the premises are true. But the logician can tell the geologist, the historian, and the musicologist whether her arguments are good or bad, independent of the particular premises.

We do have a common term for a good argument that has true premises. This is called "sound". It is a useful notion when we are applying our logic. Here is our definition:

> Sound argument: a valid argument with true premises.

A sound argument must have a true conclusion, given the definition of "valid".

3.3 Checking arguments semantically

Every element of our definition of "valid" is clear except for one. We know what "if...then..." means. We defined the semantics of the conditional in chapter 2. We have defined "argument", "premise", and "conclusion". We take *true* and *false* as primitives. But what does "necessarily" mean?

We define a valid argument as one where, necessarily, if the premises are true, then the conclusion is true. It would seem the best way to understand this is to say, there is no situation in which the premises are true but the conclusion is false. But then, what are these "situations"? Fortunately, we already have a tool that looks like it could help us: the truth table.

Remember that in the truth table, we put on the bottom left side all the possible combinations of truth values of some set of atomic sentences. Each row of the table then represents a kind of way the world could be. Using this as a way to understand "necessarily", we could rephrase our definition of valid to something like this, "In any kind of situation in which all the premises are true, the conclusion is true."

Let's try it out. We will need to use truth tables in a new way: to check an argument. That will require having not just one sentence, but several on the truth table. Consider an argument that looks like it should be valid.

> If Jupiter is more massive than Earth, then Jupiter has a stronger gravitational field than Earth. Jupiter is more massive than Earth. In conclusion, Jupiter has a stronger gravitational field than Earth.

This looks like it has the form of a valid argument, and it looks like an astrophysicist would tell us it is sound. Let's translate it to our logical language using the following translation key. (We've used up our letters, so I'm going to start over. We'll do that often: assume we are starting a new language each time we translate a new set of problems or each time we consider a new example.)

> P: Jupiter is more massive than Earth

> Q: Jupiter has a stronger gravitational field than Earth.

This way of writing out sentences of logic and sentences of English we can call a "translation key". We can use this format whenever we want to explain what our sentences mean in English.

Using this key, our argument would be formulated

$(P \rightarrow Q)$

P

———

Q

That short line is not part of our language, but rather is a handy tradition. When quickly writing down arguments, we write the premises, and then write the conclusion last, and draw a short line above the conclusion.

This is an argument: it is an ordered list of sentences, the first two of which are premises and the last of which is the conclusion.

To make a truth table, we identify all the atomic sentences that constitute these sentences. These are P and Q. There are four possible kinds of ways the world could be that matter to us then:

P	Q			
T	T			
T	F			
F	T			
F	F			

We'll write out the sentences, in the order of premises and then conclusion.

		premise	premise	conclusion
P	Q	(P → Q)	P	Q
T	T			
T	F			
F	T			
F	F			

Now we can fill in the columns for each sentence, identifying the truth value of the sentence for that kind of situation.

		premise	premise	conclusion
P	Q	(P → Q)	P	Q
T	T	T	T	T
T	F	F	T	F
F	T	T	F	T
F	F	T	F	F

We know how to fill in the column for the conditional because we can refer back to the truth table used to define the conditional, to determine what its truth value is when the first part and second part are true; and so on. P is true in those kinds of situations where P is true, and P is false in those kinds of situations where P is false. And the same is so for Q.

Now, consider all those kinds of ways the world could be such that all the premises are true. Only the first row of the truth table is one where all the premises are true. Note that the conclusion is true in that row. That means, in any kind of situation in which all the premises are true, the conclusion will be true. Or, equivalently: necessarily, if all the premises are true, then the conclusion is true.

		premise	premise	conclusion
P	Q	$(P \to Q)$	P	Q
T	*T*	*T*	*T*	*T*
T	*F*	*F*	*T*	*F*
F	*T*	*T*	*F*	*T*
F	*F*	*T*	*F*	*F*

Consider in contrast the second argument above, the invalid argument with all true premises and a true conclusion. We'll use the following translation key.

> R: Miami is the capital of Ontario

> S: Miami is in Canada

And our argument is thus

> $(R \to S)$

> ¬R

> _____

> ¬S

Here is the truth table.

		premise	premise	conclusion
R	S	$(R \to S)$	¬R	¬S
T	*T*	*T*	*F*	*F*
T	*F*	*F*	*F*	*T*
F	*T*	*T*	*T*	*F*
F	*F*	*T*	*T*	*T*

Note that there are two kinds of ways that the world could be in which all of our premises are true. These correspond to the third and fourth row of the truth table. But for the third row of the truth table, the premises are true but the conclusion is false. Yes, there is a kind of way the world could be in which all the premises are true and the conclusion is true; that is shown in the fourth row of the truth table. But we are not interested in identifying arguments that will have true conclusions if we are lucky. We are interested in valid arguments. This argument is invalid. There is a kind of way the world could be such that all the premises are true and the conclusion is false. We can highlight this.

R	S	premise $(R \rightarrow S)$	premise $\neg R$	conclusion $\neg S$
T	T	T	F	F
T	F	F	F	T
F	T	T	T	F
F	F	T	T	T

Hopefully it becomes clear why we care about validity. Any argument of the form, $(P \rightarrow Q)$ and P, therefore Q, is valid. We do not have to know what P and Q mean to determine this. Similarly, any argument of the form, $(R \rightarrow S)$ and $\neg R$, therefore $\neg S$, is invalid. We do not have to know what R and S mean to determine this. So logic can be of equal use to the astronomer and the financier, the computer scientist or the sociologist.

3.4 Returning to our historical example

We described some (not all) of the hypotheses that Semmelweis tested when he tried to identify the cause of childbed fever, so that he could save thousands of women and infants. Let us symbolize these and consider his reasoning.

The first case we considered was one where he reasoned: If childbed fever is caused by cosmic-atmospheric-terrestrial influences, then the mortality rate would be similar in the First and Second Clinics. But the mortality rate was not similar in the First and Second Clinics. So, the childbed fever is not caused by cosmic-atmospheric-terrestrial influences.

Here is a key to symbolize the argument.

T: Childbed fever is caused by cosmic-atmospheric-terrestrial influences.

U: The mortality rate is similar in the First and Second Clinics.

This would mean the argument is:

$(T \rightarrow U)$

$\neg U$

———

$\neg T$

Is this argument valid? We can check using a truth table.

		premise	premise	conclusion
T	U	$(T \rightarrow U)$	$\neg U$	$\neg T$
T	*T*	*T*	*F*	*F*
T	*F*	*F*	*T*	*F*
F	*T*	*T*	*F*	*T*
F	*F*	*T*	*T*	*T*

The last row is the only row where all the premises are true. For this row, the conclusion is true. Thus, for all the kinds of ways the world could be in which the premises are true, the conclusion is also true. This is a valid argument. If we accept his premises, then we should accept that childbed fever was not caused by cosmic-atmospheric-terrestrial influences.

The second argument we considered was the concern that fear caused the higher mortality rates, particularly the fear of the priest coming to deliver last rites. Semmelweis reasoned that if the higher rate of childbed fever is caused by fear of death resulting from the priest's approach, then the rate of childbed fever should decline if people cannot discern when the priest is coming to the Clinic. Here is a key:

V: the higher rate of childbed fever is caused by fear of death resulting from the priest's approach.

W: the rate of childbed fever will decline if people cannot discern when the priest is coming to the Clinic.

But when Semmelweis had the priest silence his bell, and take a different route, so that patients could not discern that he was coming to the First Clinic, he found no difference in the mortality rate; the First Clinic remained far worse than the second clinic. He concluded that the higher rate of childbed fever was not caused by fear of death resulting from the priest's approach.

$$(V \to W)$$

$$\neg W$$

$$\neg V$$

Is this argument valid? We can check using a truth table.

V	W	premise $(V \to W)$	premise $\neg W$	conclusion $\neg V$
T	T	T	F	F
T	F	F	T	F
F	T	T	F	T
F	F	T	T	T

Again, we see that Semmelweis's reasoning was good. He showed that it was not the case that the higher rate of childbed fever was caused by fear of death resulting from the Priest's approach.

What about Semmelweis's positive conclusion, that the higher mortality rate was caused by some contaminant from the corpses that doctors had autopsied just before they assisted in a delivery? To understand this step in his method, we need to reflect a moment on the scientific method and its relation to logic.

3.5 Other kinds of arguments 1: Scientific reasoning

Valid arguments, and the methods that we are developing, are sometimes called "deductive reasoning". This is the kind of reasoning in which necessarily our conclusions is true if our premises are true; these arguments can be shown to be good by way of our logical reasoning alone. There are other kinds of reasoning, and understanding this may help clarify the relation of logic to other endeavors. Two important, and closely related, alternatives to deductive reasoning are scientific reasoning and statistical generalizations. We'll discuss statistical generalizations in the next section.

Scientific method relies upon logic, but science is not reducible to logic: scientists do empirical research. That is, they examine and test phenomena in the world. This is a very important difference from pure logic. To understand how this difference results in a distinct method, let us review Semmelweis's important discovery.

The details and nature of scientific reasoning are somewhat controversial. I am going to provide here a basic—many philosophers would say, oversimplified—account of scientific reasoning. My goal is to indicate the relation between logic and the kind of reasoning Semmelweis may have used.

As we noted, Semmelweis learned about the death of a colleague, Professor Jakob Kolletschka. Kolletschka had been performing an autopsy, and he cut his finger. Shortly thereafter, Kolletschka died with symptoms like those of childbed fever. Semmelweis reasoned that something on the corpse caused the disease; he called this "cadaveric matter". In the First Clinic, where the mortality rate of women and babies was high, doctors were doing autopsies and then delivering babies immediately after. If he could get this cadaveric matter off the hands of the doctors, the rate of childbed fever should fall.

So, he reasoned thus: if the fever is caused by cadaveric matter on the hands of the doctors, then the mortality rate will drop when doctors wash their hands with chlorinated water before delivering babies. He forced the doctors to do this. The result was that the mortality rate dropped a very great deal, at times to below 1%.

Here is a key:

P: The fever is caused by cadaveric matter on the hands of the doctors.

Q: The mortality rate will drop when doctors wash their hands with chlorinated water before delivering babies.

And the argument appears to be something like this (as we will see, this isn't quite the right way to put it, but for now...):

$(P \rightarrow Q)$

Q

———

P

Is this argument valid? We can check using a truth table.

P	Q	premise $(P \rightarrow Q)$	premise Q	conclusion P
T	T	T	T	T
T	F	F	F	T
F	T	T	T	F
F	F	T	F	F

From this, it looks like Semmelweis has used an invalid argument!

However, an important feature of scientific reasoning must be kept in mind. There is some controversy over the details of the scientific method, but the most basic view goes something like this. Scientists formulate hypotheses about the possible causes or features of a phenomenon. They make predictions based on these hypotheses, and then they perform experiments to test those predictions. The reasoning here uses the conditional: if the hypotheses is true, then the particular prediction will be true. If the experiment shows that the prediction is false, then the scientist rejects the hypothesis.[6] But if the prediction proved to be true, then the scientist has shown that the hypothesis may be true—at least, given the information we glean from the conditional and the consequent alone.

This is very important. Scientific conclusions are about the physical world, they are not about logic. This means that scientific claims are not necessarily true, in the sense of "necessarily" that we used in our definition of "valid". Instead, science identifies claims that may be true, or (after some progress) are very likely to be true, or (after very much progress) are true.

Scientists keep testing their hypotheses, using different predictions and experiments. Very often, they have several competing hypotheses that have, so far, survived testing. To decide between these, they can use a range of criteria. In order of their importance, these include: choose the hypothesis with the most predictive power (the one that correctly predicts more kinds of phenomena); choose the hypothesis that will be most productive of other scientific theories; choose the hypothesis consistent with your other accepted hypotheses; choose the simplest hypothesis.

What Semmelweis showed was that it could be true that cadaveric matter caused the childbed fever. This hypothesis predicted more than any other hypothesis that the doctors had, and so for that reason alone this was the very best hypothesis. "But," you might reason, "doesn't that mean his conclusion was true? And don't we know now, given all that we've learned, that his conclusion must be true?" No. He was far ahead of other doctors, and his deep insights were of great service to all of humankind. But the scientific method continued to refine Semmelweis's ideas. For example, later doctors introduced the idea of microorganisms as the cause of childbed fever, and this refined and improved Semmelweis's insights: it was not because the cadaveric matter came from corpses that it caused the disease; it was because the cadaveric matter contained particular micro-organisms that it caused the disease. So, further scientific progress showed his hypothesis could be revised and improved.

To review and summarize, with the scientific method:

1. We develop a hypothesis about the causes or nature of a phenomenon.
2. We predict what (hopefully unexpected) effects are a consequence of this hypothesis.
3. We check with experiments to see if these predictions come true:

- If the predictions prove false, we reject the hypothesis;[7]
- If the predictions prove true, we conclude that the hypothesis could be true. We continue to test the hypothesis by making other predictions (that is, we

return to step 2).

This means that a hypothesis that does not make testable predictions (that is, a hypothesis that cannot possibly be proven false) is not a scientific hypothesis. Such a hypothesis is called "unfalsifiable" and we reject it as unscientific.

This method can result in more than one hypothesis being shown to be possibly true. Then, we chose between competing hypotheses by using criteria like the following (here ordered by their relative importance; "theory" can be taken to mean a collection of one or more hypotheses):

1. Predictive power: the more that a hypothesis can successfully predict, the better it is.
2. Productivity: a hypothesis that suggests more new directions for research is to be preferred.
3. Coherence with Existing Theory: if two hypotheses predict the same amount and are equally productive, then the hypothesis that coheres with (does not contradict) other successful theories is preferable to one that does contradict them.
4. Simplicity: if two hypotheses are equally predictive, productive, and coherent with existing theories, then the simpler hypothesis is preferable.

Out of respect to Ignaz Semmelweis we should tell the rest of his story, although it means we must end on a sad note. Semmelweis's great accomplishment was not respected by his colleagues, who resented being told that their lack of hygiene was causing deaths. He lost his position at the First Clinic, and his successors stopped the program of washing hands in chlorinated water. The mortality rate leapt back to its catastrophically high levels. Countless women and children died. Semmelweis continued to promote his ideas, and this caused growing resentment. Eventually, several doctors in Vienna—not one of them a psychiatrist—secretly signed papers declaring Semmelweis insane. We do not know whether Semmelweis was mentally ill at this time. These doctors took him to an asylum on the pretense of having him visit in his capacity as a doctor; when he arrived, the guards seized Semmelweis. He struggled, and the guards at the asylum beat him severely, put him in a straightjacket, and left him alone in a locked room. Neglected in isolation, the wounds from his beating became infected and he died a week later.

It was years before Semmelweis's views became widely accepted and his accomplishment properly recognized. His life teaches many lessons, including unfortunately that even the most educated among us can be evil, petty, and willfully ignorant. Let us repay Semmelweis, as those in his own time did not, by remembering and praising his scientific acumen and humanity.

3.6 Other kinds of arguments 2: Statistical reasoning

Here we can say a few words about statistical generalizations—our goal being only to provide a contrast with deductive reasoning.

In one kind of statistical generalization, we have a population of some kind that we want to make general claims about. A population could be objects or events. So, a population can be a group of organisms, or a group of weather events. "Population" just means all the events or all the things we want to make a generalization about. Often however it is impossible to examine every object or event in the population, so what we do is gather a sample. A sample is some portion of the population. Our hope is that the sample is representative of the population: that whatever traits are shared by the members of the sample are also shared by the members of the population.

For a sample to representative, it must be random and large enough. "Random" in this context means that the sample was not chosen in any way that might distinguish members of the sample from the population, other than being members of the population. In other words, every member of the population was equally likely to be in the sample. "Large enough" is harder to define. Statisticians have formal models describing this, but suffice to say we should not generalize about a whole population using just a few members.

Here's an example. We wonder if all domestic dogs are descended from wolves. Suppose we have some genetic test to identify if an organism was a descendent of wolves. We cannot give the test to all domestic dogs—this would be impractical and costly and unnecessary. We pick a random sample of domestic dogs that is large enough, and we test them. For the sample to be random, we need to select it without allowing any bias to influence our selection; all that should matter is that these are domestic dogs, and each member of the population must have an equal chance of being in the sample. Consider the alternative: if we just tested one family of dogs—say, dogs that are large—we might end up selecting dogs that differed from others in a way that matters to our test. For example, maybe large dogs are descended from wolves, but small dogs are not. Other kinds of bias can creep in less obviously. We might just sample dogs in our local community, and it might just be that people in our community prefer large dogs, and again we would have a sample bias. So, we randomly select dogs, and give them the genetic test.

Suppose the results were positive. We reason that if all the members of the randomly selected and large enough sample (the tested dogs) have the trait, then it is very likely that all the members of the population (all dogs) have the trait. Thus: we could say that it appears very likely that all dogs have the trait. (This likelihood can be estimated, so that we can also sometimes say how likely it is that all members of the population have the trait.)

This kind of reasoning obviously differs from a deductive argument very substantially. It is a method of testing claims about the world, it requires observations, and its conclusion is likely instead of being certain.

But such reasoning is not unrelated to logic. Deductive reasoning is the foundation of these and all other forms of reasoning. If one must reason using statistics in this way, one relies upon deductive methods always at some point in one's arguments. There was a conditional at the penultimate step of our reasoning, for example (we said "if all the members of the randomly selected and large enough sample have the trait, then it is very likely that all the members of the population have the trait"). Furthermore, the foundations of these methods (the most fundamental descriptions of what these methods are) are given using logic and mathematics. Logic, therefore, can be seen as the study of the most fundamental form of reasoning, which will be used in turn by all other forms of reasoning, including scientific and statistical reasoning.

3.7 Problems

1. Make truth tables to show that the following arguments are valid. Circle or highlight the rows of the truth table that show the argument is valid (that is, all the rows where all the premises are true). Note that you will need eight

rows in the truth table for problems d-f, and sixteen rows in the truth table for problems g and h.

    a. Premises: $(P \to Q)$, $\neg Q$. Conclusion: $\neg P$.
    b. Premises: $\neg P$. Conclusion: $(P \to Q)$.
    c. Premises: Q. Conclusion: $(P \to Q)$.
    d. Premises: $(P \to Q)$, $(Q \to R)$. Conclusion: $(P \to R)$.
    e. Premises: $(P \to Q)$, $(Q \to R)$, P. Conclusion: R.
    f. Premises: $(P \to Q)$, $(Q \to R)$, $\neg R$. Conclusion: $\neg P$.
    g. Premises: $(P \to Q)$, $(Q \to R)$, $(R \to S)$, P. Conclusion: S.
    h. Premises: $(P \to Q)$, $(Q \to R)$, $(R \to S)$. Conclusion: $(P \to S)$.

2. Make truth tables to show the following arguments are invalid. Circle or highlight the rows of the truth table that show the argument is invalid (that is, any row where all the premises are true but the conclusion is false).

    a. Premises: $(P \to Q)$. Conclusion: P.
    b. Premises: $(P \to Q)$. Conclusion: Q.
    c. Premises: P. Conclusion: $(P \to Q)$.
    d. Premises: $(P \to Q)$, Q. Conclusion: P.
    e. Premises: $\neg Q$. Conclusion: $(P \to Q)$.
    f. Premises: $(P \to Q)$. Conclusion: $(Q \to P)$.
    g. Premises: $(P \to Q)$, $(Q \to R)$, $\neg P$. Conclusion: $\neg R$.
    h. Premises: $(P \to Q)$, $(Q \to R)$, R. Conclusion: P.
    i. Premises: $(P \to Q)$, $(Q \to R)$. Conclusion: $(R \to P)$.
    j. Premises: $(P \to Q)$, $(Q \to R)$, $(R \to S)$. Conclusion: $(S \to P)$.

3. In normal colloquial English, write your own valid argument with at least two premises. Your argument should just be a paragraph (not an ordered list of sentences or anything else that looks like logic). Translate it into propositional logic and use a truth table to show it is valid.

4. In normal colloquial English, write your own invalid argument with at least two premises. Translate it into propositional logic and use a truth table to show it is invalid.

5. For each of the following, state whether the argument described could be: valid, invalid, sound, unsound.

a. An argument with false premises and a false conclusion.

b. An argument with true premises and a false conclusion.

c. An argument with false premises and a true conclusion.

d. An argument with true premises and a true conclusion.

---

[5] All the data cited here comes from Carter (1983) and additional biographical information comes from Carter and Carter (2008). These books are highly recommended to anyone interested in the history of science or medicine.

[6] It would be more accurate to say, if the prediction proves false, the scientist must reject either the hypothesis or some other premise of her reasoning. For example, her argument may include the implicit premise that her scientific instruments were operating correctly. She might instead reject this premise that her instruments are working correctly, change one of her instruments, and try again to test the hypothesis. See Duhem (1991). Or, to return to the case of Semmelweis, he might wonder whether he sufficiently established that there were no differences in the atmosphere between the two clinics; or he might wonder whether he sufficiently muffled the Priest's approach; or whether he recorded his results accurately; and so on. As noted, my account of scientific reasoning here is simplified.

[7] Or, as noted in note 6, we reject some other premise of the argument.

4. Proofs

4.1 A problem with semantic demonstrations of validity

Given that we can test an argument for validity, it might seem that we have a fully developed system to study arguments. However, there is a significant practical difficulty with our semantic method of checking arguments using truth tables (you may have already noted what this practical difficulty is, when you did problems 1e and 2e of chapter 3). Consider the following argument:

Alison will go to the party.

If Alison will go to the party, then Beatrice will.

If Beatrice will go to the party, then Cathy will.

If Cathy will go to the party, then Diane will.

If Diane will go to the party, then Elizabeth will.

If Elizabeth will go to the party, then Fran will.

If Fran will go to the party, then Giada will.

If Giada will go to the party, then Hilary will.

If Hillary will go to the party, then Io will.

If Io will go to the party, then Julie will.

_____

Julie will go to the party.

Most of us will agree that this argument is valid. It has a rather simple form, in which one sentence is related to the previous sentence, so that we can see the conclusion follows from the premises. Without bothering to make a translation key, we can see the argument has the following form.

P

$(P \rightarrow Q)$

$(Q \rightarrow R)$

$(R \rightarrow S)$

$(S \rightarrow T)$

$(T \rightarrow U)$

$(U \rightarrow V)$

$(V \rightarrow W)$

$(W \rightarrow X)$

$(X \rightarrow Y)$

_____

Y

However, if we are going to check this argument, then the truth table will require 1024 rows! This follows directly from our observation that for arguments or sentences composed of n atomic sentences, the truth table will require 2^n rows. This argument contains 10 atomic sentences. A truth table checking its validity must have 2^{10} rows, and $2^{10}=1024$. Furthermore, it would be trivial to extend the argument for another, say, ten steps, but then the truth table that we make would require more than a million rows!

For this reason, and for several others (which become evident later, when we consider more advanced logic), it is very valuable to develop a syntactic proof method. That is, a way to check proofs not using a truth table, but rather using rules of syntax.

Here is the idea that we will pursue. A valid argument is an argument such that, necessarily, if the premises are true, then the conclusion is true. We will start just with our premises. We will set aside the conclusion, only to remember it as a goal. Then, we will aim to find a reliable way to introduce another sentence into the argument, with the special property that, if the premises are true, then this single additional sentence to the argument must also be true. If we could find a method to do that, and if after repeated applications of this method we were able to write down our conclusion, then we would know that, necessarily, if our premises are true then the conclusion is true.

The idea is more clear when we demonstrate it. The method for introducing new sentences will be called "inference rules". We introduce our first inference rules for the conditional. Remember the truth table for the conditional:

Φ	Ψ	(Φ→Ψ)
T	T	T
T	F	F
F	T	T
F	F	T

Look at this for a moment. If we have a conditional like (P→Q) (looking at the truth table above, remember that this would meant that we let Φ be P and Ψ be Q), do we know whether any other sentence is true? From (P→Q) alone we do not. Even if (P→Q) is true, P could be false or Q could be false. But what if we have some additional information? Suppose we have as premises both (P→Q) and P. Then, we would know that if those premises were true, Q must be true. We have already checked this with a truth table.

		premise	premise	
P	Q	(P→Q)	P	Q
T	T	T	T	T
T	F	F	T	F
F	T	T	F	T
F	F	T	F	F

The first row of the truth table is the only row where all of the premises are true; and for it, we find that Q is true. This, of course, generalizes to any conditional. That is, we have that:

Φ	Ψ	premise $(\Phi \rightarrow \Psi)$	premise Φ	Ψ
T	T	T	T	T
T	F	F	T	F
F	T	T	F	T
F	F	T	F	F

We now capture this insight not using a truth table, but by introducing a rule. The rule we will write out like this:

$$(\Phi \rightarrow \Psi)$$

$$\Phi$$

———

$$\Psi$$

This is a syntactic rule. It is saying that whenever we have written down a formula in our language that has the shape of the first row (that is, whenever we have a conditional), and whenever we also have written down a formula that has the shape in the second row (that is, whenever we also have written down the antecedent of the conditional), then go ahead, whenever you like, and write down a formula like that in the third row (the consequent of the conditional). The rule talks about the shape of the formulas, not their meaning. But of course we justified the rule by looking at the meanings.

We describe this by saying that the third line is "derived" from the earlier two lines using the inference rule.

This inference rule is old. We are, therefore, stuck with its well-established, but not very enlightening, name: "modus ponens". Thus, we say, for the above example, that the third line is derived from the earlier two lines using modus ponens.

4.2 Direct proof

We need one more concept: that of a proof. Specifically, we'll start with the most fundamental kind of proof, which is called a "direct proof". The idea of a direct proof is: we write down as numbered lines the premises of our argument. Then, after this, we can write down any line that is justified by an application of an inference rule to earlier lines in the proof. When we write down our conclusion, we are done.

Let us make a proof of the simple argument above, which has premises $(P \rightarrow Q)$ and P, and conclusion Q. We start by writing down the premises and numbering them. There is a useful bit of notation that we can introduce at this point. It is known as a "Fitch bar", named after a logician Frederic Fitch, who developed this technique. We will write a vertical bar to the left, with a horizontal line indicating that the premises are above the line.

1. $(P \rightarrow Q)$
2. P

It is also helpful to identify where these steps came from. We can do that with a little explanation written out to the right.

1. $(P \rightarrow Q)$ premise
2. P   premise

Now, we are allowed to write down any line that follows from an earlier line using an inference rule.

1. $(P \rightarrow Q)$ premise
2. P   premise

3. Q

And, finally, we want a reader to understand what rule we used, so we add that into our explanation, identifying the rule and the lines used.

1. (P → Q)	premise
2. P	premise
3. Q	modus ponens, 1, 2

That is a complete direct proof.

Notice a few things. The numbering of each line, and the explanations to the right, are bookkeeping; they are not part of our argument, but rather are used to explain our argument. However, always do them because, it is hard to understand a proof without them. Also, note that our idea is that the inference rule can be applied to any earlier line, including lines themselves derived using inference rules. It is not just premises to which we can apply an inference rule. Finally, note that we have established that this argument must be valid. From the premises, and an inference rule that preserves validity, we have arrived at the conclusion. Necessarily, the conclusion is true, if the premises are true.

The long argument that we started the chapter with can now be given a direct proof.

1. P	premise
2. (P → Q)	premise
3. (Q → R)	premise
4. (R → S)	premise
5. (S → T)	premise
6. (T → U)	premise
7. (U → V)	premise
8. (V → W)	premise
9. (W → X)	premise
10. (X → Y)	premise
11. Q	modus ponens, 2, 1
12. R	modus ponens, 3, 11
13. S	modus ponens, 4, 12
14. T	modus ponens, 5, 13
15. U	modus ponens, 6, 14
16. V	modus ponens, 7, 15
17. W	modus ponens, 8, 16
18. X	modus ponens, 9, 17
19. Y	modus ponens, 10, 18

From repeated applications of modus ponens, we arrived at the conclusion. If lines 1 through 10 are true, line 19 must be true. The argument is valid. And, we completed it with 19 steps, as opposed to writing out 1024 rows of a truth table.

We can see now one of the very important features of understanding the difference between syntax and semantics. Our goal is to make the syntax of our language perfectly mirror its semantics. By manipulating symbols, we manage to say something about the world. This is a strange fact, one that underlies one of the deeper possibilities of language, and also, ultimately, of computers.

4.3 Other inference rules

We can now introduce other inference rules. Looking at the truth table for the conditional again, what else do we observe? Many have noted that if the consequent of a conditional is false, and the conditional is true, then the antecedent of the conditional must be false. Written out as a semantic check on arguments, this will be:

		premise	premise	
Φ	Ψ	$(\Phi \rightarrow \Psi)$	$\neg \Psi$	$\neg \Phi$
T	T	T	F	F
T	F	F	T	F
F	T	T	F	T
F	F	T	T	T

(Remember how we have filled out the truth table. We referred to those truth tables used to define "$\rightarrow$" and "$\neg$", and then for each row of this table above, we filled out the values in each column based on that definition.)

What we observe from this truth table is that when both $(\Phi \rightarrow \Psi)$ and $\neg \Psi$ are true, then $\neg \Phi$ is true. Namely, this can be seen in the last row of the truth table.

This rule, like the last, is old, and has a well-established name: "modus tollens". We represent it schematically with

$(\Phi \rightarrow \Psi)$

$$\neg\Psi$$

$$\overline{\qquad}$$

$$\neg\Phi$$

What about negation? If we know a sentence is false, then this fact alone does not tell us about any other sentence. But what if we consider a negated negation sentence? Such a sentence has the following truth table.

Φ	$\neg\neg\Phi$
T	T
F	F

We can introduce a rule that takes advantage of this observation. In fact, it is traditional to introduce two rules, and lump them together under a common name. The rules' name is "double negation". Basically, the rule says we can add or take away two negations any time. Here are the two schemas for the two rules:

$$\Phi$$

$$\overline{\qquad}$$

$$\neg\neg\Phi$$

and

$$\neg\neg\Phi$$

$$\overline{\qquad}$$

$$\Phi$$

Finally, it is sometimes helpful to be able to repeat a line. Technically, this is an unnecessary rule, but if a proof gets long, we often find it easier to understand the proof if we write a line over again later when we find we need it again. So we introduce the rule "repeat".

$$\Phi$$

$$\overline{\qquad}$$

Φ

4.4 An example

Here is an example that will make use of all three rules. Consider the following argument:

$(Q \rightarrow P)$

$(\neg Q \rightarrow R)$

$\neg R$

$$\overline{\qquad}$$

P

We want to check this argument to see if it is valid.

To do a direct proof, we number the premises so that we can refer to them when using inference rules.

1. $(Q \rightarrow P)$	premise
2. $(\neg Q \rightarrow R)$	premise
3. $\neg R$	premise

And, now, we apply our inference rules. Sometimes, it can be hard to see how to complete a proof. In the worst case, where you are uncertain of how to proceed, you can apply all the rules that you see are applicable and then, assess if you have gotten closer to the conclusion; and repeat this process. Here in any case is a direct proof of the sought conclusion.

1. $(Q \rightarrow P)$	premise
2. $(\neg Q \rightarrow R)$	premise
3. $\neg R$	premise
4. $\neg\neg Q$	modus tollens, 2, 3
5. Q	double negation, 4
6. P	modus ponens, 1, 5

Developing skill at completing proofs merely requires practice. You should strive to do as many problems as you can.

4.5 Problems

1. Complete a direct derivation (also called a "direct proof") for each of the following arguments, showing that it is valid. You will need the rules modus ponens, modus tollens, and double negation.

    a. Premises: $(P \rightarrow Q)$, $\neg\neg P$. Show: $\neg\neg Q$.

    b. Premises: Q, $(\neg P \rightarrow \neg Q)$. Show: P.

    c. Premises: $\neg Q$, $(\neg Q \rightarrow S)$. Show: S.

    d. Premises: $\neg S$, $(\neg Q \rightarrow S)$. Show: Q.

    e. Premises: $(S \rightarrow \neg Q)$, $(P \rightarrow S)$, $\neg\neg P$. Show: $\neg Q$.

    f. Premises: $(T \rightarrow P)$, $(Q \rightarrow S)$, $(S \rightarrow T)$, $\neg P$. Show: $\neg Q$.

    g. Premises: R, P, $(P \rightarrow (R \rightarrow Q))$. Show: Q.

    h. Premises: $((R \rightarrow S) \rightarrow Q)$, $\neg Q$, $(\neg(R \rightarrow S) \rightarrow V)$. Show: V.

    i. Premises: $(P \rightarrow (Q \rightarrow R))$, $\neg(Q \rightarrow R)$. Show: $\neg P$.

    j. Premises: $(\neg(Q \rightarrow R) \rightarrow P)$, $\neg P$, Q. Show: R.

    k. Premises: P, $(P \rightarrow R)$, $(P \rightarrow (R \rightarrow Q))$. Show: Q.

    l. Premises: $\neg R$, $(S \rightarrow R)$, P, $(P \rightarrow (T \rightarrow S))$. Show: $\neg T$.

    m. Premises: P, $(P \rightarrow Q)$, $(P \rightarrow R)$, $(Q \rightarrow (R \rightarrow S))$. Show: S.

    n. Premises: $(P \rightarrow (Q \rightarrow R))$, P, $((Q \rightarrow R) \rightarrow \neg S))$, $((T \rightarrow V) \rightarrow S)$. Show: $\neg(T \rightarrow V)$.

2. In normal colloquial English, write your own valid argument with at least two premises. Your argument should just be a paragraph (not an ordered list of sen-

tences or anything else that looks like logic). Translate it into propositional logic and use a direct proof to show it is valid.

3. In normal colloquial English, write your own valid argument with at least three premises. Your argument should just be a paragraph (not an ordered list of sentences or anything else that looks like logic). Translate it into propositional logic and use a direct proof to show it is valid.

4. Make your own key to translate into propositional logic the portions of the following argument that are in bold. Using a direct proof, prove that the resulting argument is valid.

> Inspector Tarski told his assistant, Mr. Carroll, "**If Wittgenstein had mud on his boots, then he was in the field. Furthermore, if Wittgenstein was in the field, then he is the prime suspect for the murder of Dodgson. Wittgenstein did have mud on his boots. We conclude, Wittgenstein is the prime suspect for the murder of Dodgson.**"

5. "And"

5.1 The conjunction

To make our logical language more easy and intuitive to use, we can now add to it elements that make it able to express the equivalents of other sentences from a natural language like English. Our translations will not be exact, but they will be close enough that: first, we will have a way to more quickly understand the language we are constructing; and, second, we will have a way to speak English more precisely when that is required of us.

Consider the following expressions. How would we translate them into our logical language?

> Tom will go to Berlin and Paris.

> The number a is evenly divisible by 2 and 3.

> Steve is from Texas but not from Dallas.

We could translate each of these using an atomic sentence. But then we would have lost—or rather we would have hidden—information that is clearly there in the English sentences. We can capture this information by introducing a new connective; one that corresponds to our "and".

To see this, consider whether you will agree that these sentences above are equivalent to the following sentences.

> Tom will go to Berlin and Tom will go to Paris.

> The number a is evenly divisible by 2 and the number a is evenly divisible by 3.

> Steve is from Texas and it is not the case that Steve is from Dallas.

Once we grant that these sentences are equivalent to those above, we see that we can treat the "and" in each sentence as a truth functional connective.

Suppose we assume the following key.

P: Tom will go to Berlin.

Q: Tom will go to Paris.

R: *a* is evenly divisible by 2.

S: *a* is evenly divisible by 3.

T: Steve is from Texas

U: Steve is from Dallas.

A partial translation of these sentences would then be:

P and Q

R and S

T and ¬U

Our third sentence above might generate some controversy. How should we understand "but"? Consider that in terms of the truth value of the connected sentences, "but" is the same as "and". That is, if you say "P but Q" you are asserting that both P and Q are true. However, in English there is extra meaning; the English "but" seems to indicate that the additional sentence is unexpected or counterintuitive. "P but Q" seems to say, "P is true, and you will find it surprising or unexpected that Q is true also." That extra meaning is lost in our logic. We will not be representing surprise or expectations. So, we can treat "but" as being the same as "and". This captures the truth value of the sentence formed using "but", which is all that we require of our logic.

Following our method up until now, we want a symbol to stand for "and". In recent years the most commonly used symbol has been "^".

The syntax for "^" is simple. If Φ and Ψ are sentences, then

(Φ^Ψ)

is a sentence. Our translations of our three example sentences should thus look like this:

(P^Q)

(R^S)

(T^¬U)

Each of these is called a "conjunction". The two parts of a conjunction are called "conjuncts".

The semantics of the conjunction are given by its truth table. Most people find the conjunction's semantics obvious. If I claim that both Φ and Ψ are true, normal usage requires that if Φ is false or Ψ is false, or both are false, then I spoke falsely also.

Consider an example. Suppose your employer says, "After one year of employment you will get a raise and two weeks vacation". A year passes. Suppose now that this employer gives you a raise but no vacation, or a vacation but no raise, or neither a raise nor a vacation. In each case, the employer has broken his promise. The sentence forming the promise turned out to be false.

Thus, the semantics for the conjunction are given with the following truth table. For any sentences Φ and Ψ:

Φ	Ψ	(Φ^Ψ)
T	T	T
T	F	F
F	T	F
F	F	F

5.2 Alternative phrasings, and a different "and"

We have noted that in English, "but" is an alternative to "and", and can be translated the same way in our propositional logic. There are other phrases that have a similar meaning: they are best translated by conjunctions, but they convey (in English) a sense of surprise or failure of expectations. For example, consider the following sentence.

Even though they lost the battle, they won the war.

Here "even though" seems to do the same work as "but". The implication is that it is surprising—that one might expect that if they lost the battle then they lost the war. But, as we already noted, we will not capture expectations with our logic. So, we would take this sentence to be sufficiently equivalent to:

They lost the battle and they won the war.

With the exception of "but", it seems in English there is no other single word that is an alternative to "and" that means the same thing. However, there are many ways that one can imply a conjunction. To see this, consider the following sentences.

Tom, who won the race, also won the championship.

The star Phosphorous, that we see in the morning, is the Evening Star.

The Evening Star, which is called "Hesperus", is also the Morning Star.

While Steve is tall, Tom is not.

Dogs are vertebrate terrestrial mammals.

Depending on what elements we take as basic in our language, these sentences all include implied conjunctions. They are equivalent to the following sentences, for example:

Tom won the race and Tom won the championship.

Phosphorous is the star that we see in the morning and Phosphorous is the Evening Star.

The Evening Star is called "Hesperus" and the Evening Star is the Morning Star.

Steve is tall and it is not the case that Tom is tall.

Dogs are vertebrates and dogs are terrestrial and dogs are mammals.

Thus, we need to be sensitive to complex sentences that are conjunctions but that do not use "and" or "but" or phrases like "even though".

Unfortunately, in English there are some uses of "and" that are not conjunctions. The same is true for equivalent terms in some other natural languages. Here is an example.

> Rochester is between Buffalo and Albany.

The "and" in this sentence is not a conjunction. To see this, note that this sentence is not equivalent to the following:

> Rochester is between Buffalo and Rochester is between Albany.

That sentence is not even semantically correct. What is happening in the original sentence?

The issue here is that "is between" is what we call a "predicate". We will learn about predicates in chapter 11, but what we can say here is that some predicates take several names in order to form a sentence. In English, if a predicate takes more than two names, then we typically use the "and" to combine names that are being described by that predicate. In contrast, the conjunction in our propositional logic only combines sentences. So, we must say that there are some uses of the English "and" that are not equivalent to our conjunction.

This could be confusing because sometimes in English we put "and" between names and there is an implied conjunction. Consider:

> Steve is older than Joe and Karen.

Superficially, this looks to have the same structure as "Rochester is between Buffalo and Albany". But this sentence really is equivalent to:

> Steve is older than Joe and Steve is older than Karen.

The difference, however, is that there must be three things in order for one to be between the other two. There need only be two things for one to be older than the other. So, in the sentence "Rochester is between Buffalo and Albany", we need all three names ("Rochester", "Buffalo", and "Albany) to make a single proper atomic sentence with "between". This tells us that the "and" is just being used to combine these names, and not to combine implied sentences (since there can be no implied sentence about what is "between", using just two or just one of these names).

That sounds complex. Do not despair, however. The use of "and" to identify names being used by predicates is less common than "and" being used for a conjunction. Also, after we discuss predicates in chapter 11, and after you have practiced translating different kinds of sentences, the distinction between these uses of "and" will become easy to identify in almost all cases. In the meantime, we shall pick examples that do not invite this confusion.

5.3 Inference rules for conjunctions

Looking at the truth table for the conjunction should tell us two things very clearly. First, if a conjunction is true, what else must be true? The obvious answer is that both of the parts, the conjuncts, must be true. We can introduce a rule to capture this insight. In fact, we can introduce two rules and call them by the same name, since the order of conjuncts does not affect their truth value. These rules are often called "simplification".

$(\Phi \wedge \Psi)$

———

Φ

And:

$(\Phi \wedge \Psi)$

———

Ψ

In other words, if $(\Phi \wedge \Psi)$ is true, then Φ must be true; and if $(\Phi \wedge \Psi)$ is true, then Ψ must be true.

We can also introduce a rule to show a conjunction, based on what we see from the truth table. That is, it is clear that there is only one kind of condition in which $(\Phi \wedge \Psi)$ is true, and that is when Φ is true and when Ψ is true. This suggests the following rule:

Φ

$$\Psi$$

$$(\Phi{\wedge}\Psi)$$

We might call this rule "conjunction", but to avoid confusion with the name of the sentences, we will call this rule "adjunction".

5.4 Reasoning with conjunctions

It would be helpful to consider some examples of reasoning with conjunctions. Let's begin with an argument in a natural language.

Tom and Steve will go to London. If Steve goes to London, then he will ride the Eye. Tom will ride the Eye too, provided that he goes to London. So, both Steve and Tom will ride the Eye.

We need a translation key.

T: Tom will go to London.

S: Steve will go to London.

U: Tom will ride the Eye.

V: Steve will ride the Eye.

Thus our argument is:

$$(T{\wedge}S)$$

$$(S \rightarrow U)$$

$$(T \rightarrow V)$$

$$(V{\wedge}U)$$

Our direct proof will look like this.

1. (T ∧ S)	premise
2. (S → U)	premise
3. (T → V)	premise
4. T	simplification, 1
5. V	modus ponens, 3, 4
6. S	simplification, 1
7. U	modus ponens, 2, 6
8. (V ∧ U)	adjunction, 5, 7

Now an example using just our logical language. Consider the following argument.

(Q → ¬S)

(P → (Q^R))

(T → ¬R)

P

———

(¬S^¬T)

Here is one possible proof.

1. (Q → ¬S)	premise
2. (P → (Q ∧ R))	premise
3. (T → ¬R)	premise
4. P	premise
5. (Q ∧ R)	modus ponens, 2, 4
6. Q	simplification, 5
7. ¬S	modus ponens, 1, 6
8. R	simplification, 5
9. ¬¬R	double negation, 8
10. ¬T	modus tollens, 3, 9
11. (¬S ∧ ¬T)	adjunction, 7, 10

5.5 Alternative symbolizations for the conjunction

Alternative notations for the conjunction include the symbols "&" and the symbol "·". Thus, the expression (P^Q) would be written in these different styles, as:

(P&Q)

(P·Q)

5.6 Complex sentences

Now that we have three different connectives, this is a convenient time to consider complex sentences. The example that we just considered required us to symbolize complex sentences, which use several different kinds of connectives. We want to avoid confusion by being clear about the nature of these sentences. We also want to be able to understand when such sentences are true and when they are false. These two goals are closely related.

Consider the following sentences.

$\neg(P \to Q)$

$(\neg P \to Q)$

$(\neg P \to \neg Q)$

We want to understand what kinds of sentences these are, and also when they are true and when they are false. (Sometimes people wrongly assume that there is some simple distribution law for negation and conditionals, so there is some additional value to reviewing these particular examples.) The first task is to determine what kinds of sentences these are. If the first symbol of your expression is a negation, then you know the sentence is a negation. The first sentence above is a negation. If the first symbol of your expression is a parenthesis, then for our logical language we know that we are dealing with a connective that combines two sentences.

The way to proceed is to match parentheses. Generally people are able to do this by eye, but if you are not, you can use the following rule. Moving left to right, the last "(" that you encounter always matches the first ")" that you encounter. These form a sentence that must have two parts combined with a connective. You can identify the two parts because each will be an atomic sentence, a negation sentence, or a more complex sentence bound with parentheses on each side of the connective.

In our propositional logic, each set of paired parentheses forms a sentence of its own. So, when we encounter a sentence that begins with a parenthesis, we find that if we match the other parentheses, we will ultimately end up with two sentences as constituents, one on each side of a single connective. The connective that combines these two parts is called the "main connective", and it tells us what kind of sentence this is. Thus, above we have examples of a negation, a conditional, and a conditional.

How should we understand the meaning of these sentences? Here we can use truth tables in a new, third way (along with defining a connective and checking arguments). Our method will be this.

First, write out the sentence on the right, leaving plenty of room. Identify what kind of sentence this is. If it is a negation sentence, you should add just to the left a column for the non-negated sentence. This is because the truth table defining negation tells us what a negated sentence means in relation to the non-negated sentence that forms the sentence. If the sentence is a conditional, make two columns to the left, one for the antecedent and one for the consequent. If the sentence is a conjunction, make two columns to the left, one for each conjunct. Here again, we do this because the semantic definitions of these connectives tell us what the truth value of the sentence is, as a function of the truth value of its two parts. Continue this process until the parts would be atomic sentences. Then, we stipulate all possible truth values for the atomic sentences. Once we have done this, we can fill out the truth table, working left to right.

Let's try it for $\neg(P \rightarrow Q)$. We write it to the right.

¬(P → Q)

This is a negation sentence, so we write to the left the sentence being negated.

(P → Q)	¬(P → Q)

This sentence is a conditional. Its two parts are atomic sentences. We put these to the left of the dividing line, and we stipulate all possible combinations of truth values for these atomic sentences.

P	Q	(P → Q)	¬(P → Q)
T	T		
T	F		
F	T		
F	F		

Now, we can fill out each column, moving left to right. We have stipulated the values for P and Q, so we can identify the possible truth values of (P → Q). The semantic definition for "→" tells us how to do that, given that we know for each row the truth value of its parts.

P	Q	$(P \rightarrow Q)$	$\neg(P \rightarrow Q)$
T	T	T	
T	F	F	
F	T	T	
F	F	T	

This column now allows us to fill in the last column. The sentence in the last column is a negation of $(P \rightarrow Q)$, so the definition of "$\neg$" tell us that $\neg(P \rightarrow Q)$ is true when $(P \rightarrow Q)$ is false, and $\neg(P \rightarrow Q)$ is false when $(P \rightarrow Q)$ is true.

P	Q	$(P \rightarrow Q)$	$\neg(P \rightarrow Q)$
T	T	T	F
T	F	F	T
F	T	T	F
F	F	T	F

This truth table tells us what $\neg(P \rightarrow Q)$ means in our propositional logic. Namely, if we assert $\neg(P \rightarrow Q)$ we are asserting that P is true and Q is false.

We can make similar truth tables for the other sentences.

P	Q	$\neg P$	$(\neg P \rightarrow Q)$
T	T	F	T
T	F	F	T
F	T	T	T
F	F	T	F

How did we make this table? The sentence $(\neg P \rightarrow Q)$ is a conditional with two parts, $\neg P$ and Q. Because Q is atomic, it will be on the left side. We make a row for $\neg P$. The sentence $\neg P$ is a negation of P, which is atomic, so we put P also on the left. We fill in the columns, going left to right, using our definitions of the connectives.

And:

P	Q	¬P	¬Q	(¬P → ¬Q)
T	T	F	F	T
T	F	F	T	T
F	T	T	F	F
F	F	T	T	T

Such a truth table is very helpful in determining when sentences are, and are not, equivalent. We have used the concept of equivalence repeatedly, but have not yet defined it. We can offer a semantic, and a syntactic, explanation of equivalence. The semantic notion is relevant here: we say two sentences Φ and Ψ are "equivalent" or "logically equivalent" when they must have the same truth value. (For the syntactic concept of equivalence, see section 9.2). These truth tables show that these three sentences are not equivalent, because it is not the case that they must have the same truth value. For example, if P and Q are both true, then ¬(P → Q) is false but (¬P → Q) is true and (¬P → ¬Q) is true. If P is false and Q is true, then (¬P → Q) is true but (¬P → ¬Q) is false. Thus, each of these sentences is true in some situation where one of the others is false. No two of them are equivalent.

We should consider an example that uses conjunction, and which can help in some translations. How should we translate "Not both Steve and Tom will go to Berlin"? This sentence tells us that it is not the case that both Steve will go to Berlin and Tom will go to Berlin. The sentence does allow, however, that one of them will go to Berlin. Thus, let U mean *Steve will go to Berlin* and V mean *Tom will go to Berlin*. Then we should translate this sentence, ¬(U∧V). We should not translate the sentence (¬U∧¬V). To see why, consider their truth tables.

U	V	(U∧V)	¬(U∧V)	¬U	¬V	(¬U∧¬V)
T	T	T	F	F	F	F
T	F	F	T	F	T	F
F	T	F	T	T	F	F
F	F	F	T	T	T	T

We can see that ¬(U∧V) and (¬U∧¬V) are not equivalent. Also, note the following. Both ¬(U∧V) and (¬U∧¬V) are true if Steve does not go to Berlin and Tom does not go to Berlin. This is captured in the last row of this truth table, and this is consistent with the meaning of the English sentence. But, now note: it is true that not both Steve and Tom will go to Berlin, if Steve goes and Tom does not. This is captured in the second row of this truth table. It is true that not both Steve and Tom will go to Berlin, if Steve does not go but Tom does. This is captured in the third row of this truth table. In both kinds of cases (in both rows of the truth table), ¬(U^V) is true but (¬U^¬V) is false. Thus, we can see that ¬(U^V) is the correct translation of "Not both Steve and Tom will go to Berlin".

Let's consider a more complex sentence that uses all of our connectives so far: ((P^¬Q) → ¬(P → Q)). This sentence is a conditional. The antecedent is a conjunction. The consequent is a negation. Here is the truth table, completed.

P	Q	¬Q	(P→Q)	(P^¬Q)	¬(P→Q)	((P^¬Q) → ¬(P→Q))
T	T	F	T	F	F	T
T	F	T	F	T	T	T
F	T	F	T	F	F	T
F	F	T	T	F	F	T

This sentence has an interesting property: it cannot be false. That is not surprising, once we think about what it says. In English, the sentence says: If P is true and Q is false, then it is not the case that P implies Q. That must be true: if it were the case that P implies Q, then if P is true then Q is true. But the antecedent says P is true and Q is false.

Sentences of the propositional logic that must be true are called "tautologies". We will discuss them at length in later chapters.

Finally, note that we can combine this method for finding the truth conditions for a complex sentence with our method for determining whether an argument is valid using a truth table. We will need to do this if any of our premises or the conclusion are complex. Here is an example. We'll start with an argument in English:

> If whales are mammals, then they have vestigial limbs. If whales are mammals, then they have a quadrupedal ancestor. Therefore, if whales are mammals then they have a quadrupedal ancestor and they have vestigial limbs.

We need a translation key.

P: Whales are mammals.

Q: Whales have have vestigial limbs.

R: Whales have a quadrupedal ancestor.

The argument will then be symbolized as:

$(P \rightarrow Q)$

$(P \rightarrow R)$

_____

$(P \rightarrow (R \wedge Q))$

Here is a semantic check of the argument.

			premise	premise		conclusion
P	Q	R	$(P \rightarrow Q)$	$(P \rightarrow R)$	$(R \wedge Q)$	$(P \rightarrow (R \wedge Q))$
T	T	T	T	T	T	T
T	T	F	T	F	F	F
T	F	T	F	T	F	F
T	F	F	F	F	F	F
F	T	T	T	T	T	T
F	T	F	T	T	F	T
F	F	T	T	T	F	T
F	F	F	T	T	F	T

We have highlighted the rows where the premises are all true. Note that for these, the conclusion is true. Thus, in any kind of situation in which all the premises are true, the conclusion is true. This is equivalent, we have noted, to our definition of valid: necessarily, if all the premises are true, the conclusion is true. So this is a valid argument. The third column of the analyzed sentences (the column for $(R \wedge Q)$) is there so that we can identify when the conclusion is true. The conclusion is a conditional, and we needed to know, for each kind of situation, if its antecedent P, and if its consequent $(R \wedge Q)$, are true. The third column tells us the situations in which the consequent is true. The stipulations on the left tell us in what kind of situation the antecedent P is true.

5.6 Problems

1. Translate the following sentences into our logical language. You will need to create your own key to do so.

    a. Ulysses, who is crafty, is from Ithaca.
    b. Ulysses, who isn't crafty, is from Ithaca.
    c. Ulysses, who is crafty, isn't from Ithaca.
    d. Ulysses isn't both crafty and from Ithaca.
    e. Ulysses will go home only if he's from Ithaca and not Troy.
    f. Ulysses is not both from Ithaca and Troy, though he is crafty.
    g. If Ulysses outsmarts both Circes and the Cyclops, then he can go home.
    h. If Ulysses outsmarts Circes but not the Cyclops, then he will be eaten.
    i. Though he won't outsmart Circe, Ulysses will outsmart the Cyclops, even given that he is from Ithaca.
    j. Ulysses won't outsmart both Circes and the Cyclops, but he won't be eaten and will go home even though he is from Ithaca.

2. Prove the following arguments are valid, using a direct derivation.

    a. Premise: $((P \rightarrow Q) \wedge \neg Q)$. Conclusion: $\neg P$.
    b. Premises: $(((P \rightarrow Q) \wedge (Q \rightarrow R)) \wedge P)$. Conclusion: R.
    c. Premises: $((P \rightarrow Q) \wedge (R \rightarrow S)), (\neg Q \wedge \neg S)$. Conclusion: $(\neg P \wedge \neg R)$.
    d. Premises: $((R \wedge S) \rightarrow T), (Q \wedge \neg T)$. Conclusion: $\neg(R \wedge S)$.
    e. Premises: $(P \rightarrow (Q \rightarrow R)), (Q \wedge P)$. Conclusion: R.
    f. Premises: $(P \rightarrow (Q \rightarrow R)), (\neg R \wedge P)$. Conclusion: $\neg Q$.
    g. Premises: $((P \wedge Q) \rightarrow (R \rightarrow S)), (Q \wedge (P \wedge \neg S))$. Conclusion: $(\neg R \wedge Q)$.
    h. Premises: $((P \rightarrow Q) \wedge (R \rightarrow S)), (P \wedge R)$. Conclusion: $((P \wedge Q) \wedge (R \wedge S))$.

3. Make truth tables for the following complex sentences. Identify which are tautologies.

    a. $\neg(P \wedge Q)$

b. ¬(¬P → ¬Q)

c. (P ∧ ¬P)

d. ¬(P ∧ ¬P)

e. (((P → Q)∧ ¬Q) → ¬P)

f. (((P → Q)∧ ¬P) → ¬Q)

g. (((P → Q)∧ P) → Q)

h. (((P → Q)∧ Q) → P)

4. Make truth tables to show when the following sentences are true and when they are false. State which of these sentences are equivalent. Also, can you identify if any have the same truth table as some of our connectives?

a. ¬(P∧Q)

b. (¬P∧¬Q)

c. ¬(¬P∧¬Q)

d. ¬(P → Q)

e. (P∧¬Q)

f. (¬P∧Q)

g. ¬(P → ¬Q)

h. ¬(¬P → ¬Q)

i. (P ∧ (Q ∧ R))

j. ((P ∧ Q) ∧ R))

k. (P → (Q → R))

l. ((P → Q) → R))

5. Write a valid argument in normal colloquial English with at least two premises, one of which is a conjunction or includes a conjunction. Your argument should just be a paragraph (not an ordered list of sentences or anything else that looks like formal logic). Translate the argument into propositional logic. Prove it is valid.

6. Write a valid argument in normal colloquial English with at least three premises, one of which is a conjunction or includes a conjunction and one of which is a conditional or includes a conditional. Translate the argument into propositional logic. Prove it is valid.

7. Often in a natural language like English, there are many implicit conjunctions in descriptions and other phrases. Here are some passages from litera-

ture. Translate them into our propositional logic. You will want to make a separate key for each particular problem.

   a. "But Achilles the son of Peleus again shouted at Agamemnon the son of Atreus, for he was still in a rage."
      (Homer, *The Illiad*)

   b. "Socrates is an evil-doer, and a curious person, who searches into things under the earth and in heaven, and he makes the worse appear the better cause...." (Plato, *The Apology*)

   c. "Incensed with indignation, Satan stood Unterrified...." (Milton, *Paradise Lost*)

   d. "Teiresias, seer who comprehends all...
      You know, though thy blind eyes see nothing,
      What plague infects our city Thebes." (Sophocles, *Oedipus Rex*)

   e. "Scrooge! a squeezing, wrenching, grasping, scraping, clutching, covetous, old sinner!" (Charles Dickens, "A Christmas Carrol")

   f. "When I wrote the following pages, or rather the bulk of them, I lived alone, in the woods, a mile from any neighbor, in a house which I had built myself, on the shore of Walden Pond, in Concord, Massachusetts, and earned my living by the labor of my hands only." [Here one can substitute "Thoreau" for "I" in the translation, if helpful.]. (Henry David Thoreau, *Walden*)

   g. "In appearance Shatov was in complete harmony with his convictions: he was short, awkward, had a shock of flaxen hair, broad shoulders, thick lips, very thick overhanging white eyebrows, a wrinkled forehead, and a hostile, obstinately downcast, as it were shamefaced, expression in his eyes." (Fyodor Dostoevsky, *The Possessed*)

8. Make your own key to translate the following argument into our propositional logic. Translate only the parts in bold. Prove the argument is valid.

   "I suspect Dr. Kronecker of the crime of stealing Cantor's book," Inspector Tarski said. His assistant, Mr. Carroll, waited patiently for his reasoning. "For," Tarski said, "The thief left cigarette ashes on the table. The thief also did not wear shoes, but slipped silently into the room. Thus, **If Dr. Kronecker smokes and is in his stocking feet, then he most likely stole Cantor's book.**" At this point, Tarski pointed at Kronecker's feet. "**Dr. Kronecker is in his stocking feet.**" Tarski reached forward and pulled from Kronecker's pocket a gold cigarette case. "And **Kronecker smokes.**"

Mr. Carroll nodded sagely, "Your conclusion is obvious: **Dr. Kronecker most likely stole Cantor's book.**"

6. Conditional Derivations

6.1 An argument from Hobbes

In his great work, *Leviathan*, the philosopher Thomas Hobbes (1588-1679) gives an important argument for government. Hobbes begins by claiming that without a common power, our condition is very poor indeed. He calls this state without government, "the state of nature", and claims

> Hereby it is manifest that during the time men live without a common power to keep them all in awe, they are in that condition which is called war; and such a war as is of every man against every man.... In such condition there is no place for industry, because the fruit thereof is uncertain: and consequently no culture of the earth; no navigation, nor use of the commodities that may be imported by sea; no commodious building; no instruments of moving and removing such things as require much force; no knowledge of the face of the earth; no account of time; no arts; no letters; no society; and which is worst of all, continual fear, and danger of violent death; and the life of man, solitary, poor, nasty, brutish, and short.[8]

Hobbes developed what is sometimes called "contract theory". This is a view of government in which one views the state as the product of a rational contract. Although we inherit our government, the idea is that in some sense we would find it rational to choose the government, were we ever in the position to do so. So, in the passage above, Hobbes claims that in this state of nature, we have absolute freedom, but this leads to universal struggle between all people. There can be no property, for example, if there is no power to enforce property rights. You are free to take other people's things, but they are also free to take yours. Only violence can discourage such theft. But, a common power, like a king, can enforce rules, such as property rights. To have this common power, we must give up some freedoms. You are (or should be, if it were ever up to you) willing to give up those freedoms because of the benefits that you get from this. For example, you are willing to give up the freedom to just seize people's goods, because you like even more that other people cannot seize your goods.

We can reconstruct Hobbes's defense of government, greatly simplified, as being something like this:

> If we want to be safe, then we should have a state that can protect us.
>
> If we should have a state that can protect us, then we should give up some freedoms.
>
> Therefore, if we want to be safe, then we should give up some freedoms.

Let us use the following translation key.

> P: We want to be safe.
>
> Q: We should have a state that can protect us.
>
> R: We should give up some freedoms.

The argument in our logical language would then be:

> $(P \rightarrow Q)$
>
> $(Q \rightarrow R)$
>
> _____
>
> $(P \rightarrow R)$

This is a valid argument. Let's take the time to show this with a truth table.

P	Q	R	premise $(P \rightarrow Q)$	premise $(Q \rightarrow R)$	conclusion $(P \rightarrow R)$
T	T	T	T	T	T
T	T	F	T	F	F
T	F	T	F	T	T
T	F	F	F	T	F
F	T	T	T	T	T
F	T	F	T	F	T
F	F	T	T	T	T
F	F	F	T	T	T

The rows in which all the premises are true are the first, fifth, seventh, and eighth rows. Note that in each such row, the conclusion is true. Thus, in any kind of situation where the premises are true, the conclusion is true. This is our semantics for a valid argument.

What syntactic method can we use to prove this argument is valid? Right now, we have none. Other than double negation, we cannot even apply any of our inference rules using these premises.

Some logic systems introduce a rule to capture this inference; this rule is typically called the "chain rule". But, there is a more general principle at stake here: we need a way to show conditionals. So we want to take another approach to showing this argument is valid.

6.2 Conditional derivation

As a handy rule of thumb, we can think of the inference rules as providing a way to either show a kind of sentence, or to make use of a kind of sentence. For example, adjunction allows us to show a conjunction. Simplification allows us to make use of a conjunction. But this pattern is not complete: we have rules to make use of a conditional (modus ponens and modus tollens), but no rule to show a conditional.

We will want to have some means to prove a conditional, because sometimes an argument will have a conditional as a conclusion. It is not clear what rule we should introduce, however. The conditional is true when the antecedent is false, or if both the antecedent and the consequent are true. That's a rather messy affair for making an inference rule.

However, think about what the conditional asserts: if the antecedent is true, then the consequent is true. We can make use of this idea not with an inference rule, but rather in the very structure of a proof. We treat the proof as embodying a conditional relationship.

Our idea is this: let us assume some sentence, Φ. If we can then prove another sentence Ψ, we will have proved that if Φ is true then Ψ is true. The proof structure will thus have a shape like this:

$$\begin{array}{c|l} & \quad\phi \\ & \quad\vdots \\ & \quad\psi \\ \triangleright & (\phi \to \psi) \end{array}$$

The last line of the proof is justified by the shape of the proof: by assuming that Φ is true, and then using our inference rules to prove Ψ, we know that if Φ is true then Ψ is true. And this is just what the conditional asserts.

This method is sometimes referred to as an application of the deduction theorem. In chapter 17 we will prove the deduction theorem. Here, instead, we shall think of this as a proof method, traditionally called "conditional derivation".

A conditional derivation is like a direct derivation, but with two differences. First, along with the premises, you get a single special assumption, called "the assumption for conditional derivation". Second, you do not aim to show your conclusion, but rather the consequent of your conclusion. So, to show (Φ → Ψ) you will always assume Φ and try to show Ψ. Also, in our logical system, a conditional derivation will always be a subproof. A subproof is a proof within another proof. We always start with a direct proof, and then do the conditional proof within that direct proof.

Here is how we would apply the proof method to prove the validity of Hobbes's argument, as we reconstructed it above.

1. (P → Q)	premise
2. (Q → R))	premise
3. P	assumption for conditional derivation
4 Q	modus ponens, 1, 3
5. R	modus ponens, 2, 4
6. (P → R)	conditional derivation, 3-5

Our Fitch bars make clear what is a sub-proof here; they let us see this as a direct derivation with a conditional derivation embedded in it. This is an important concept: we can have proofs within proofs.

An important principle is that once a subproof is done, we cannot use any of the lines in the subproof. We need this rule because conditional derivation allowed us to make a special assumption that we use only temporarily. Above, we assumed **P**. Our goal is only to show that if **P** is true, then **R** is true. But perhaps **P** isn't true. We do not want to later make use of **P** for some other purpose. So, we have the rule that when a subproof is complete, you cannot use the lines that occur in the subproof. In this case, that means that we cannot use lines 3, 4, or 5 for any other purpose than to show the conditional **(P → R)**. We cannot now cite those individual lines again. We can, however, use line 6, the conclusion of the subproof.

The Fitch bars—which we have used before now in our proofs only to separate the premises from the later steps—now have a very beneficial use. They allow us to set aside a conditional derivation as a subproof, and they help remind us that we cannot cite the lines in that subproof once the subproof is complete.

It might be helpful to give an example of why this is necessary. That is, it might be helpful to give an example of an argument made invalid because it makes use of lines in a finished subproof. Consider the following argument.

If you are Pope, then you have a home in the Vatican.

If you have a home in the Vatican, then you hear church bells often.

———

If you are Pope, then you hear church bells often.

That is a valid argument, with the same form as the argument we adopted from Hobbes. However, if we broke our rule about conditional derivations, we could prove that you are Pope. Let's use this key:

S: You are Pope.

T: You have a home in the Vatican.

U: You hear church bells often.

Now consider this "proof":

```
 1. (S → T)                                    premise
 2. (T → U))                                   premise


     3. S                                      assumption for conditional derivation

     4 T                                       modus ponens, 1, 3
     5. U                                      modus ponens, 2, 4
 6. (S → U)                                    conditional derivation, 3-5
 7. S                                          repeat, 3
```

And, thus, we have proven that you are Pope. But, of course, you are not the Pope. From true premises, we ended up with a false conclusion, so the argument is obviously invalid. What went wrong? The problem was that after we completed the conditional derivation that occurs in lines 3 through 5, and used that conditional derivation to assert line 6, we can no longer use those lines 3 through 5. But on line 7 we made use of line 3. Line 3 is not something we know to be true; our reasoning from lines 3 through line 5 was to ask, if S were true, what else would be true? When we are done with that conditional derivation, we can use only the conditional that we derived, and not the steps used in the conditional derivation.

6.3 Some additional examples

Here are a few kinds of arguments that help illustrate the power of the conditional derivation.

This argument makes use of conjunctions.

$(P \rightarrow Q)$

$(R \rightarrow S)$

_____

$((P \wedge R) \rightarrow (Q \wedge S))$

We always begin by constructing a direct proof, using the Fitch bar to identify the premises of our argument, if any.

| 1. $(P \rightarrow Q)$ | premise |
| 2. $(R \rightarrow S)$ | premise |

Because the conclusion is a conditional, we assume the antecedent and show the consequent.

1. $(P \rightarrow Q)$	premise
2. $(R \rightarrow S)$	premise
3. $(P \wedge R)$	assumption for conditional derivation
4 P	simplification, 3
5. Q	modus ponens, 1, 4
6. R	simplification, 3
7. S	modus ponens, 2, 6
8. $(Q \wedge S)$	adjunction, 5, 7
9. $((P \wedge R) \rightarrow (Q \wedge S))$	conditional derivation, 3-8

Here's another example. Note that the following argument is valid.

$(P \rightarrow (S \rightarrow R))$

$(P \rightarrow (Q \rightarrow S))$

_____

$(P \rightarrow (Q \rightarrow R))$

The proof will require several embedded subproofs.

```
  │ 1. (P → (S → R))                      premise
  │ 2. (P → (Q → S))                      premise
  │
  │ │ 3. P                                assumption for conditional derivation
  │ │
  │ │ │ 4. Q                              assumption for conditional derivation
  │ │ │ 5. (Q → S)                        modus ponens, 2, 3
  │ │ │ 6. S                              modus ponens, 5, 4
  │ │ │ 7. (S → R)                        modus ponens, 1, 3
  │ │ │ 8. R                              modus ponens, 7, 6
  │ │ 9. (Q → R)                          conditional derivation, 4-8
  │ 10. (P → (Q → R))                     conditional derivation, 3-9
```

6.4 Theorems

Conditional derivation allows us to see an important new concept. Consider the following sentence:

$$((P \to Q) \to (\neg Q \to \neg P))$$

This sentence is a tautology. To check this, we can make its truth table.

P	Q	¬Q	¬P	(P → Q)	(¬Q → ¬P)	((P → Q) → (¬Q → ¬P))
T	T	F	F	T	T	T
T	F	T	F	F	F	T
F	T	F	T	T	T	T
F	F	T	T	T	T	T

This sentence is true in every kind of situation, which is what we mean by a "tautology".

Now reflect on our definition of "valid": necessarily, if the premises are true, then the conclusion is true. What about an argument in which the conclusion is a tautology? By our definition of "valid", an argument with a conclusion that must be true must be a valid argument—no matter what the premises are! (If this confuses you, look back at the truth table for the conditional. Our definition of valid includes the conditional: if the premises are true, then the conclusion is true. Suppose now our conclusion must be true. Any conditional with a true consequent is true. So the definition of "valid" must be true of any argument with a tautology as a conclusion.) And, given that, it would seem that it is irrelevant whether we have any premises at all, since any will do. This suggests that there can be valid arguments with no premises.

Conditional derivation lets us actually construct such arguments. First, we will draw our Fitch bar for our main argument to indicate that we have no premises. Then, we will construct a conditional derivation. It will start like this:

1. (P → Q)   assumption for conditional derivation

But what now? Well, we have assumed the antecedent of our sentence, and we should strive now to show the consequent. But note that the consequent is a conditional. So, we will again do a conditional derivation.

1. (P → Q)   assumption for conditional derivation

2. ¬Q   assumption for conditional derivation

3. ¬P   modus tollens, 1, 2

4. (¬Q → ¬P)   conditional derivation, 2-3

5. ((P → Q) → (¬Q → ¬P))   conditional derivation, 1-4

This is a proof, without premises, of ((P→Q)→(¬Q→¬P)). The top of the proof shows that we have no premises. Our conclusion is a conditional, so, on line 1, we assumed the antecedent of the conditional. We now have to show the consequent of the conditional; but the consequent of the conditional is also a conditional, so we assumed its antecedent on line 2. Line 4 is the result of the conditional derivation from lines 2 to 3. Lines 1 through 4 tell us that if (P→Q) is true, then (¬Q→¬P) is true. And that is what we conclude on line 5.

We call a sentence that can be proved without premises a "theorem". Theorems are special because they reveal the things that follow from logic alone. It is a very great benefit of our propositional logic that all the theorems are tautologies. It is an equally great benefit of our propositional logic that all the tautologies are theorems. Nonetheless, these concepts are different. "Tautology" refers to a semantic concept: a tautology is a sentence that must be true. "Theorem" refers to a concept of syntax and derivation: a theorem is a sentence that can be derived without premises.

Theorem: a sentence that can be proved without premises.

Tautology: a sentence of the propositional logic that must be true.

6.5 Problems

1. Prove the following arguments are valid. This will require conditional derivation.

    a. Premise: (¬Q → ¬P). Conclusion: (P → Q).
    b. Premise: (P→Q), (Q→R). Conclusion: (P→R).
    c. Premises: (P → (Q → R)), Q. Conclusion: (P→R).
    d. Premise: (P→Q), (S→R). Conclusion: ((¬Q ∧ ¬R) → (¬P ∧ ¬S)).
    e. Premise: (P→Q). Conclusion: ((P ∧ R) → Q).
    f. Premise: ((R∧Q) → S), (¬P → (R∧Q)). Conclusion: (¬S → P).
    g. Premise: (P → ¬Q). Conclusion: (Q → ¬P).
    h. Premises: (P→Q), (P→R). Conclusion:(P→(Q∧R))).
    i. Premises: (P→ (Q ∧ S)), (Q → R), (S → T). Conclusion: (P→ (R ∧ T)).
    j. Premises: (P → (Q → R)), (P → (S → T)),(Q ∧ S). Conclusion: (P→ (R ∧ T)).

2. Prove the following theorems.

    a. (P→P).
    b. ((P → Q) → ((R → P) → (R → Q))).
    c. ((P → (Q → R)) → ((P → Q) → (P → R)).
    d. ((¬P → Q) → (¬Q → P)).
    e. (((P → Q) ∧ (P → R)) → (P → (Q∧R))).

3. Make a truth table for each of the following complex sentences, in order to see when it is true or false. Identify which are tautologies. Prove the tau-

tologies.

    a. $((P \to Q) \to Q)$.
    b. $(P \to (Q \to Q))$.
    c. $((P \to Q) \to P)$.
    d. $(P \to (Q \to P))$.
    e. $(P \to (P \to Q))$.
    f. $((P \to P) \to Q))$.
    g. $(P \to \neg P)$.
    h. $(P \to \neg\neg P)$.
    i. $((P \to Q) \to (P \wedge Q))$.
    j. $((P \wedge Q) \to (P \to Q))$.

4. In normal colloquial English, write your own valid argument with at least two premises and with a conclusion that is a conditional. Your argument should just be a paragraph (not an ordered list of sentences or anything else that looks like formal logic). Translate it into propositional logic and prove it is valid.

5. Translate the following passage into our propositional logic. Prove the argument is valid.

> Either Beneke or Mill is the culprit who burned the Logician's Club. Also, if Beneke did it, then he bought the flares. But if Beneke bought the flares, he was at the Mariner's Shop yesterday. Thus, if Beneke was not at the Mariner's Shop yesterday, Mill did it.

---

[8] Hobbes (1886: 64).

7. "Or"

7.1 A historical example: The Euthryphro argument

The philosopher Plato (who lived from approximately 427 BC to 347 BC) wrote a series of great philosophical texts. Plato was the first philosopher to deploy argument in a vigorous and consistent way, and in so doing he showed how philosophy takes logic as its essential method. We think of Plato as the principal founder of Western philosophy. The American philosopher Alfred Whitehead (1861-1947) in fact once famously quipped that philosophy is a "series of footnotes to Plato".

Plato's teacher was Socrates (c. 469-399 B.C.), a gadfly of ancient Athens who made many enemies by showing people how little they knew. Socrates did not write anything, but most of Plato's writings are dialogues, which are like small plays, in which Socrates is the protagonist of the philosophical drama that ensues. Several of the dialogues are named after the person who will be seen arguing with Socrates. In the dialogue *Euthyphro*, Socrates is standing in line, awaiting his trial. He has been accused of corrupting the youth of Athens. A trial in ancient Athens was essentially a debate before the assembled citizen men of the city. Before Socrates in line is a young man, Euthyphro. Socrates asks Euthyphro what his business is that day, and Euthyphro proudly proclaims he is there to charge his own father with murder. Socrates is shocked. In ancient Athens, respect for one's father was highly valued and expected. Socrates, with characteristic sarcasm, tells Euthyphro that he must be very wise to be so confident. Here are two profound and conflicting duties: to respect one's father, and to punish murder. Euthyphro seems to find it very easy to decide which is the greater duty. Euthyphro is not bothered. To him, these ethical matters are simple: one should be pious. When Socrates demands a definition of piety that applies to all pious acts, Euthyphro says,

> Piety is that which is loved by the gods and impiety is that which is not loved by them.

Socrates observes that this is ambiguous. It could mean, an act is good because the gods love that act. Or it could mean, the gods love an act because it is good. We have, then, an "or" statement, which logicians call a "disjunction":

> Either an act is good because the gods love that act, or the gods love an act because it is good.

Might the former be true? This view—that an act is good because the gods love it—is now called "divine command theory", and theists have disagreed since Socrates's time about whether it is true. But, Socrates finds it absurd. For, if tomorrow the gods love, say, murder, then, tomorrow murder would be good.

Euthyphro comes to agree that it cannot be that an act is good because the gods love that act. Our argument so far has this form:

> Either an act is good because the gods love that act, or the gods love an act because it is good.

> It is not the case that an act is good because the gods love it.

Socrates concludes that the gods love an act because it is good.

> Either an act is good because the gods love that act, or the gods love an act because it is good.

> It is not the case that an act is good because the gods love it.

> _____

> The gods love an act because it is good.

This argument is one of the most important arguments in philosophy. Most philosophers consider some version of this argument both valid and sound. Some who disagree with it bite the bullet and claim that if tomorrow God (most theistic philosophers alive today are monotheists) loved puppy torture, adultery, random acts of cruelty, pollution, and lying, these would all be good things. (If you are inclined to say, "That is not fair, God would never love those things", then you have already agreed with Socrates. For, the reason you believe that God would never love these kinds of acts is because these kinds of acts are bad. But then, being bad or good is something independent of the love of God.) But most philosophers agree with Socrates: they find it absurd to believe that random acts of cruelty and other such acts could be good. There is something inherently bad to these acts, they believe. The importance of the Euthyphro argument is not that it helps illustrate that divine command theory is an enormously strange and costly position to hold (though that is an important outcome), but rather that the argument shows ethics can be studied independently of theology. For, if there is something about acts that makes them good or bad independently of a god's will, then we do not have to study a god's will to study what makes those acts good or bad.

Of course, many philosophers are atheists so they already believed this, but for most of philosophy's history, one was obliged to be a theist. Even today, lay people tend to think of ethics as an extension of religion. Philosophers believe instead that ethics is its own field of study. The Euthyphro argument explains why, even if you are a theist, you can study ethics independently of studying theology.

But is Socrates's argument valid? Is it sound?

7.2 The disjunction

We want to extend our language so that it can represent sentences that contain an "or". Sentences like

> Tom will go to Berlin or Paris.

> We have coffee or tea.

> This web page contains the phrase "Mark Twain" or "Samuel Clemens."

Logicians call these kinds of sentences "disjunctions". Each of the two parts of a disjunction is called a "disjunct". The idea is that these are really equivalent to the following sentences:

> Tom will go to Berlin or Tom will go to Paris.

> We have coffee or we have tea.

> This web page contains the phrase "Mark Twain" or this web page contains the phrase "Samuel Clemens."

We can, therefore, see that (at least in many sentences) the "or" operates as a connective between two sentences.

It is traditional to use the symbol "v" for "or". This comes from the Latin "vel," meaning (in some contexts) *or*.

The syntax for the disjunction is very basic. If Φ and Ψ are sentences, then

$$(\Phi \text{ v } \Psi)$$

is a sentence.

The semantics is a little more controversial. This much of the defining truth table, most people find obvious:

Φ	Ψ	(ΦvΨ)
T	T	
T	F	T
F	T	T
F	F	F

Consider: if I promise that I will bring you roses or lilacs, then it seems that I told the truth either if I have brought you roses but not lilacs, or if I brought you lilacs but not roses. Similarly, the last row should be intuitive, also. If I promise I will bring you roses or lilacs, and I bring you nothing, then I spoke falsely.

What about the first row? Many people who are not logicians want it to be the case that we define this condition as false. The resulting meaning would correspond to what is sometimes called the "exclusive 'or'". Logicians disagree. They favor the definition where a disjunction is true if its two parts are true; this is sometimes called the "inclusive 'or'". Of course, all that matters is that we pick a definition and stick with it, but we can offer some reasons why the "inclusive 'or'", as we call it, is more general than the "exclusive 'or'".

Consider the first two sentences above. It seems that the first sentence—"Tom will go to Berlin or Paris"—should be true if Tom goes to both. Or consider the second sentence, "We have coffee or tea." In most restaurants, this means they have both coffee and they have tea, but they expect that you will order only one of these. After all, it would be strange to be told that they have coffee or tea, and then be told that it is false that they have both coffee and tea. Or, similarly, suppose the waiter said, "We have coffee or tea", and then you said "I'll have both", and the waiter replied "We don't have both". This would seem strange. But if you find it strange, then you implicitly agree that the disjunction should be interpreted as the inclusive "or".

Examples like these suggest to logicians that the inclusive "or" (where the first row of the table is true) is the default case, and that the context of our speech tells us when not both disjuncts are true. For example, when a restaurant has a fixed price menu—where you pay one fee and then get either steak or lobster—it is understood by the context that this means you can have one or the other but not both. But that is not logic, that is social custom. One must know about restaurants to determine this.

Thus, it is customary to define the semantics of the disjunction as

Φ	Ψ	$(\Phi \lor \Psi)$
T	T	T
T	F	T
F	T	T
F	F	F

We haven't lost the ability to express the exclusive "or". We can say, "one or the other but not both", which is expressed by the formula "$((\Phi \lor \Psi) \land \neg(\Phi \land \Psi))$". To check, we can make the truth table for this complex expression:

Φ	Ψ	$(\Phi \land \Psi)$	$(\Phi \lor \Psi)$	$\neg(\Phi \land \Psi)$	$((\Phi \lor \Psi) \land \neg(\Phi \land \Psi))$
T	T	T	T	F	F
T	F	F	T	T	T
F	T	F	T	T	T
F	F	F	F	T	F

Note that this formula is equivalent to the exclusive "or" (it is true when Φ is true or Ψ is true, but not when both are true or both are false). So, if we need to say something like the exclusive "or", we can do so.

7.3 Alternative forms

There do not seem to be many alternative expressions in English equivalent to the "or". We have

P or Q

Either P or Q

These are both expressed in our logic with (P v Q).

One expression that does arise in English is "neither...nor...". This expression seems best captured by simply making it into "not either... or...". Let's test this proposal. Consider the sentence

Neither Smith nor Jones will go to London.

This sentence expresses the idea that Smith will not go to London, and that Jones will not go to London. So, it would surely be a mistake to express it as

Either Smith will not go to London or Jones will not go to London.

Why? Because this latter sentence would be true if one of them went to London and one of them did not. Consider the truth table for this expression to see this. Use the following translation key.

P: Smith will go to London.

Q: Jones will go to London.

Then suppose we did (wrongly) translate "Neither Smith nor Jones will go to London" with

(¬P v ¬Q)

Here is the truth table for this expression.

P	Q	¬Q	¬P	(¬P∨¬Q)
T	*T*	*F*	*F*	*F*
T	*F*	*T*	*F*	*T*
F	*T*	*F*	*T*	*T*
F	*F*	*T*	*T*	*T*

Note that this sentence is true if P is true and Q is false, or if Q is true and P is false. In other words, it is true if one of the two goes to London. That's not what we mean in English by that sentence claiming that neither of them will go to London.

The better translation is ¬(P∨Q).

P	Q	(P∨Q)	¬(P∨Q)
T	*T*	*T*	*F*
T	*F*	*T*	*F*
F	*T*	*T*	*F*
F	*F*	*F*	*T*

This captures the idea well: it is only true if each does not go to London. So, we can simply translate "neither...nor..." as "It is not the case that either... or...".

7.4 Reasoning with disjunctions

How shall we reason with the disjunction? Looking at the truth table that defines the disjunction, we find that we do not know much if we are told that, say, (P ∨ Q). P could be true, or it could be false. The same is so for Q. All we know is that they cannot both be false.

This does suggest a reasonable and useful kind of inference rule. If we have a disjunction, and we discover that half of it is false, then we know that the other half must be true. This is true for either disjunct. This means we have two rules, but we can group together both rules with a single name and treat them as one rule:

$$(\Phi \lor \Psi)$$

$$\neg\Phi$$

———

$$\Psi$$

and

$$(\Phi \lor \Psi)$$

$$\neg\Psi$$

———

$$\Phi$$

This rule is traditionally called "modus tollendo ponens".

What if we are required to show a disjunction? One insight we can use is that if some sentence is true, then any disjunction that contains it is true. This is so whether the sentence makes up the first or second disjunct. Again, then, we would have two rules, which we can group together under one name:

$$\Phi$$

———

$$(\Phi \lor \Psi)$$

and

$$\Psi$$

———

$$(\Phi \lor \Psi)$$

This rule is often called "addition".

The addition rule often confuses students. It seems to be a cheat, as if we are getting away with something for free. But a moment of reflection will help clarify that just the opposite is true. We lose information when we use the addition rule.

If you ask me where John is, and I say, "John is in New York", I told you more than if I answered you, "John is either in New York or in New Jersey". Just so, when we go from some sentence P to (PvQ), we did not get something for free.

This rule does have the seemingly odd consequence that from, say, 2+2=4 you can derive that either 2+2=4 or 7=0. But that only seems odd because in normal speech, we have a number of implicit rules. The philosopher Paul Grice (1913-1988) described some of these rules, and we sometimes call the rules he described "Grice's Maxims".[9] He observed that in conversation we expect people to give all the information required but not more; to try to be truthful; to say things that are relevant; and to be clear and brief and orderly. So, in normal English conversations, if someone says, "Tom is in New York or New Jersey," they would be breaking the rule to give enough information, and to say what is relevant, if they knew that Tom was in New York. This also means that we expect people to use a disjunction when they have reason to believe that either or both disjuncts could be true. But our logical language is designed only to be precise, and we have been making the language precise by specifying when a sentence is true or false, and by specifying the relations between sentences in terms of their truth values. We are thus not representing, and not putting into our language, Grice's maxims of conversation. It remains true that if you knew Tom is in New York, but answered my question "Where is Tom?" by saying "Tom is in New York or New Jersey", then you have wasted my time. But you did not say something false.

We are now in a position to test Socrates's argument. Using the following translation key, we can translate the argument into symbolic form.

P: An act is good because the gods love that act.

Q: The gods love an act because it is good.

Euthyphro had argued

| 1. (P ∨ Q) | premise |

Socrates had got Euthryphro to admit that

```
| 1. (P ∨ Q)                    premise
| 2. ¬P                         premise
```

And so we have a simple direct derivation:

```
| 1. (P ∨ Q)                    premise
| 2. ¬P                         premise
| 3. Q                          modus tollendo ponens, 1, 2
```

Socrates's argument is valid. I will leave it up to you to determine whether Socrates's argument is sound.

Another example might be helpful. Here is an argument in our logical language.

(P v Q)

¬P

(¬P → (Q → R))

———

(R v S)

This will make use of the addition rule, and so is useful to illustrating that rule's application. Here is one possible proof.

```
| 1. (P ∨ Q)                    premise
| 2. ¬P                         premise
| 3. (¬P → (Q → R))             premise
| 4. Q                          modus tollendo ponens, 1, 2
| 5. (Q → R)                    modus ponens, 3, 2
| 6. R                          modus ponens, 5, 4
| 7. (R ∨ S)                    addition, 6
```

7.5 Alternative symbolizations of disjunction

We are fortunate that there have been no popular alternatives to the use of "v" as a symbol for disjunction. Perhaps the second most widely used alternative symbol was "||", such that (P v Q) would be symbolized:

(P || Q)

7.6 Problems

1. Prove the following using a derivation.

   a. Premises: (PvQ), (Q → S), (¬S^T). Conclusion: (T^P).
   b. Premises: ((P → ¬Q) ^ (R → S)), (Q v R). Conclusion: (P → S).
   c. Premises: ((P^Q) v R), ((P^Q) → S), ¬S. Conclusion: R.
   d. Premises: (RvS), ((S → T) ^ V), ¬T, ((R^V) → P). Conclusion: (PvQ).
   e. Premises: ((P → Q) v (¬R → S)), ((P → Q) → T), (¬T ^ ¬S). Conclusion: (R v V).
   f. Premises: (P v S), (T → ¬S), T. Conclusion: ((P v Q) v R).
   g. Conclusion: (P → (PvQ)).
   h. Conclusion: ((PvQ) → (¬P → Q)).
   i. Conclusion: ((PvQ) → (¬Q → P)).
   j. Conclusion: (((PvQ) ^ (¬Q v ¬R)) → (R → P)).

2. Consider the following four cards in figure 7.1. Each card has a letter on one side, and a shape on the other side.

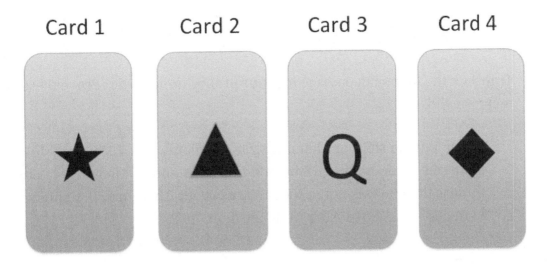

Card 1   Card 2   Card 3   Card 4

Figure 7.1

For each of the following claims, determine (1) the minimum number of cards you must turn over to check the claim, and (2) what those cards are, in order to determine if the claim is true of all four cards.

    a. If there is a P or Q on the letter side of the card, then there is a diamond on the shape side of the card.

    b. If there is a Q on the letter side of the card, then there is either a diamond or a star on the shape side of the card.

3. In normal colloquial English, write your own valid argument with at least two premises, at least one of which is a disjunction. Your argument should just be a paragraph (not an ordered list of sentences or anything else that looks like formal logic). Translate it into propositional logic and prove it is valid.

4. Translate the following passage into our propositional logic. Prove the argument is valid.

> Either Dr. Kronecker or Bishop Berkeley killed Colonel Cardinality. If Dr. Kronecker killed Colonel Cardinality, then Dr. Kronecker was in the kitchen. If Bishop Berkeley killed Colonel Cardinality, then he was in the drawing room. If Bishop Berkeley was in the drawing room, then he was

wearing boots. But Bishop Berkeley was not wearing boots. So, Dr. Kronecker killed the Colonel.

5. Translate the following passage into our propositional logic. Prove the argument is valid.

Either Wittgenstein or Meinong stole the diamonds. If Meinong stole the diamonds, then he was in the billiards room. But if Meinong was in the library, then he was not in the billiards room. Therefore, if Meinong was in the library, Wittgenstein stole the diamonds.

---

[9] Grice (1975).

8. Reductio ad Absurdum

8.1 A historical example

In his book, *The Two New Sciences*,[10] Galileo Galilea (1564-1642) gives several arguments meant to demonstrate that there can be no such thing as actual infinities or actual infinitesimals. One of his arguments can be reconstructed in the following way. Galileo proposes that we take as a premise that there is an actual infinity of natural numbers (the natural numbers are the positive whole numbers from 1 on):

$$\{1, \quad 2, \quad 3, \quad 4, \quad 5, \quad 6, \quad 7, \; ....\}$$

He also proposes that we take as a premise that there is an actual infinity of the squares of the natural numbers.

$$\{1, \quad 4, \quad 9, \quad 16, \quad 25, \quad 36, \quad 49, \; ....\}$$

Now, Galileo reasons, note that these two groups (today we would call them "sets") have the same size. We can see this because we can see that there is a one-to-one correspondence between the two groups.

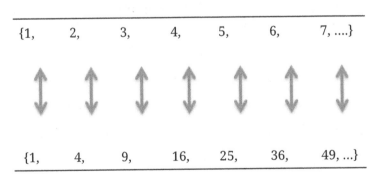

If we can associate every natural number with one and only one square number, and if we can associate every square number with one and only one natural number, then these sets must be the same size.

But wait a moment, Galileo says. There are obviously very many more natural numbers than there are square numbers. That is, every square number is in the list of natural numbers, but many of the natural numbers are not in the list of square numbers. The following numbers are all in the list of natural numbers but not in the list of square numbers.

$$\{2, \quad 3, \quad 5, \quad 6, \quad 7, \quad 8, \quad 10, \ldots\}$$

So, Galileo reasons, if there are many numbers in the group of natural numbers that are not in the group of the square numbers, and if there are no numbers in the group of the square numbers that are not in the naturals numbers, then the natural numbers is bigger than the square numbers. And if the group of the natural numbers is bigger than the group of the square numbers, then the natural numbers and the square numbers are not the same size.

We have reached two conclusions: the set of the natural numbers and the set of the square numbers are the same size; and, the set of the natural numbers and the set of the square numbers are not the same size. That's contradictory.

Galileo argues that the reason we reached a contradiction is because we assumed that there are actual infinities. He concludes, therefore, that there are no actual infinities.

8.2 Indirect proofs

Our logic is not yet strong enough to prove some valid arguments. Consider the following argument as an example.

$(P \rightarrow (Q \lor R))$

$\neg Q$

$\neg R$

_____

$\neg P$

This argument looks valid. By the first premise we know: if P were true, then so would (Q v R) be true. But then either Q or R or both would be true. And by the second and third premises we know: Q is false and R is false. So it cannot be that (Q v R) is true, and so it cannot be that P is true.

We can check the argument using a truth table. Our table will be complex because one of our premise is complex.

P	Q	R	(QvR)	premise (P→(QvR))	premise ¬Q	premise ¬R	conclusion ¬P
T	T	T	T	T	F	F	F
T	T	F	T	T	F	T	F
T	F	T	T	T	T	F	F
T	F	F	F	F	T	T	F
F	T	T	T	T	F	F	T
F	T	F	T	T	F	T	T
F	F	T	T	T	T	F	T
F	F	F	F	T	T	T	T

In any kind of situation in which all the premises are true, the conclusion is true. That is: the premises are all true only in the last row. For that row, the conclusion is also true. So, this is a valid argument.

But take a minute and try to prove this argument. We begin with

1. $(P \rightarrow (Q \vee R))$ premise
2. $\neg Q$ premise
3. $\neg R$ premise

And now we are stopped. We cannot apply any of our rules. Here is a valid argument that we have not made our reasoning system strong enough to prove.

There are several ways to rectify this problem and to make our reasoning system strong enough. One of the oldest solutions is to introduce a new proof method, traditionally called "reductio ad absurdum", which means *a reduction to absurdity*. This method is also often called an "indirect proof" or "indirect derivation".

The idea is that we assume the denial of our conclusion, and then show that a contradiction results. A contradiction is shown when we prove some sentence Ψ, and its negation ¬Ψ. This can be any sentence. The point is that, given the principle of bivalence, we must have proven something false. For if Ψ is true, then ¬Ψ is false;

and if ¬Ψ is true, then Ψ is false. We don't need to know which is false (Ψ or ¬Ψ); it is enough to know that one of them must be.

Remember that we have built our logical system so that it cannot produce a falsehood from true statements. The source of the falsehood that we produce in the indirect derivation must, therefore, be some falsehood that we added to our argument. And what we added to our argument is the denial of the conclusion. Thus, the conclusion must be true.

The shape of the argument is like this:

$$
\begin{array}{ll}
& \quad \neg\phi \\
& \quad \vdots \\
& \quad \psi \\
& \quad \neg\psi \\
\triangleright & \phi
\end{array}
$$

Traditionally, the assumption for indirect derivation has also been commonly called "the assumption for reductio".

As a concrete example, we can prove our perplexing case.

$$
\begin{array}{lll}
1. & (P \rightarrow (Q \vee R)) & \text{premise} \\
2. & \neg Q & \text{premise} \\
3. & \neg R & \text{premise} \\
\\
4. & \neg\neg P & \text{assumption for indirect derivation} \\
\\
5. & P & \text{double negation, 4} \\
6. & (Q \vee R) & \text{modus ponens, 1, 5} \\
7. & R & \text{modus tollendo ponens, 6, 2} \\
8. & \neg R & \text{repeat, 3} \\
\\
9. & \neg P & \text{indirect derivation, 4-8}
\end{array}
$$

We assumed the denial of our conclusion on line 4. The conclusion we believed was correct was ¬P, and the denial of this is ¬¬P. In line 7, we proved R. Technically, we are done at that point, but we would like to be kind to anyone trying to understand our proof, so we repeat line 3 so that the sentences R and ¬R are side by side, and it is very easy to see that something has gone wrong. That is, if we have proven both R and ¬R, then we have proven something false.

Our reasoning now goes like this. What went wrong? Line 8 is a correct use of repetition; line 7 comes from a correct use of modus tollendo ponens; line 6 from a correct use of modus ponens; line 5 from a correct use of double negation. So, we did not make a mistake in our reasoning. We used lines 1, 2, and 3, but those are premises that we agreed to assume are correct. This leaves line 4. That must be the source of my contradiction. It must be false. If line 4 is false, then ¬P is true.

Some people consider indirect proofs less strong than direct proofs. There are many, and complex, reasons for this. But, for our propositional logic, none of these reasons apply. This is because it is possible to prove that our propositional logic is consistent. This means, it is possible to prove that our propositional logic cannot prove a falsehood unless one first introduces a falsehood into the system. (It is generally not possible to prove that more powerful and advanced logical or mathematical systems are consistent, from inside those systems; for example, one cannot prove in arithmetic that arithmetic is consistent.) Given that we can be certain of the consistency of the propositional logic, we can be certain that in our propositional logic an indirect proof is a good form of reasoning. We know that if we prove a falsehood, we must have put a falsehood in; and if we are confident about all the other assumptions (that is, the premises) of our proof except for the assumption for indirect derivation, then we can be confident that this assumption for indirect derivation must be the source of the falsehood.

A note about terminology is required here. The word "contradiction" gets used ambiguously in most logic discussions. It can mean a situation like we see above, where two sentences are asserted, and these sentences cannot both be true. Or it can mean a single sentence that cannot be true. An example of such a sentence is (P∧¬P). The truth table for this sentence is:

P	¬P	(P ∧ ¬P)
T	F	F
F	T	F

Thus, this kind of sentence can never be true, regardless of the meaning of P.

To avoid ambiguity, in this text, we will always call a single sentence that cannot be true a "contradictory sentence". Thus, (P∧¬P) is a contradictory sentence. Situations where two sentences are asserted that cannot both be true will be called a "contradiction".

8.3 Our example, and other examples

We can reconstruct a version of Galileo's argument now. We will use the following key.

P: There are actual infinities (including the natural numbers and the square numbers).

Q: There is a one-to-one correspondence between the natural numbers and the square numbers.

R: The size of the set of the natural numbers and the size of the set of the square numbers are the same.

S: All the square numbers are natural numbers.

T: Some of the natural numbers are not square numbers.

U: There are more natural numbers than square numbers.

With this key, the argument will be translated:

$(P \rightarrow Q)$

$(Q \rightarrow R)$

$(P \rightarrow (S \wedge T))$

$((S \wedge T) \rightarrow U)$

$(U \rightarrow \neg R)$

———

$\neg P$

And we can prove this is a valid argument by using indirect derivation:

1. $(P \rightarrow Q)$		premise
2. $(Q \rightarrow R)$		premise
3. $(P \rightarrow (S \wedge T))$		premise
4. $((S \wedge T) \rightarrow U)$		premise
5. $(U \rightarrow \neg R)$		premise
	6. $\neg\neg P$	assumption for indirect derivation
	7. P	double negation, 6
	8. Q	modus ponens, 1, 7
	9. R	modus ponens, 2, 8
	10. $(S \wedge T)$	modus ponens, 3, 7
	11. U	modus ponens, 4, 10
	12. $\neg R$	modus ponens, 5, 11
	13. R	repeat, 9
14. $\neg P$		indirect derivation, 6-13

On line 6, we assumed ¬¬P because Galileo believed that ¬P and aimed to prove that ¬P. That is, he believed that there are no actual infinities, and so assumed that it was false to believe that it is not the case that there are no actual infinities. This falsehood will lead to other falsehoods, exposing itself.

For those who are interested: Galileo concluded that there are no actual infinities but there are potential infinities. Thus, he reasoned, it is not the case that all the natural numbers exist (in some sense of "exist"), but it is true that you could count natural numbers forever. Many philosophers before and after Galileo held this view; it is similar to a view held by Aristotle, who was an important logician and philosopher writing nearly two thousand years before Galileo.

Note that in an argument like this, you could reason that not the assumption for indirect derivation, but rather one of the premises was the source of the contradiction. Today, most mathematicians believe this about Galileo's argument. A logician and mathematician named Georg Cantor (1845-1918), the inventor of set theory, argued that infinite sets can have proper subsets of the same size. That is, Cantor denied premise 4 above: even though all the square numbers are natural numbers, and not all natural numbers are square numbers, it is not the case that these two sets are of different size. Cantor accepted however premise 2 above, and, therefore, believed that the size of the set of natural numbers and the size of the set of square numbers is the same. Today, using Cantor's reasoning, mathematicians and logicians study infinity, and have developed a large body of knowledge about the nature of infinity. If this interests you, see section 17.5.

Let us consider another example to illustrate indirect derivation. A very useful set of theorems are today called "De Morgan's Theorems", after the logician Augustus De Morgan (1806–1871). We cannot state these fully until chapter 9, but we can state their equivalent in English: DeMorgan observed that ¬(PvQ) and (¬P∧¬Q) are equivalent, and also that ¬(P∧Q) and (¬Pv¬Q) are equivalent. Given this, it should be a theorem of our language that (¬(PvQ)→(¬P∧¬Q)). Let's prove this.

The whole formula is a conditional, so we will use a conditional derivation. Our proof must thus begin:

| 1. ¬(P ∨ Q) | assumption for conditional derivation |

To complete the conditional derivation, we must prove (¬P∧¬Q). This is a conjunction, and our rule for showing conjunctions is adjunction. Since using this rule might be our best way to show (¬P∧¬Q), we can aim to show ¬P and then show ¬Q, and then perform adjunction. But, we obviously have very little to work with—just line 1, which is a negation. In such a case, it is typically wise to attempt an indirect proof. Start with an indirect proof of ¬P.

1. ¬(P ∨ Q)	assumption for conditional derivation
2. ¬¬P	assumption for indirect derivation
3. P	double negation, 2

We now need to find a contradiction—any contradiction. But there is an obvious one already. Line 1 says that neither P nor Q is true. But line 3 says that P is true. We must make this contradiction explicit by finding a formula and its denial. We can do this using addition.

1. ¬(P ∨ Q)	assumption for conditional derivation
2. ¬¬P	assumption for indirect derivation
3. P	double negation, 2
4. (P ∨ Q)	addition, 3
5. ¬(P ∨ Q)	repeat, 1
6. ¬P	indirect derivation 2-5

To complete the proof, we will use this strategy again.

1. ¬(P ∨ Q)	assumption for conditional derivation
2. ¬¬P	assumption for indirect derivation
3. P	double negation, 2
4. (P ∨ Q)	addition, 3
5. ¬(P ∨ Q)	repeat, 1
6. ¬P	indirect derivation 2-5
7. ¬¬Q	assumption for indirect derivation
8. Q	double negation, 7
9. (P ∨ Q)	addition, 8
10. ¬(P ∨ Q)	repeat, 1
11. ¬Q	indirect derivation 7-10
12. (¬P ∧ ¬Q)	adjunction, 6, 11
13. (¬(P ∨ Q) → (¬P ∧ ¬Q))	conditional derivation 1-12

We will prove De Morgan's theorems as problems for chapter 9.

Here is a general rule of thumb for doing proofs: When proving a conditional, always do conditional derivation; otherwise, try direct derivation; if that fails, then, try indirect derivation.

8.4 Problems

1. Complete the following proofs. Each will require an indirect derivation. The last two are challenging.

a. Premises: $(P \to R)$, $(Q \to R)$, $(P \lor Q)$. Conclusion: R.

b. Premises: $((P \lor Q) \to R)$, $\neg R$. Conclusion: $\neg P$.

c. Premise: $(\neg P \land \neg Q)$. Conclusion: $\neg(P \lor Q)$.

d. Premise: $\neg(P \land Q)$. Conclusion: $(\neg P \lor \neg Q)$.

e. Premise: $(\neg P \lor \neg Q)$. Conclusion: $\neg(P \land Q)$.

f. Premise: $(P \to R)$, $(Q \to S)$, $\neg(R \land S)$. Conclusion: $\neg(P \land Q)$.

g. Premise: $\neg R$, $((P \to R) \lor (Q \to R))$. Conclusion: $(\neg P \lor \neg Q)$.

h. Premise: $\neg(R \lor S)$, $(P \to R)$, $(Q \to S)$. Conclusion: $\neg(P \lor Q)$.

2. Prove the following are theorems.

a. $\neg(P \land \neg P)$.

b. $(\neg P \to \neg(P \land Q))$.

c. $((P \land \neg Q) \to \neg(P \to Q))$.

d. $((P \to Q) \to \neg(P \land \neg Q))$.

e. $(\neg(P \lor Q) \to \neg P)$.

f. $((\neg P \land \neg Q) \to \neg(P \lor Q))$.

g. $((\neg P \lor \neg Q) \to \neg(P \land Q))$.

h. $(\neg(P \land Q) \to (\neg P \lor \neg Q))$.

i. $\neg((P \to \neg P) \land (\neg P \to P))$.

j. $(P \lor \neg P)$.

3. In normal colloquial English, write your own valid argument with at least two premises. Your argument should just be a paragraph (not an ordered list of sentences or anything else that looks like formal logic). Translate it into propositional logic and prove it is valid using an indirect derivation.

4. Translate the following argument into English, and then prove it is valid using an indirect proof.

Either Beneke or Meinong conned Dodgson with marked cards. But either Beneke didn't do it or the marked cards are in the car. But also, if Meinong did it, the marked cards are in the car. So, regardless of whether Beneke or Meinong conned Dodgson, the cards are in the car.

[10] This translation of the title of Galileo's book has become the most common, although a more literal one would have been *Mathematical Discourses and Demonstrations.* Translations of the book include Drake (1974).

9. "... if and only if ...", Using Theorems

9.1 A historical example

The philosopher David Hume (1711-1776) is remembered for being a brilliant skeptical empiricist. A person is a skeptic about a topic if that person both has very strict standards for what constitutes knowledge about that topic and also believes we cannot meet those strict standards. Empiricism is the view that we primarily gain knowledge through experience, particular experiences of our senses. In his book, *An Inquiry Concerning Human Understanding*, Hume lays out his principles for knowledge, and then advises us to clean up our libraries:

> When we run over libraries, persuaded of these principles, what havoc must we make? If we take in our hand any volume of divinity or school metaphysics, for instance, let us ask, Does it contain any abstract reasoning concerning quantity or number? No. Does it contain any experimental reasoning concerning matter of fact and existence? No. Commit it then to the flames, for it can contain nothing but sophistry and illusion.[11]

Hume felt that the only sources of knowledge were logical or mathematical reasoning (which he calls above "abstract reasoning concerning quantity or number") or sense experience ("experimental reasoning concerning matter of fact and existence"). Hume is led to argue that any claims not based upon one or the other method is worthless.

We can reconstruct Hume's argument in the following way. Suppose *t* is some topic about which we claim to have knowledge. Suppose that we did not get this knowledge from experience or logic. Written in English, we can reconstruct his argument in the following way:

> We have knowledge about *t* if and only if our claims about *t* are learned from experimental reasoning or from logic or mathematics.

> Our claims about *t* are not learned from experimental reasoning.

Our claims about t are not learned from logic or mathematics.

———

We do not have knowledge about t.

on the unit

What does that phrase "if and only if" mean? Philosophers think that it, and several synonymous phrases, are used often in reasoning. Leaving "if and only" unexplained for now, we can use the following translation key to write up the argument in a mix of our propositional logic and English.

P: We have knowledge about t.

Q: Our claims about t are learned from experimental reasoning.

R: Our claims about t are learned from logic or mathematics.

And so we have:

P if and only if **(QvR)**

¬Q

¬R

———

¬P

Our task is to add to our logical language an equivalent to "if and only if". Then we can evaluate this reformulation of Hume's argument.

9.2 The biconditional

(?) better known

Before we introduce a symbol synonymous with "if and only if", and then lay out its syntax and semantics, we should start with an observation. A phrase like "P if and only if Q" appears to be an abbreviated way of saying "P if Q and P only if Q". Once we notice this, we do not have to try to discern the meaning of "if and only if" using our expert understanding of English. Instead, we can discern the meaning of "if and only if" using our already rigorous definitions of "if", "and", and "only if". Specifically, "P if Q and P only if Q" will be translated "$((Q \to P) \wedge (P \to Q))$". (If this is unclear to you, go back and review section 2.2.) Now, let us make a truth table for this formula.

P	Q	$(Q \to P)$	$(P \to Q)$	$((Q \to P) \wedge (P \to Q))$
T	T	T	T	T
T	F	T	F	F
F	T	F	T	F
F	F	T	T	T

We have settled the semantics for "if and only if". We can now introduce a new symbol for this expression. It is traditional to use the double arrow, "$\leftrightarrow$". We can now express the syntax and semantics of "$\leftrightarrow$".

If Φ and Ψ are sentences, then

$$(\Phi \leftrightarrow \Psi)$$

is a sentence. This kind of sentence is typically called a "biconditional".

The semantics is given by the following truth table.

Φ	Ψ	$(\Phi \leftrightarrow \Psi)$
T	T	T
T	F	F
F	T	F
F	F	T

One pleasing result of our account of the biconditional is that it allows us to succinctly explain the syntactic notion of logical equivalence. We say that two sentences Φ and Ψ are "equivalent" or "logically equivalent" if $(\Phi \leftrightarrow \Psi)$ is a theorem.

9.3 Alternative phrases

In English, it appears that there are several phrases that usually have the same meaning as the biconditional. Each of the following sentences would be translated as $(P \leftrightarrow Q)$.

P if and only if Q.

P just in case Q.

P is necessary and sufficient for Q.

P is equivalent to Q.

9.4 Reasoning with the biconditional

How can we reason using a biconditional? At first, it would seem to offer little guidance. If I know that $(P \leftrightarrow Q)$, I know that P and Q have the same truth value, but from that sentence alone I do not know if they are both true or both false. Nonetheless, we can take advantage of the semantics for the biconditional to observe that if we also know the truth value of one of the sentences constituting the biconditional, then we can derive the truth value of the other sentence. This suggests a straightforward set of rules. These will actually be four rules, but we will group them together under a single name, "equivalence":

$(\Phi \leftrightarrow \Psi)$

Φ

_____

Ψ

and

$(\Phi \leftrightarrow \Psi)$

$$\Psi$$

$$\overline{\hphantom{xxx}}$$

$$\Phi$$

and

$$(\Phi \leftrightarrow \Psi)$$

$$\neg\Phi$$

$$\overline{\hphantom{xxx}}$$

$$\neg\Psi$$

and

$$(\Phi \leftrightarrow \Psi)$$

$$\neg\Psi$$

$$\overline{\hphantom{xxx}}$$

$$\neg\Phi$$

What if we instead are trying to show a biconditional? Here we can return to the insight that the biconditional $(\Phi \leftrightarrow \Psi)$ is equivalent to $((\Phi \to \Psi) \wedge (\Psi \to \Phi))$. If we could prove both $(\Phi \to \Psi)$ and $(\Psi \to \Phi)$, we will know that $(\Phi \leftrightarrow \Psi)$ must be true.

We can call this rule "bicondition". It has the following form:

$$(\Phi \to \Psi)$$

$$(\Psi \to \Phi)$$

$$\overline{\hphantom{xxx}}$$

$$(\Phi \leftrightarrow \Psi)$$

This means that often when we aim to prove a biconditional, we will undertake two conditional derivations to derive two conditionals, and then use the bicondition rule. That is, many proofs of biconditionals have the following form:

$$
\begin{array}{l}
\quad\quad \phi \\
\quad\quad \vdots \\
\quad\quad \psi \\
\triangleright \quad (\phi \rightarrow \psi) \\
\quad\quad \psi \\
\quad\quad \vdots \\
\quad\quad \phi \\
\triangleright \quad (\psi \rightarrow \phi) \\
\quad\quad (\phi \leftrightarrow \psi)
\end{array}
$$

9.5 Returning to Hume

We can now see if we are able to prove Hume's argument. Given now the new biconditional symbol, we can begin a direct proof with our three premises.

1. $(P \leftrightarrow (Q \lor R))$	premise
2. $\neg Q$	premise
3. $\neg R$	premise

We have already observed that we think (QvR) is false because ¬Q and ¬R. So let's prove ¬(QvR). This sentence cannot be proved directly, given the premises we have; and it cannot be proven with a conditional proof, since it is not a conditional. So let's try an indirect proof. We believe that ¬(QvR) is true, so we'll assume the denial of this and show a contradiction.

1. $(P \leftrightarrow (Q \lor R))$	premise
2. $\neg Q$	premise
3. $\neg R$	premise
4. $\neg\neg(Q \lor R)$	assumption for indirect derivation
5. $(Q \lor R)$	double negation, 4
6. R	modus tollendo ponens, 5, 2
7. $\neg R$	repetition, 3
8. $\neg(Q \lor R)$	indirect proof, 4-7
9. $\neg P$	equivalence, 1, 8

Hume's argument, at least as we reconstructed it, is valid.

Is Hume's argument sound? Whether it is sound depends upon the first premise above (since the second and third premises are abstractions about some topic *t*). Most specifically, it depends upon the claim that we have knowledge about something just in case we can show it with experiment or logic. Hume argues we should distrust—indeed, we should burn texts containing—claims that are not from experiment and observation, or from logic and math. But consider this claim: we have knowledge about a topic *t* if and only if our claims about *t* are learned from experiment or our claims about *t* are learned from logic or mathematics.

Did Hume discover this claim through experiments? Or did he discover it through logic? What fate would Hume's book suffer, if we took his advice?

9.6 Some examples

It can be helpful to prove some theorems that make use of the biconditional, in order to illustrate how we can reason with the biconditional.

Here is a useful principle. If two sentences have the same truth value as a third sentence, then they have the same truth value as each other. We state this as $(((P \leftrightarrow Q) \land (R \leftrightarrow Q)) \rightarrow (P \leftrightarrow R))$. To illustrate reasoning with the biconditional, let us prove this theorem.

This theorem is a conditional, so it will require a conditional derivation. The consequent of the conditional is a biconditional, so we will expect to need two conditional derivations, one to prove $(P \rightarrow R)$ and one to prove $(R \rightarrow P)$. The proof will look like this. Study it closely.

1. $((P \leftrightarrow Q) \wedge (R \leftrightarrow Q))$	assumption for conditional derivation
2. $(P \leftrightarrow Q)$	simplification, 1
3. $(R \leftrightarrow Q)$	simplification, 1
4. P	assumption for conditional derivation
5. Q	equivalence, 2, 4
6. R	equivalence, 3, 5
7. $(P \rightarrow R)$	conditional derivation, 4-6
8. R	assumption for conditional derivation
9. Q	equivalence, 3, 8
10. P	equivalence, 2, 9
11. $(R \rightarrow P)$	conditional derivation, 8-10
12. $(P \leftrightarrow R)$	bincondition, 7, 11
13. $(((P \leftrightarrow Q) \wedge (R \leftrightarrow Q)) \rightarrow (P \leftrightarrow R))$	conditional derivation 1-12

We have mentioned before the principles that we associate with the mathematician Augustus De Morgan (1806-1871), and which today are called "De Morgan's Laws" or the "De Morgan Equivalences". These are the recognition that ¬(PvQ) and (¬P∧¬Q) are equivalent, and also that ¬(P∧Q) and (¬Pv¬Q) are equivalent. We can now express these with the biconditional. The following are theorems of our logic:

$(\neg(PvQ) \leftrightarrow (\neg P \wedge \neg Q))$

$(\neg(P \wedge Q) \leftrightarrow (\neg Pv\neg Q))$

We will prove the second of these theorems. This is perhaps the most difficult proof we have seen; it requires nested indirect proofs, and a fair amount of cleverness in finding what the relevant contradiction will be.

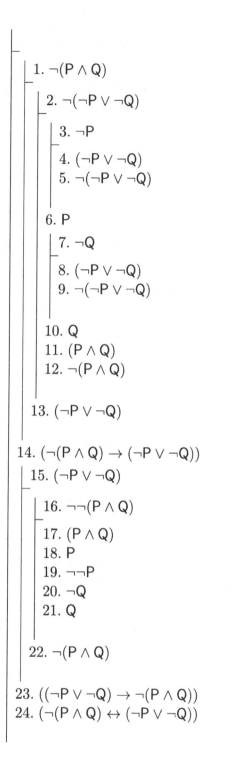

1. ¬(P ∧ Q)   assumption for conditional derivation

2. ¬(¬P ∨ ¬Q)   assumption for indirect derivation

3. ¬P   assumption for indirect derivation

4. (¬P ∨ ¬Q)   addition, 3
5. ¬(¬P ∨ ¬Q)   repeat, 2

6. P   indirect derivation, 3-5

7. ¬Q   assumption for indirect derivation

8. (¬P ∨ ¬Q)   addition, 7
9. ¬(¬P ∨ ¬Q)   repeat, 2

10. Q   indirect derivation, 6-9
11. (P ∧ Q)   adjunction, 6, 10
12. ¬(P ∧ Q)   repeat, 1

13. (¬P ∨ ¬Q)   indirect derivation, 2-12

14. (¬(P ∧ Q) → (¬P ∨ ¬Q))   conditional derivation, 1-13
15. (¬P ∨ ¬Q)   assumption for conditional derivation

16. ¬¬(P ∧ Q)   assumption for indirect derivation

17. (P ∧ Q)   double negation 16
18. P   simplification, 17
19. ¬¬P   double negation, 18
20. ¬Q   modus tollendo ponens, 15, 19
21. Q   simplification, 17

22. ¬(P ∧ Q)   indirect derivation 16-21

23. ((¬P ∨ ¬Q) → ¬(P ∧ Q))   conditional derivation, 15-22
24. (¬(P ∧ Q) ↔ (¬P ∨ ¬Q))   bicondition, 14, 23

9.7 Using theorems

Every sentence of our logic is, in semantic terms, one of three kinds. It is either a tautology, a contradictory sentence, or a contingent sentence. We have already defined "tautology" (a sentence that must be true) and "contradictory sentence" (a sentence that must be false). A contingent sentence is a sentence that is neither a tautology nor a contradictory sentence. Thus, a contingent sentence is a sentence that might be true, or might be false.

Here is an example of each kind of sentence:

$(P \lor \neg P)$

$(P \leftrightarrow \neg P)$

P

The first is a tautology, the second is a contradictory sentence, and the third is contingent. We can see this with a truth table.

P	¬P	(P∨¬P)	(P ↔ ¬P)	P
T	F	T	F	T
F	T	T	F	F

Notice that the negation of a tautology is a contradiction, the negation of a contradiction is a tautology, and the negation of a contingent sentence is a contingent sentence.

$\neg(P \lor \neg P)$

$\neg(P \leftrightarrow \neg P)$

$\neg P$

P	¬P	(P∨¬P)	¬(P∨¬P)	(P ↔ ¬P)	¬(P ↔ ¬P)
T	F	T	F	F	T
F	T	T	F	F	T

A moment's reflection will reveal that it would be quite a disaster if either a contradictory sentence or a contingent sentence were a theorem of our propositional logic. Our logic was designed to produce only valid arguments. Arguments that have no premises, we observed, should have conclusions that must be true (again, this follows because a sentence that can be proved with no premises could be proved with any premises, and so it had better be true no matter what premises we use). If a theorem were contradictory, we would know that we could prove a falsehood. If a theorem were contingent, then sometimes we could prove a falsehood (that is, we could prove a sentence that is under some conditions false). And, given that we have adopted indirect derivation as a proof method, it follows that once we have a contradiction or a contradictory sentence in an argument, we can prove anything.

Theorems can be very useful to us in arguments. Suppose we know that neither Smith nor Jones will go to London, and we want to prove, therefore, that Jones will not go to London. If we allowed ourselves to use one of De Morgan's theorems, we could make quick work of the argument. Assume the following key.

P: Smith will go to London.

Q: Jones will go to London.

And we have the following argument:

1. $\neg(P \vee Q)$	premise
2. $(\neg(P \vee Q) \leftrightarrow (\neg P \wedge \neg Q))$	theorem
3. $(\neg P \wedge \neg Q)$	equivalence, 2, 1
4. $\neg Q$	simplification, 3

This proof was made very easy by our use of the theorem at line 2.

There are two things to note about this. First, we should allow ourselves to do this, because if we know that a sentence is a theorem, then we know that we could prove that theorem in a subproof. That is, we could replace line 2 above with a long subproof that proves $(\neg(P \vee Q) \leftrightarrow (\neg P \wedge \neg Q))$, which we could then use. But if we are certain that $(\neg(P \vee Q) \leftrightarrow (\neg P \wedge \neg Q))$ is a theorem, we should not need to do this proof again and again, each time that we want to make use of the theorem.

The second issue that we should recognize is more subtle. There are infinitely many sentences of the form of our theorem, and we should be able to use those also. For example, the following sentences would each have a proof identical to our proof of the theorem $(\neg(P \vee Q) \leftrightarrow (\neg P \wedge \neg Q))$, except that the letters would be different:

$(\neg(R \vee S) \leftrightarrow (\neg R \wedge \neg S))$

$(\neg(T \vee U) \leftrightarrow (\neg T \wedge \neg U))$

$(\neg(V \vee W) \leftrightarrow (\neg V \wedge \neg W))$

This is hopefully obvious. Take the proof of $(\neg(P \vee Q) \leftrightarrow (\neg P \wedge \neg Q))$, and in that proof replace each instance of P with R and each instance of Q with S, and you would have a proof of $(\neg(R \vee S) \leftrightarrow (\neg R \wedge \neg S))$.

But here is something that perhaps is less obvious. Each of the following can be thought of as similar to the theorem $(\neg(P \vee Q) \leftrightarrow (\neg P \wedge \neg Q))$.

$(\neg((P \wedge Q) \vee (R \wedge S)) \leftrightarrow (\neg(P \wedge Q) \wedge \neg(R \wedge S)))$

$(\neg(T \vee (Q \vee V)) \leftrightarrow (\neg T \wedge \neg(Q \vee V)))$

$(\neg((Q \leftrightarrow P) \vee (\neg R \to \neg Q)) \leftrightarrow (\neg(Q \leftrightarrow P) \wedge \neg(\neg R \to \neg Q)))$

For example, if one took a proof of $(\neg(P \vee Q) \leftrightarrow (\neg P \wedge \neg Q))$ and replaced each initial instance of P with $(Q \leftrightarrow P)$ and each initial instance of Q with $(\neg R \to \neg Q)$, then one would have a proof of the theorem $(\neg((Q \leftrightarrow P) \vee (\neg R \to \neg Q)) \leftrightarrow (\neg(Q \leftrightarrow P) \wedge \neg(\neg R \to \neg Q)))$.

We could capture this insight in two ways. We could state theorems of our metalanguage and allow that these have instances. Thus, we could take $(\neg(\Phi \vee \Psi) \leftrightarrow (\neg \Phi \wedge \neg \Psi))$ as a metalanguage theorem, in which we could replace each Φ with a sentence and each Ψ with a sentence and get a particular instance of a theorem. An alternative is to allow that from a theorem we can produce other theorems through substitution. For ease, we will take this second strategy.

Our rule will be this. Once we prove a theorem, we can cite it in a proof at any time. Our justification is that the claim is a theorem. We allow substitution of any atomic sentence in the theorem with any other sentence if and only if we replace each initial instance of that atomic sentence in the theorem with the same sentence.

Before we consider an example, it is beneficial to list some useful theorems. There are infinitely many theorems of our language, but these ten are often very helpful. A few we have proved. The others can be proved as an exercise.

T1 $(P \vee \neg P)$

T2 $(\neg(P \rightarrow Q) \leftrightarrow (P \wedge \neg Q))$

T3 $(\neg(P \vee Q) \leftrightarrow (\neg P \wedge \neg Q))$

T4 $((\neg P \vee \neg Q) \leftrightarrow \neg(P \wedge Q))$

T5 $(\neg(P \leftrightarrow Q) \leftrightarrow (P \leftrightarrow \neg Q))$

T6 $(\neg P \rightarrow (P \rightarrow Q))$

T7 $(P \rightarrow (Q \rightarrow P))$

T8 $((P \rightarrow (Q \rightarrow R)) \rightarrow ((P \rightarrow Q) \rightarrow (P \rightarrow R)))$

T9 $((\neg P \rightarrow \neg Q) \rightarrow ((\neg P \rightarrow Q) \rightarrow P))$

T10 $((P \rightarrow Q) \rightarrow (\neg Q \rightarrow \neg P))$

Some examples will make the advantage of using theorems clear. Consider a different argument, building on the one above. We know that neither is it the case that if Smith goes to London, he will go to Berlin, nor is it the case that if Jones goes to London he will go to Berlin. We want to prove that it is not the case that Jones will go to Berlin. We add the following to our key:

R: Smith will go to Berlin.

S: Jones will go to Berlin.

And we have the following argument:

1. ¬((P → R) ∨ (Q → S))	premise
2. (¬((P → R) ∨ (Q → S)) ↔ (¬(P → R) ∧ ¬(Q → S)))	theorem T3
3. (¬(P → R) ∧ ¬(Q → S))	equivalence, 2, 1
4. ¬(Q → S)	simplification, 3
5. (¬(Q → S) ↔ (Q ∧ ¬S))	theorem T2
6. (Q ∧ ¬S)	equivalence, 5, 4
7. ¬S	simplification, 6

Using theorems made this proof much shorter than it might otherwise be. Also, theorems often make a proof easier to follow, since we recognize the theorems as tautologies—as sentences that must be true.

9.8 Problems

1. Prove each of the following arguments is valid.

    a. Premises: ((P^Q) ↔ R), (P ↔ S), (S ^ Q). Conclusion: R.
    b. Premises: (P ↔ Q). Conclusion: ((P → Q) ^ (Q → P)).
    c. Premises: P, ¬Q. Conclusion: ¬(P ↔ Q).
    d. Premises: (¬PvQ), (Pv¬Q). Conclusion: (P ↔ Q).
    e. Premises: (P ↔ Q), (R ↔ S). Conclusion: ((P^R) ↔ (Q^S)).
    f. Premises: ((PvQ) ↔ R), ¬(P ↔ Q). Conclusion: R.
    g. Conclusion: ((P ↔ Q) ↔ (¬P ↔ ¬Q)).
    h. Conclusion: ((P → Q) ↔ (¬P v Q)).

2. Prove each of the following theorems.

    a. T2
    b. T3
    c. T5
    d. T6
    e. T7
    f. T8
    g. T9

h. $((P \wedge Q) \leftrightarrow \neg(\neg P \vee \neg Q))$

i. $((P \to Q) \leftrightarrow \neg(P \wedge \neg Q))$

3. Here are some passages from literature, philosophical works, and important political texts. Hopefully you recognize some of them. Find the best translation into propositional logic. Because these are from diverse texts you will find it easiest to make a new key for each sentence.

    a. "Neither a borrower nor a lender be." (Shakespeare, *Hamlet*.)

    b. "My copy-book was the board fence, brick wall, and pavement." (Frederick Douglass, *Narrative of the Life of Frederick Douglass*.)

    c. "The bourgeoisie has torn away from the family its sentimental veil, and has reduced the family relation to a mere money relation." (Marx and Engels, *The Communist Manifesto*.)

    d. "The Senate shall chuse their other Officers, and also a President pro tempore, in the Absence of the Vice President, or when he shall exercise the Office of President of the United States." (The Constitution of the United States.)

    e. "Excessive bail shall not be required, nor excessive fines imposed, nor cruel and unusual punishments inflicted." (The Constitution of the United States.)

    f. "Annual income twenty pounds, annual expenditure nineteen nineteen and six, result happiness. Annual income twenty pounds, annual expenditure twenty pounds ought and six, result misery." (Charles Dickens, *Great Expectations*.)

    g. "Thou shalt get kings, though thou be none." (Shakespeare, *Macbeth*.)

    h. "If a faction consists of less than a majority, relief is supplied by the republican principle, which enables the majority to defeat its sinister views by regular vote." (Federalist Papers.)

4. In normal colloquial English, write your own valid argument with at least two premises, at least one of which is a biconditional. Your argument should just be a paragraph (not an ordered list of sentences or anything else that looks like formal logic). Translate it into propositional logic and prove it is valid.

5. In normal colloquial English, write your own valid argument with at least two premises, and with a conclusion that is a biconditional. Your argument

should just be a paragraph (not an ordered list of sentences or anything else that looks formal like logic). Translate it into propositional logic and prove it is valid.

6. Here is a passage from Aquinas's reflections on the law, The Treatise on the Laws. Symbolize this argument and prove it is valid.

> A law, properly speaking, regards first and foremost the order to the common good. Now if a law regards the order to the common good, then its making belongs either to the whole people, or to someone who is the viceregent of the whole people. And therefore the making of a law belongs either to the whole people or to the viceregent of the whole people.

---

[11] From Hume's *Enquiry Concerning Human Understanding*, p.161 in Selby-Bigge and Nidditch (1995 [1777]).

10. Summary of Propositional Logic

10.1 Elements of the language

- Principle of Bivalence: each sentence is either true or false, never both, never neither.
- Each atomic sentence is a sentence.
- Syntax: if Φ and Ψ are sentences, then the following are also sentences
  - $\neg\Phi$
  - $(\Phi \rightarrow \Psi)$
  - $(\Phi \wedge \Psi)$
  - $(\Phi \vee \Psi)$
  - $(\Phi \leftrightarrow \Psi)$
- Semantics: if Φ and Ψ are sentences, then the meanings of the connectives are fully given by their truth tables. These truth tables are:

Φ	$\neg\Phi$
T	F
F	T

Φ	Ψ	$(\Phi \rightarrow \Psi)$
T	T	T
T	F	F
F	T	T
F	F	T

Φ	Ψ	(Φ ∧ Ψ)
T	T	T
T	F	F
F	T	F
F	F	F

Φ	Ψ	(Φ ∨ Ψ)
T	T	T
T	F	T
F	T	T
F	F	F

Φ	Ψ	(Φ ↔ Ψ)
T	T	T
T	F	F
F	T	F
F	F	T

- A sentence of the propositional logic that must be true is a tautology.
- A sentence that must be false is a contradictory sentence.
- A sentence that is neither a tautology nor a contradictory sentence is a contingent sentence.
- Two sentences Φ and Ψ are equivalent, or logically equivalent, when (Φ ↔ Ψ) is a theorem.

10.2 Reasoning with the language

- An argument is an ordered list of sentences, one sentence of which we call the "conclusion" and the others of which we call the "premises".
- A valid argument is an argument in which: necessarily, if the premises are true, then the conclusion is true.
- A sound argument is a valid argument with true premises.
- Inference rules allow us to write down a sentence that must be true, assuming that certain other sentences are true. We say that the new sentence is "derived from" those other sentences using the inference rule.
- Schematically, we can write out the inference rules in the following way (think of these as saying, if you have written the sentence(s) above the line, then you can write the sentence below the line):

Modus ponens	Modus tollens	Double negation	Double negation
$(\Phi \rightarrow \Psi)$	$(\Phi \rightarrow \Psi)$		
Φ	$\neg\Psi$	Φ	$\neg\neg\Phi$
——	——	——	——
Ψ	$\neg\Phi$	$\neg\neg\Phi$	Φ

Addition	Addition	Modus tollendo ponens	Modus tollendo ponens
		$(\Phi \lor \Psi)$	$(\Phi \lor \Psi)$
Φ	Ψ	$\neg\Phi$	$\neg\Psi$
——	——	——	——
$(\Phi \lor \Psi)$	$(\Phi \lor \Psi)$	Ψ	Φ

Adjunction	Simplification	Simplification	Bicondition
Φ			$(\Phi \rightarrow \Psi)$
Ψ	$(\Phi \land \Psi)$	$(\Phi \land \Psi)$	$(\Psi \rightarrow \Phi)$
——	——	——	——
$(\Phi \land \Psi)$	Φ	Ψ	$(\Phi \leftrightarrow \Psi)$

Equivalence	Equivalence	Equivalence	Equivalence
$(\Phi \leftrightarrow \Psi)$	$(\Phi \leftrightarrow \Psi)$	$(\Phi \leftrightarrow \Psi)$	$(\Phi \leftrightarrow \Psi)$
Φ	Ψ	$\neg\Phi$	$\neg\Psi$
——	——	——	——
Ψ	Φ	$\neg\Psi$	$\neg\Phi$

- A proof (or derivation) is a syntactic method for showing an argument is valid. Our system has three kinds of proof (or derivation): direct, conditional, and indirect.
- A direct proof (or direct derivation) is an ordered list of sentences in which every sentence is either a premise or is derived from earlier lines using an inference rule. The last line of the proof is the conclusion.
- A conditional proof (or conditional derivation) is an ordered list of sentences in which every sentence is either a premise, is the special assumption for conditional derivation, or is derived from earlier lines using an inference rule. If the assumption for conditional derivation is Φ, and we derive as some step in the proof Ψ, then we can write after this $(\Phi \rightarrow \Psi)$ as our conclusion.

- An indirect proof (or indirect derivation, and also known as a reductio ad absurdum) is: an ordered list of sentences in which every sentence is either 1) a premise, 2) the special assumption for indirect derivation (also sometimes called the "assumption for reductio"), or 3) derived from earlier lines using an inference rule. If our assumption for indirect derivation is ¬Φ, and we derive as some step in the proof Ψ and also as some step of our proof ¬Ψ, then we conclude that Φ.
- We can use Fitch bars to write out the three proof schemas in the following way:

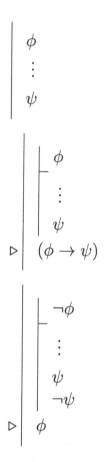

- A sentence that we can prove without premises is a theorem.
- Suppose Φ is a theorem, and it contains the atomic sentences $P_1...P_n$. If we replace each and every occurrence of one of those atomic sentences P_i in Φ with another sentence Ψ, the resulting sentence is also a theorem. This can be repeated for any atomic sentences in the theorem.

PART II: FIRST ORDER LOGIC

11. Names and predicates

11.1 A limitation of the propositional logic

The propositional logic is a perfect language for what it does. It is rigorously precise and easy to use. But it is not the only kind of logic that philosophers developed. The philosopher Aristotle (384-322 BC) wrote several books on logic, and famously, he used the following argument as one of his examples.

> All men are mortal.
>
> Socrates is a man.
>
> ____
>
> Socrates is mortal.

Aristotle considered this an example of a valid argument. And it appears to be one. But let us translate it into our propositional logic. We have three atomic sentences. Our translation key would look something like this:

> P: All men are mortal.
>
> Q: Socrates is a man.
>
> R: Socrates is mortal.

And the argument, written in propositional logic, would be

> P
>
> Q
>
> ____
>
> R

This argument is obviously invalid. What went wrong? Somehow, between Aristotle's argument and our translation, essential information was lost. This information was required in order for the argument to be valid. When we lost it, we ended up with an argument where the conclusion could be false (as far as we can tell from the shape of the argument alone).

It seems quite clear what we lost in the translation. There are parts of the first premise that are shared by the other two: something to do with being a man, and being mortal. There is a part of the second sentence shared with the conclusion: the proper name "Socrates". And the word "All" seems to be playing an important role here.

Note that all three of these things (those adjective phrases, a proper name, and "all") are themselves not sentences. To understand this argument of Aristotle's, we will need to break into the atomic sentences, and begin to understand their parts. Doing this proved to be very challenging—most of all, making sense of that "all" proved challenging. As a result, for nearly two thousand years, we had two logics working in parallel: the propositional logic and Aristotle's logic. It was not until late in the nineteenth century that we developed a clear and precise understanding of how to combine these two logics into one, which we will call "first order logic" (we will explain later what "first order" means).

Our task will be to make sense of these parts: proper names, adjective phrases, and the "all". We can begin with names.

11.2 Symbolic terms: proper names

The first thing we want to add to our expanded language are names. We will take proper names (such as, "Abraham Lincoln") as our model. General names (such as "Americans") we will handle in a different way, to be discussed later. We will call these proper names of our language, "names".

Recall that we want our language to have no vagueness, and no ambiguity. A name would be vague if it might or might not pick out an object. So we will require that each name pick out an object. That is, a name may not be added to our language if it refers to nothing, or only refers to something under some conditions. A name would be ambiguous if it pointed at more than one thing. "John Smith" is a name that points at thousands of people. We will not allow this in our language. Each name points at only one thing.

We might decide also that each thing that our language talks about has only one name. Some philosophers have thought that such a rule would be very helpful. However, it turns out it is often very hard to know if two apparent things are the same thing, and so in a natural language we often have several names for the same thing. A favorite example of philosophers, taken from the philosopher and mathematician Gottlob Frege (1848-1925), is "Hesperus" and "Phosphorus." These are both names for Venus, although some who used these names did not know that. Thus, for a while, some people did not know that Hesperus was Phosphorus. And, of course, we would not have been able to use just one name for both, if we did not know that these names pointed at the same one thing. Thus, if we want to model scientific problems, or other real world problems, using our logic, then a rule that each thing have one and only one name would demand too much: it would require us to solve all our mysteries before we got started. In any case, there is no ambiguity in a thing having several names.

Names refer to things. But when we say *a* refers to such and such an object, then if someone asked, "What do you mean by 'refer'?", we would be hard pressed to do anything more than offer a list of synonyms: *a* points at the object, *a* names the object, *a* indicates the object, *a* picks out the object. "Refer" is another primitive that we are adding to our language. We cannot in this book explain what reference is; in fact, philosophers vigorously debate this today, and there are several different and (seemingly) incompatible theories about how names work. However, taking "refer" as a primitive will not cause us difficulties, since we all use names and so we all have a working understanding of names and how they refer.

In our language, we will use lower case letters, from the beginning of the alphabet, for names. Thus, the following are names:

a

b

c

...

In a natural language, there is more meaning to a name than what it points at. Gottlob Frege was intrigued by the following kinds of cases.

a=a

a=b

Hesperus is Hesperus.

Hesperus is Phosphorus.

What is peculiar in these four sentences is that the first and third are trivial. We know that they must be true. The second and fourth sentences, however, might be surprising, even if true. Frege observed that reference cannot constitute all the meaning of a name, for if it did, and if *a* is *b*, then the second sentence above should have the same meaning as the first sentence. And, if Hesperus is Phosphorus, the third and fourth sentences should have the same meaning. But obviously they don't. The meaning of a name, he concluded, is more than just what it refers to. He called this extra meaning *sense* (*Sinn*, in his native German).

We won't be able to explore these subtleties. We're going to reduce the meaning of our names down to their referent. This is another case where we see that a natural language like English is very powerful, and contains subtleties that we avoid and simplify away in order to develop our precise language.

Finally, let us repeat that we are using the word "name" in a very specific sense. A name picks out a single object. For this reason, although it may be true that "cat" is a kind of name in English, it cannot be properly translated to a name in our logical language. Thus, when considering whether some element of a natural language is a proper name, just ask yourself: is there a single thing being referred to by this element? If the answer is no, then that part of the natural language is not like a name in our logical language.

11.3 Predicates

Another element of Aristotle's argument above that we want to capture is phrases like "is a man" and "is mortal". These adjective phrases are called by philosophers "predicates". They tell us about properties or relations had by the things our language is about. In our sentence "Socrates is a man", the predicate ("... is a man") identifies a property of Socrates. We want to introduce into our logical language a way to express these predicates. But before we do this, we need to clarify how predicates relate to the objects we are talking about, and we want to be sure that we introduce predicates in such a way that their meaning is precise (they are not vague or ambiguous).

Our example of "... is a man" might lead us to think that predicates identify properties of individual objects. But consider the following sentences.

> Tom is tall.

> Tom is taller than Jack.

> 7 is odd.

> 7 is greater than or equal to 5.

The first and third sentence are quite like the ones we've seen before. "Tom" and "7" are names. And "...is tall" and "...is odd" are predicates. These are similar (at least in terms of their apparent syntax) to "Socrates" and "... is a man".

But what about those other two sentences? The predicates in these sentences express relations between two things. And, although in English it is rare that a predicate expresses a relation of more than two things, in our logical language a predicate could identify a relation between any number of things. We need, then, to be aware that each predicate identifies a relation between a specific number of things. This is important, because the predicates in the first and second sentence above are not the same. That is, "...is tall" and "... is taller than..." are not the same predicate.

Logicians have a slang for this; they call it the "arity" of the predicate. This odd word comes from taking the "ary" on words like "binary" and "trinary", and making it into a noun. So, we can say the following: each predicate has an arity. The arity of a predicate is the minimum number of things that can have the property or relation. The predicate "... is tall" is arity one. One thing alone can be tall. The predicate "... is taller than..." is arity two. You need at least two things for one to be taller than the other.

Thus, consider the following sentence.

> Stefano, Margarita, Aletheia, and Lorena are Italian.

There is a predicate here, "... are Italian." It has been used to describe four things. Is it an arity four predicate? We could treat it as one, but that would make our language deceptive. Our test should be the following principle: what is the minimum number of things that can have that property or relation? In that case, "... are Italian" should be an arity one predicate because one thing alone can be Italian. Thus, the sentence above should be understood as equivalent to:

Stefano is Italian and Margarita is Italian and Aletheia is Italian and Lorena is Italian.

This is formed using conjunctions of atomic sentences, each containing the same arity one predicate. Consider also the following sentence.

Stefano is older than Aletheia and Lorena.

There are three names here. Is the predicate then an arity three predicate? No. The minimum number of things such that one can be older than the other is two. From this fact, we know that "... is older than..." is an arity two predicate. This sentence is thus equivalent to:

Stefano is older than Aletheia and Stefano is older than Lorena.

This is formed using a conjunction of atomic sentences, each containing the same arity two predicate.

Note an important difference we need to make between our logical language and a natural language like English. In a natural language like English, we have a vast range of kinds of names and kinds of predicates. Some of these could be combined to form sentences without any recognizable truth value. Consider:

Jupiter is an odd number.

America is taller than Smith.

7 is older than Jones.

These expressions are semantic nonsense, although they are syntactically well formed. The predicate "...is an odd number" cannot be true or false of a planet. America does not have a height to be compared. Numbers do not have an age. And so on.

We are very clever speakers in our native languages. We naturally avoid these kinds of mistakes (most of the time). But our logic is being built to avoid such mistakes always; it aims to make them impossible. Thus, each first order logical language must have what we will call its "domain of discourse". The domain of discourse is the set of things that our first order logic is talking about. If we want to talk about numbers, people, and nations, we will want to make three different languages with three different sets of predicates and three different domains of discourse.

We can now state our rule for predicates precisely. A predicate of arity n must be true or false, never both, never neither, of each n objects from our domain of discourse.

This will allow us to avoid predicates that are vague or ambiguous. A vague predicate might include, "...is kind of tall." It might be obviously false of very short people, but it is not going to have a clear truth value with respect to people who are of height slightly above average. If a predicate were ambiguous, we would again not be able to tell in some cases whether the predicate were true or false of some of the things in our domain of discourse. An example might include, "...is by the pen." It could mean *is by the writing implement,* or it could mean *is by the children's playpen.* Not knowing which, we would not be able to tell whether a sentence like "Fido is by the pen" were true or false. Our rule for predicates explicitly rules out either possibility.

When we say, "a predicate of arity n is true or false of each n objects from our domain of discourse", what we mean is that an arity one predicate must be true or false of each thing in the domain of discourse; and an arity two predicate must be true or false of every possible ordered pair of things from the domain of discourse; and an arity three predicate must be true or false of every possible ordered triple of things from our domain of discourse; and so on.

We will use upper case letters from F on to represent predicates of our logical language. Thus,

F

G

H

I

J

K

...

are predicates.

11.4 First order logic sentences

We can now explain what a sentence is in our first order logic.

We need to decide how names and predicates will be combined. Different methods have been used, but most common is what is called "prefix notation". This means we put the predicate before names. So, if we had the sentences

Tom is tall.

Tom is taller than Steve.

And we had the following translation key,

Fx: x is tall

Gxy: x is taller than y

a: Tom

b: Steve

Then our translations would be

F*a*

G*ab*

I did something new in the translation key: I used variables to identify places in a predicate. This is not any part of our language, but just a handy bit of bookkeeping we can use in explaining our predicates. The advantage is that if we write simply:

G: is greater than

there could be ambiguity about which name should come first after the predicate (the greater than name, or the less than name). We avoid this ambiguity by putting variables into the predicate and the English in the translation key. But the variables are doing no other work. Don't think of a predicate as containing variables.

The sentence above that we had

Stefano is Italian and Margarita is Italian and Aletheia is Italian and Lorena is Italian.

can be translated with the following key:

Ix: x is Italian.

c: Stefano

d: Margarita

e: Aletheia

f: Lorena

And in our language would look like this:

$((Ic \wedge Id) \wedge (Ie \wedge If))$

We have not yet given a formal syntax for atomic sentences of first order logic. We will need a new concept of syntax—the well formed formula that is not a sentence—and for this reason we will put off the specification of the syntax for the next chapter.

11.5 Problems

1. Translate the following sentences into our first order logic. Provide a trans-

lation key that identifies the names and predicates.

    a. Bob is a poriferan.
    b. Bob is neither a cnidarian nor female.
    c. Bob is a male poriferan.
    d. Bob is not a male poriferan.
    e. Bob is a poriferan if and only if he is not a cnidarian.
    f. Pat is not both a poriferan and a cnidarian.
    g. Pat is not a poriferan, though he is male.
    h. Pat and Bob are male.
    i. Bob is older than Pat.
    j. Pat is not older than both Sandi and Bob.

2. Identify the predicate of the following sentences, and identify its arity.

    a. Aletheia and Lorena are tall.
    b. Aletheia and Lorena are taller than Stefano and Margarita.
    c. Margarita is younger than Aletheia, Lorena, and Stefano.
    d. Margarita and Stefano live in Rome and Aletheia and Lorena live in Milan.
    e. Lorena stands between Stefano and Aletheia.

3. Make your own translation key for the following sentences. Use your key to write the English equivalents.

    a. Fa.
    b. ¬Fa.
    c. Gab.
    d. ¬Gab.
    e. (Gab ∧ Fb).
    f. ¬(Gab ∧ Fb).
    g. (¬Gab ∧ Fb).
    h. ¬(Gab v Fb).
    i. (Gab ↔ Gac).
    j. (Fa ∧ Fb).

12. "All" and "some"

12.1 The challenge of translating "all" and "some"

We are still not able to translate fully Aristotle's argument. It began:

> All men are mortal.

What does this "all" mean?

Let's start with a simpler example. Suppose for a moment we consider the sentence

> All is mortal.

Or, equivalently,

> Everything is mortal.

How should we understand this "all" or "everything"? This is a puzzle that stumped many generations of logicians. The reason is that, at first, it seems obvious how to handle this case. "All", one might conclude, is a special name. It is a name for everything in my domain of discourse. We could then introduce a special name for this, with the following translation key.

> ε: all (or everything)

> Mx: x is mortal

And, so we translate the sentence

> $M\varepsilon$

So far, so good. But now, what about our first sentence? Let's add to our translation key

> Hx: x is human

Now how shall we translate "all men are mortal"? Most philosophers think this should be captured with a conditional (we will see why below), but look at this sentence:

$$(H\varepsilon \rightarrow M\varepsilon)$$

That does not at all capture what we meant to say. That sentence says: if everything is a human, then everything is mortal. We want to say just that all the humans are mortal.

Using a different connective will not help.

$$(H\varepsilon \wedge M\varepsilon)$$

$$(H\varepsilon \vee M\varepsilon)$$

$$(H\varepsilon \leftrightarrow M\varepsilon)$$

All of these fail to say what we want to say. The first says everything is human and everything is mortal. The second, that everything is human or everything is mortal. The third that everything is human if and only if everything is mortal.

The problem is even worse for another word that seems quite similar in its use to "all": the word "some". This sentence is surely true:

Some men are mortal.

Suppose we treat "some" as a name, since it also appears to act like one. We might have a key like this:

σ: some

And suppose, for a moment, that this meant, *at least one thing in our domain of discourse*. And then translate our example sentence, at least as a first attempt, as

$$(H\sigma \wedge M\sigma)$$

This says that some things are human, and some things are mortal. It might seem at first to work. But now consider a different sentence.

Some things are human and some things are crabs.

That's true. Let us introduce the predicate Kx for x is a crab. Then, it would seem we should translate this

$$(H\sigma \wedge K\sigma)$$

But that does not work. For σ, if it is a name, must refer to the same thing. But, then something is both a human and a crab, which is false.

"All" and "some" are actually subtle. They look and (in some ways) act like names, but they are different than names. So, we should not treat them as names.

~~ε: all (or everything)~~

~~σ: some~~

This perplexed many philosophers and mathematicians, but finally a very deep thinker whom we have already mentioned—Gottlob Frege—got clear about what is happening here, and developed what we today call the "quantifier".

The insight needed for the quantifier is that we need to treat "all" and "some" as special operators that can "bind" or "reach into" potentially several of the arity places in one or more predicates. To see the idea, consider first the simplest case. We introduce the symbol ∀ for all. However, we also introduce a variable—in this case we will use x—to be a special kind of place holder. (Or: you could think of ∀ as meaning *every* and x as meaning *thing*, and then ∀x means *everything*.) Now, to say "everything is human", we would write

$$\forall x Hx$$

Think of this sentence as saying, *you can take any object from our domain of discourse, and that thing has property H.* In other words, if ∀xHx is true, then Ha is true, and Hb is true, and Hc is true, and so on, for all the objects of our domain of discourse.

So far, this is not much different than using a single name to mean "everything". But there is a very significant difference when we consider a more complex formula. Consider "All men are mortal". Most logicians believe this means that "Everything is such that, if it is human, then it is mortal". We can write

$$\forall x(Hx \rightarrow Mx)$$

So, if $\forall x(Hx \to Mx)$ is true, then $(Ha \to Ma)$ and $(Hb \to Mb)$ and $(Hc \to Mc)$ and so on are true.

This captures exactly what we want. We did not want to say *if everything is human, then everything is mortal.* We wanted to say, *for each thing, if it is human, then it is mortal.*

A similar approach will work for "some". Let "∃" be our symbol for "some". Then we can translate

Some men are mortal

With

$\exists x(Hx \wedge Mx)$

(We will discuss in section 13.3 below why we do not use a conditional here; at this point, we just want to focus on the meaning of the "∃".) Read this as saying, for this example, *there is at least one thing from our domain of discourse that has properties H and M.* In other words, either $(Ha \wedge Ma)$ is true or $(Hb \wedge Mb)$ is true or $(Hc \wedge Mc)$ is true or etc.

These new elements to our language are called "quantifiers". The symbol "∀" is called the "universal quantifier". The symbol "∃" is called the "existential quantifier" (to remember this, think of it as saying, "there exists at least one thing such that..."). We say that they "quantify over" the things that our language is about (that is, the things in our domain of discourse).

We are now ready to provide the syntax for terms, predicates, and quantifiers.

12.2 A new syntax

For the propositional logic, our syntax was always trivial. For the first order logic our syntax will be more complex. We will need a new concept, the concept of a "well-formed formula". And we will need to make more explicit use of the fact that our syntax is a recursive syntax, which means that our rules must be stated with a first case, and then a way to repeatedly apply our syntactic rules. We are, also, going to change one feature of our metalanguage. The symbol Φ will no longer mean a sentence. Instead, it is any well-formed expression of our language. We can write $\Phi(a)$ to mean that the name a appears in Φ; this does not mean that Φ is an arity-one predicate with the single name a. Φ can be very complex. For example, Φ could be the expression $((Fa \leftrightarrow Gbc) \wedge Hd)$.

A symbolic term is either a name, an indefinite name, an arbitrary term, or a variable (we will explain what indefinite terms and arbitrary terms are later). Names are a, b, c, d.... Indefinite names are p, q, r.... Variables are u, v, w, x, y, z. Arbitrary terms are u', v', w', x', y', z'.

A predicate of arity n followed by n symbolic terms is a well-formed formula.

If Φ and Ψ are well-formed formulas, and α is a variable, then the following are well-formed formulas:

$\neg\Phi$

$(\Phi \rightarrow \Psi)$

$(\Phi \wedge \Psi)$

$(\Phi \vee \Psi)$

$(\Phi \leftrightarrow \Psi)$

$\forall\alpha\Phi$

$\exists\alpha\Phi$

If the expression $\Phi(\alpha)$ contains no quantifiers, and α is a variable, then we say that α is a "free variable" in $\Phi(\alpha)$. If the expression $\Phi(\alpha)$ contains no quantifiers, and α is a variable, then we say that α is "bound" in $\forall\alpha\Phi(\alpha)$ and α is "bound" in $\exists\alpha\Phi(\alpha)$. A variable that is bound is not free.

If Φ is a well-formed formula with no free variables, then it is a sentence.

If Φ and Ψ are sentences, then the following are sentences:

$\neg\Phi$

$(\Phi \rightarrow \Psi)$

$(\Phi \wedge \Psi)$

$(\Phi \lor \Psi)$

$(\Phi \leftrightarrow \Psi)$

This way of expressing ourselves is precise; but, for some of us, when seeing it for the first time, it is hard to follow. Let's take it a step at a time. Let's suppose that F is a predicate of arity one, that G is a predicate of arity two, and that H is a predicate of arity three. Then the following are all well-formed formulas.

Fx

Fy

Fa

Gxy

Gyx

Gab

Gax

Hxyz

Haxc

Hczy

And, if we combine these with connectives, they form well-formed formulas. All of these are well-formed formulas:

¬Fx

$(Fx \rightarrow Fy)$

$(Fa \wedge Gxy)$

$(Gyx \lor Gab)$

$(Gax \leftrightarrow Hxyz)$

∀xHaxc

∃zHczy

For these formulas, we say that *x* is a free variable in each of the first five well-formed formulas. The variable *x* is bound in the sixth well-formed formula. The variable *z* is bound in the last well-formed formula, but *y* is free in that formula.

For the following formulae, there are no free variables.

∀xFx

∃zGza

F*a*

G*bc*

Each of these four well-formed formulas is, therefore, a sentence. If combined using our connectives, these would make additional sentences. For example, these are all sentences:

¬∀xFx

(∀xFx → ∃zGza)

(F*a* ∧ G*bc*)

(G*bc* ↔ ∃zGza)

(G*bc* ∨ ∃zGza)

The basic idea is that in addition to sentences, we recognize formulae that have the right shape to be a sentence, if only they had names instead of variables in certain places in the formula. These then become sentences when combined with a quantifier binding that variable, because now the variable is no longer a meaningless placeholder, and instead stands for any or some object in our language.

What about the semantics for the quantifiers? This will, unfortunately, have to remain intuitive during our development of first order logic. We need set theory to develop a semantics for the quantifiers; truth tables will not work. In chapter 17, you can read a little about how to construct a proper semantics for the quantifiers. Here, let us simply understand the universal quantifier, "∀", as meaning *every object in our domain of discourse*; and understand the existential quantifier, "∃", as meaning *at least one object in our domain of discourse*.

A note about the existential quantifier. "Some" in English does not often mean *at least one*. If you ask your friend for some of her french fries, and she gives you exactly one, you will feel cheated. However, we will likely agree that there is no clear norm for the number of french fries that she must give you, in order to satisfy your request. In short, the word "some" is vague in English. This is a useful vagueness—we don't want to have to say things like, "Give me 11 french fries, please". But, our logical language must be precise, and so, it must have no vagueness. For this reason, we interpret the existential quantifier to mean *at least one*.

12.3 Common sentence forms for quantifiers

Formulas using quantifiers can have very complex meanings. However, translating from English to first order logic expressions is usually surprisingly easy, because in English many of our phrases using "all" or "some" or similar phrases are of eight basic forms. Once we memorize those forms, we can translate these kinds of phrases from English into logic.

Here are examples of the eight forms, using some hypothetical sentences.

Everything is human.

Something is human.

Something is not human.

Nothing is human.

All humans are mortal.

Some humans are mortal.

Some humans are not mortal.

No humans are mortal.

Our goal is to decide how best to translate each of these. Then, we will generalize. Let us use our key above, in which "Hx" means *x is human*, and "Mx" means *x is mortal*.

The first two sentences are straightforward. The following are translations.

$$\forall xHx$$

$$\exists xHx$$

What about the third sentence? It is saying there is something, and that thing is not human. A best translation of that would be to start with the "something".

$$\exists x\neg Hx$$

That captures what we want. At least one thing is not human. Contrast this with the next sentence. We can understand it as saying, *It is not the case that something is human.* That is translated:

$$\neg\exists xHx$$

(It turns out that "$\exists x\neg Hx$" and "$\neg\forall xHx$" are equivalent and "$\neg\exists xHx$" and "$\forall x\neg Hx$" are equivalent; so we could also translate "Something is not human" with "$\neg\forall xHx$", and "Nothing is human" with "$\forall x\neg Hx$". However, this author finds these less close to the English in syntactic form.)

The next four are more subtle. "All humans are mortal" seems to be saying, if anything is human, then that thing is mortal. That tells us directly how to translate the expression:

$$\forall x(Hx \to Mx)$$

What about "some humans are mortal"? This is properly translated with:

$$\exists x(Hx \wedge Mx)$$

Many students suspect there is some deep similarity between "all humans are mortal" and "some humans are mortal", and so want to translate "some humans are mortal" as $\exists x(Hx \to Mx)$. This would be a mistake. Remember the truth table for the conditional; if the antecedent is false, then the conditional is true. Thus, the formula $\exists x(Hx \rightarrow Mx)$ would be true if there were no humans, and it would be true if there were no humans and no mortals.

That might seem a bit abstract, so let's leave off our language about humans and mortality, and consider a different first order logic language, this one about numbers. Our domain of discourse, let us suppose, is the natural numbers (1, 2, 3, ...). Let "Fx" mean "x is even" and "Gx" mean "x is odd". Now consider the following formula:

Some even number is odd.

We can agree that, for the usual interpretation of "odd" and "even", this sentence is false. But now suppose we translated it as

$\exists x(Fx \rightarrow Gx)$

This sentence is true. That's because there is at least one object in our domain of discourse for which it is true. For example, consider the number 3 (or any odd number). Suppose that in our logical language, a means 3. Then, the following sentence is true:

$(Fa \rightarrow Ga)$

This sentence is true because the antecedent is false, and the consequent is true. That makes the whole conditional true.

Clearly, "$\exists x(Fx \rightarrow Gx)$" cannot be a good translation of "Some even number is odd", because whereas "Some even number is odd" is false, "$\exists x(Fx \rightarrow Gx)$" is true. The better translation is

$\exists x(Fx \wedge Gx)$

This says, some number is both even and odd. That's clearly false, matching the truth value of the English expression.

To return to our language about humans and mortality. The sentence "some human is mortal" should be translated

$\exists x(Hx \wedge Mx)$

And this makes clear how we can translate, "some human is not mortal":

$∃x(Hx ∧ ¬Mx)$

The last sentence, "No humans are mortal" is similar to "Nothing is human". We can read it as meaning *It is not the case that some humans are mortal*, which we can translate:

$¬∃x(Hx∧Mx)$

(It turns out that this sentence is equivalent to, "all humans are not mortal". Thus, we could also translate the sentence with:

$∀x(Hx → ¬Mx)$.)

We need to generalize these eight forms. Let $Φ$ and $Ψ$ be expressions (these can be complex). Let $α$ be any variable. Then, we can give the eight forms schematically in the following way.

Everything is $Φ$

$∀αΦ(α)$

Something is $Φ$

$∃αΦ(α)$

Something is not $Φ$

$∃α¬Φ(α)$

Nothing is $Φ$

$¬∃αΦ(α)$

All $Φ$ are $Ψ$

$∀α(Φ(α) → Ψ(α))$

Some $Φ$ are $Ψ$

$∃α(Φ(α) ∧ Ψ(α))$

Some $Φ$ are not $Ψ$

$∃α(Φ(α) ∧ ¬Ψ(α))$

No Φ are Ψ

¬∃α (Φ(α)^ Ψ(α))

These eight forms include the most common forms of sentences that we encounter in English that use quantifiers. This may not, at first, seem plausible, but, when we recognize that these generalized forms allow that the expression Φ or Ψ can be complex, then, we see that the following are examples of the eight forms, given in the same order:

Everything is a female human from Texas.

Something is a male human from Texas.

Something is not a female human computer scientist from Texas.

Nothing is a male computer scientist from Texas.

All male humans are mortal mammals.

Some female humans are computer scientists who live in Texas.

Some female humans are not computer scientists who live in Texas.

No male human is a computer scientist who lives in Texas.

The task in translating such sentences is to see, when we refer back to our schemas, that Φ and Ψ can be complex. Thus, if we add to our key the following predicates:

Fx: x is female

Gx: x is male

Tx: x is from Texas

Sx: x is a computer scientist

Lx: x is a mammal

Then, we can see that the following are translations of the eight English sentences, and they utilize the eight forms.

∀x((Fx^Hx) ^ Tx)

$\exists x((Gx \land Hx) \land Tx)$

$\exists x \neg((Fx \land Hx) \land (Sx \land Tx))$

$\neg \exists x((Gx \land Sx) \land Tx)$

$\forall x((Gx \land Hx) \rightarrow (Mx \land Lx))$

$\exists x((Fx \land Hx) \land (Sx \land Tx))$

$\exists x((Fx \land Hx) \land \neg(Sx \land Tx))$

$\neg \exists x((Gx \land Hx) \land (Sx \land Tx))$

Another important issue to be aware of when translating expressions with quantifiers is that "only" plays a special role in some English expressions. Consider the following sentences.

All sharks are fish.

Only sharks are fish.

The first of these is true; the second is false. We will start a new logical language and key. Let Fx mean that *x is a fish*, and Sx mean that *x is a shark*. We know how to translate the first sentence.

$\forall x(Sx \rightarrow Fx)$

However, how shall we translate "Only sharks are fish"? This sentence tells us that the only things that are fish are the sharks. But then, all fish are sharks. That is, the translation is:

$\forall x(Fx \rightarrow Sx)$

It would also be possible to combine these claims:

All and only sharks are fish.

Which should be translated:

$\forall x(Sx \leftrightarrow Fx)$

This indicates two additional schemas for translation that may be useful. First, sentences of the form "Only Φ are Ψ" should be translated:

$$\forall a(\Psi(a) \to \Phi(a))$$

Second, sentences of the form "all and only Φ are Ψ" should be translated in the following way:

$$\forall a(\Phi(a) \leftrightarrow \Psi(a))$$

12.4 Problems

1. Which of the following expressions has a free variable? Identify the free variable if there is one. Assume F is an arity one predicate, and G is an arity two predicate.

   a. Fa
   b. Fx
   c. Gxa
   d. ∃xFx
   e. ∀xGxa
   f. ∀xGxy
   g. ∀x(Fx → Gxa)
   h. (∀xFx → Gxa)
   i. (∀xFx → ∀xGxa)
   j. ∀x(Fx → Gxy)

2. Provide a key and translate the following expressions into first order logic. Assume the domain of discourse is Terrestrial organisms. Thus, ∀xFx would mean *all Terrestrial organisms are* F, and ∃xFx would mean *at least one Terrestrial organisms is* F. Don't be concerned that some of these sentences are obviously false.

   a. All horses are mammals.
   b. Some horses are mammals.

c. No horses are mammals.

d. Some horses are not mammals.

e. Some mammals lay eggs, and some mammals do not.

f. Some chestnut horses are mammals that don't lay eggs.

g. No chestnut horses are mammals that lay eggs.

h. Some egg-laying mammals are not horses.

i. There are no horses.

j. There are some mammals.

k. Only horses are mammals.

l. All and only horses are mammals.

3. Provide a key and translate the following expressions into first order logic. Assume the domain of discourse is all humans.

   a. Steve is taller than Dave.

   b. Dave is not taller than Steve.

   c. Everyone is taller than Dave.

   d. Someone is taller than Steve.

   e. Someone is not taller than Steve.

   f. No one is taller than Steve.

   g. Steve is taller than everyone.

   h. Steve is taller than someone.

4. Translating from natural languages can sometimes be challenging. Here are some passages from literature, philosophy, and some political texts. Hopefully you recognize some of these passages. Find the best translation into first order logic using our eight forms. You will need to make a new key for each sentence, and tell us what the domain of discourse is.

   a. "A single man in possession of a good fortunate must be in want of a wife." (Jane Austen, *Pride and Prejudice*)

   b. "Everything is lawful." (Dostoevsky, *The Brothers Karamazov*)

   c. "All mimsy were the borogoves,
      And the mome raths outgrabe." (Lewis Carroll, "Jabberwocky")

   d. "A law is unjust if it is inflicted on a minority that... had no part in enacting or devising the law." (Martin Luther King, "Letter from a Birmingham Jail")

   e. "All men are created equal... endowed by their Creator with certain unalienable Rights." (Declaration of Independence)

f. "All men and women are created equal… endowed by their Creator with certain inalienable rights."
("Declaration of Sentiments and Resolutions from Seneca Falls")

g. "No man is allowed to be a judge in his own cause." (Federalist Papers 10)

h. "STATES NEITHER LOSE ANY OF THEIR RIGHTS, NOR ARE DISCHARGED FROM ANY OF THEIR OBLIGATIONS, BY A CHANGE IN THE FORM OF THEIR CIVIL GOVERNMENT." (Federalist Papers 84)

i. "None of us cared for Kate." (William Shakespeare, *The Tempest*)

j. "Men only disagree,
Of creatures rational" (Milton, *Paradise Lost*)

k. "Some of them lived nobly and showed great qualities of soul, nevertheless they have lost their empire or have been killed by subjects who have conspired against them." (Machiavelli, *The Prince*)

l. "There are some who remain proud and fierce even in hell." (Fyodor Dostoevsky, *The Brothers Karamazov*)

m. "The first question that offers itself is, whether the general form and aspect of the government be strictly republican. It is evident that no other form would be reconcilable with the genius of the people of America." (Federalist Papers 39)

n. "Some are born great, some achieve greatness, and some have greatness thrust upon them." (Shakespeare, *Twelfth Night*)

5. Provide your own key and translate the following expressions of first order logic into natural sounding English sentences. All the predicates here are meant to be arity one. Do not worry if some of your sentences are obviously false; you rather want to show you can translate from logic to normal sounding English.

a. $\forall x((Fx \wedge Gx) \rightarrow Hx)$

b. $\forall x(Fx \rightarrow \neg Hx)$

c. $\exists x((Fx \wedge (Gx \wedge Hx))$

d. $\exists x((Fx \wedge \neg(Gx \wedge Hx))$

e. $\neg \exists x(Fx \wedge Gx)$

13. Reasoning with quantifiers

13.1 Using the universal quantifier

How shall we construct valid arguments using the existential and the universal quantifier? The semantics for the quantifiers must remain intuitive. However, they are sufficiently clear for us to introduce some rules that will obviously preserve validity. In this chapter, we will review three inference rules, ordering them from the easiest to understand to the more complex.

The easiest case to begin with is the universal quantifier. Recall Aristotle's argument:

> All men are mortal.
>
> Socrates is a man.
>
> ____
>
> Socrates is mortal.

We now have the tools to represent this argument.

> $\forall x(Hx \rightarrow Mx)$
>
> Ha
>
> ____
>
> Ma

But, how can we show that this argument is valid?

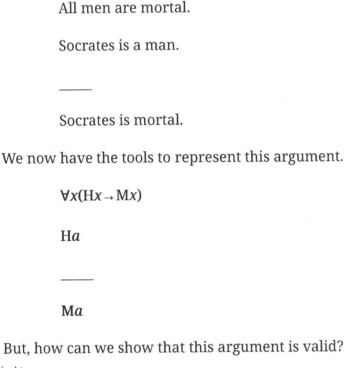

The important insight here concerns the universal quantifier. We understand the first sentence as meaning, for any object in my domain of discourse, if that object is human, then that object is mortal. That means we could remove the quantifier, put any name in our language into the free x slots in the resulting formula, and we would have a true sentence: $(Ha \rightarrow Ma)$ and $(Hb \rightarrow Mb)$ and $(Hc \rightarrow Mc)$ and $(Hd \rightarrow Md)$ and so on would all be true.

We need only make this semantic concept into a rule. We will call this, "universal instantiation". To remember this rule, just remember that it is taking us from a general and universal claim, to a specific instance. That's what we mean by "instantiation". We write the rule, using our metalanguage, in the following way. Let α be any variable, and let β be any symbolic term.

$$\forall \alpha \Phi(\alpha)$$

$$\overline{}$$

$$\Phi(\beta)$$

^{remv}
^{quantifier.}
This is a very easy rule to understand. One removes the quantifier, and replaces every free instance of the formerly bound variable with a single symbolic term (this is important: the instance that replaces your variable must be the same symbolic term throughout—you cannot instantiate $\forall x(Hx \rightarrow Mx)$ to $(Ha \rightarrow Mb)$, for example).

With this rule, we can finally prove Aristotle's argument is valid.

1. $\forall x(Hx \rightarrow Mx)$	premise
2. Ha	premise
3. $(Ha \rightarrow Ma)$	universal instantiation, 1
4. Ma	modus ponens, 3, 2

13.2 Showing the existential quantifier

Consider the following argument.

> All men are mortal.
>
> Socrates is a man.
>
> _____
>
> Something is mortal.

This looks to be an obviously valid argument, a slight variation on Aristotle's original syllogism. Consider: if the original argument, with the same two premises, was valid, then the conclusion that Socrates is mortal must be true if the premises are true. But, if it must be true that Socrates is mortal, then it must be true that something is mortal. Namely, at least Socrates is mortal (recall that we interpret the existential quantifier to mean *at least one*).

We can capture this reasoning with a rule. If a particular object has a property, then, something has that property. Written in our meta-language, where β is some symbolic term and α is a variable:

$$\Phi(\beta)$$

$$\overline{}$$

$$\exists\alpha\Phi(\alpha)$$

This rule is called "existential generalization". It takes an instance and then generalizes to a general claim.

We can now show that the variation on Aristotle's argument is valid.

1. $\forall x(Hx \rightarrow Mx)$	premise
2. Ha	premise
3. $(Ha \rightarrow Ma)$	universal instantiation, 1
4. Ma	modus ponens, 3, 2
5. $\exists xMx$	existential generalization, 4

13.3 Using the existential quantifier

Consider one more variation of Aristotle's argument.

All men are mortal.

Something is a man.

_____

Something is mortal.

This, too, looks like it must be a valid argument. If the first premise is true, then any human being you could find would be mortal. And, the second premise tells us that something is a human being. So, this something must be mortal.

But, this argument confronts us with a special problem. The argument does not tell us which thing is a human being. This might seem trivial, but it really is only trivial in our example (because you know that there are many human beings). In mathematics, for example, there are many very surprising and important proofs that some number with some strange property exists, but no one has been able to show specifically which number. So, it can happen that we know that there is something with a property, but, not know what thing.

Logicians have a solution to this problem. We will introduce a special kind of name, which refers to something, but we know not what. Call this an "indefinite name". We will use *p, q, r*... as these special names (we know these are not atomic sentences because they are lowercase). Then, where χ is some indefinite name and α is a variable, our rule is:

$\exists \alpha \Phi(\alpha)$

_____

$\Phi(\chi)$

where χ is an indefinite name that does not appear above in an open proof

This rule is called "existential instantiation". By "open proof" we mean a sub-proof that is not yet complete.

The last clause is important. It requires us to introduce indefinite names that are new. If an indefinite name is already being used in your proof, then you must use a new indefinite name if you do existential instantiation. This rule is a little bit stronger than is required in all cases, but it is by far the easiest way to avoid a kind of mistake that would produce invalid arguments. To see why this is so, let us drop the clause for the sake of an example. In this example, we will prove that the Pope is the President of the United States. We need only the following key.

Hx: x is the President of the United States.

Jx: x is the Pope.

Here are two very plausible premises, which I believe that you will grant: there is a President of the United States, and there is a Pope. So, here is our proof:

1. $\exists x H x$	premise
2. $\exists x J x$	premise
3. $H p$	existential instantiation, 1
4. $J p$	existential instantiation, 2
5. $(H p \wedge J p)$	adjunction, 3, 4
6. $\exists x (H x \wedge J x)$	existential generalization, 5

Thus, we have just proved that there is a President of the United States who is Pope.

But that's false. We got a false conclusion from true premises—that is, we constructed an invalid argument. What went wrong? We ignored the clause on our existential instantiation rule that requires that the indefinite name used when we apply the existential instantiation rule cannot already be in use in the proof. In line 4, we used the indefinite name "p" when it was already in use in line 3.

Instead, if we had followed the rule, we would have a very different proof:

1. $\exists x H x$	premise
2. $\exists x J x$	premise
3. $H p$	existential instantiation, 1
4. $J q$	existential instantiation, 2
5. $(H p \wedge J q)$	adjunction, 3, 4

Because we cannot assume that the two unknowns are the same thing, we give them each a temporary name that is different. Since existential generalization replaces only one symbolic term, from line five you can only generalize to $\exists x (H x \wedge J q)$ or to $\exists x (H p \wedge J x)$—or, if we performed existential generalization twice, to something like $\exists x \exists y (H x \wedge J y)$. Each of these three sentences would be true if the Pope and the President were different things, which in fact they are.

We can now prove that the variation on Aristotle's argument, given above, is valid.

$$1.\ \forall x(Hx \rightarrow Mx) \quad\quad\quad\quad\quad \text{premise}$$
$$2.\ \exists x Hx \quad\quad\quad\quad\quad\quad\quad\quad \text{premise}$$

$$3.\ Hp \quad\quad\quad\quad\quad\quad\quad\quad\quad \text{existential instantiation, 2}$$
$$4.\ (Hp \rightarrow Mp) \quad\quad\quad\quad\quad \text{universal instantiation, 1}$$
$$5.\ Mp \quad\quad\quad\quad\quad\quad\quad\quad\quad \text{modus ponens, 4, 3}$$
$$6.\ \exists x Mx \quad\quad\quad\quad\quad\quad\quad\quad \text{existential generalization, 5}$$

A few features of this proof are noteworthy. We did existential instantiation first, in order to obey the rule that our temporary name is new: "*p*" does not appear in any line in the proof before line 3. But, then, we are permitted to do universal instantiation to "*p*", as we did on line 4. A universal claim is true of every object in our domain of discourse, including the I-know-not-what.

We can consider an example that uses all three of these rules for quantifiers. Consider the following argument.

> All whales are mammals. Some whales are carnivorous. All carnivorous organisms eat other animals. Therefore, some mammals eat other animals.

We could use the following key.

Fx: x is a whale.

Gx: x is a mammal.

Hx: x is carnivorous.

Ix: x eats other animals.

Which would give us:

$$\forall x(Fx \rightarrow Gx)$$

$$\exists x(Fx \wedge Hx)$$

$$\forall x(Hx \rightarrow Ix)$$

$$\underline{\quad\quad\quad\quad}$$

$$\exists x(Gx \wedge Ix)$$

Here is one proof that the argument is valid.

1. $\forall x(Fx \to Gx)$	premise
2. $\exists x(Fx \land Hx)$	premise
3. $\forall x(Hx \to Ix)$	premise
4. $(Fp \land Hp)$	existential instantiation, 2
5. Fp	simplification, 4
6. $(Fp \to Gp)$	universal instantiation, 1
7. Gp	modus ponens, 6, 5
8. Hp	simplification, 4
9. $(Hp \to Ip)$	universal instantiation, 3
10. Ip	modus ponens, 9, 8
11. $(Gp \land Ip)$	adjunction, 7, 10
12. $\exists x(Gx \land Ix)$	existential generalization, 11

13.4 Problems

1. Prove the following arguments are valid. Note that, in addition to the new rules for reasoning with quantifiers, you will still have to use techniques like conditional derivation (when proving a conditional) and indirect derivation (when proving something that is not a conditional, and for which you cannot find a direct derivation). These will require universal instantiation.

    a. Premises: $\forall x(Fx \to Gx)$, Fa, Fb. Conclusion: $(Ga \land Gb)$.

    b. Premises: $\forall x(Hx \leftrightarrow Fx)$, ¬Fc. Conclusion: ¬Hc.

    c. Premises: $\forall x(Gx \lor Hx)$, ¬Hb. Conclusion: Gb.

    d. Premises: $\forall x(Fx \to Gx)$, $\forall x(Gx \to Hx)$. Conclusion: $(Fa \to Ha)$.

    e. Premises: $\forall x(Gx \lor Ix)$, $\forall x(Gx \to Jx)$, $\forall x(Ix \to Jx)$. Conclusion: Jb.

2. Prove the following arguments are valid. These will require existential generalization.

    a. Premises: $\forall xFx$. Conclusion: $\exists xFx$.

    b. Premises: $\forall x(Fx \leftrightarrow Gx)$, Gd. Conclusion: $\exists x(Gx \land Fx)$.

    c. Premises: $(Ga \land Fa)$, $\forall x(Fx \leftrightarrow Hx)$, $\forall x(¬Gx \lor Jx)$. Conclusion: $\exists x(Hx \land Jx)$.

d. Premises: ¬(Fa ∧ Ga). Conclusion: ∃x(¬Fx ∨ ¬Gx).

e. Conclusion: ∃x(Fx ∨ ¬Fx)

f. Conclusion: ¬∃x(Fx ∧ ¬Fx)

3. Prove the following arguments are valid. These will require existential instantiation.

   a. Premises: ∃xFx. Conclusion: ¬∀x¬Fx.

   b. Premises: ∃x¬Fx. Conclusion: ¬∀xFx.

   c. Premises: ∀x¬Fx. Conclusion: ¬∃xFx.

   d. Premises: ∀xFx. Conclusion: ¬∃x¬Fx.

   e. Premises: ∃x¬(Fx ∧ Gx). Conclusion: ∃x(¬Fx ∨ ¬Gx).

   f. Premises: ∃x(Fx ∧ Gx), ∀x(¬Gx ∨ Kx), ∀x(Fx → Hx). Conclusion: ∃x(Hx ∧ Kx).

   g. Conclusion: (∀x(Fx → Gx) → (∃xFx → ∃xGx))

   h. Conclusion: (∀x(Fx → Gx) → (∃x¬Gx → ∃x¬Fx))

4. In normal colloquial English, write your own valid argument with at least two premises, and where at least one premise is an existential claim. Your argument should just be a paragraph (not an ordered list of sentences or anything else that looks like formal logic). Translate it into first order logic and prove it is valid.

5. In normal colloquial English, write your own valid argument with at least two premises and with a conclusion that is an existential claim. Your argument should just be a paragraph (not an ordered list of sentences or anything that looks like formal logic). Translate it into first order logic and prove it is valid.

6. In normal colloquial English, write your own valid argument with at least two premises, and where at least one premise is a universal claim. Your argument should just be a paragraph (not an ordered list of sentences or anything else that looks like formal logic). Translate it into first order logic and prove it is valid.

7. Some philosophers have developed arguments attempting to prove that there is a god. One such argument, which was very influential until Darwin,

is the Design Argument. The Design Argument has various forms, with subtle differences, but here is one (simplified) version of a design argument.

> Anything with complex independently interrelated parts was designed. If something is designed, then there is an intelligent designer. All living organisms have complex independently interrelated parts. There are living organisms. Therefore, there is an intelligent designer.

Symbolize this argument, and prove that it is valid. (The second sentence is perhaps best symbolized not using one of the eight forms, but rather using a conditional, where both the antecedent and the consequent are existential sentences.) Do you believe this argument is sound? Why do you think Darwin's work was considered a significant challenge to the claim that the argument is sound?

8. Philosophical arguments are often complex because they can use more advanced logic, but also because they tend to leave unstated those premises that one might consider obvious. An argument with unstated but presumably obvious premises is called an "enthymeme". Consider the following argument from Descartes's Meditations, which he gives as reason to believe the mind and body are two different kinds of substances.

> To commence this examination accordingly, I here remark, in the first place, that there is a vast difference between mind and body, in respect that body, from its nature, is always divisible, and that mind is entirely indivisible.... This would be sufficient to teach me that the mind or soul of man is entirely different from the body, if I had not already been apprised of it on other grounds.

The missing premise here seems to be: if every body is divisible and every mind is indivisible, then mind and body are different substances. Assume our domain of discourse is substances. Using the following translation key, translate Descartes's premises, as described in the passage; and also translate the implicit premise. For simplicity, we will include a proposition in the key.

Translation Key	
Logic	English
Fx	x is a mind.
Gx	x is divisible.
Hx	x is a body.
P	Mind and body are different substances.

9. Legal opinions, when they include arguments, are often also enthymemes. An enthymeme is an argument where some premises are implied, usually because they are obvious. Consider this passage from the decision in Brown v. The Board of Education.

> We conclude that, in the field of public education, the doctrine of "separate but equal" has no place. Separate educational facilities are inherently unequal. Therefore, we hold that the plaintiffs and others similarly situated for whom the actions have been brought are, by reason of the segregation complained of, deprived of the equal protection of the laws guaranteed by the Fourteenth Amendment.

This first sentence is our conclusion. Presumably "has no place" means here "is unconstitutional." Also, there is also an implicit premise (unstated because obvious) that if an institution is inherently unequal and deprives students of equal protection of the law guaranteed by the Fourteenth Amendment, then it is unconstitutional.

Symbolize this argument. The domain of discourse seems to be institutions, and in particular, schools. Here is one plausible translation key, if you feel stumped creating your own:

	Translation Key	
Logic	English	
Fx	x is a public school.	
Gx	x is segregated (or "separate").	
Hx	x is inherently unequal.	
Ix	x deprives students of equal protection of the laws guaranteed by the Fourteenth Amendment.	
Jx	x is acting in an unconstitutional way.	

14. Universal derivation

14.1 An example: the Meno

In one of Plato's dialogues, the *Meno*, Socrates uses questions and prompts to direct a young slave boy in the process of making a square that has twice the area of a given square, by using the diagonal of the given square as a side in the new square. Socrates draws a square 1 foot on a side in the dirt. The young boy at first just suggests that to double its area, the two sides of the square should be doubled, but Socrates shows him that this would result in a square that is four times the area of the given square; that is, a square of the size four square feet. Next, Socrates takes this 2×2 square, which has four square feet, and shows the boy how to make a square double its size.

> **Socrates:** Tell me, boy, is not this a square of four feet that I have drawn?
> **Boy:** Yes.
> **Socrates:** And now I add another square equal to the former one?
> **Boy:** Yes.
> **Socrates:** And a third, which is equal to either of them?
> **Boy:** Yes.
> **Socrates:** Suppose that we fill up the vacant corner?
> **Boy:** Very good.
> **Socrates:** Here, then, there are four equal spaces?
> **Boy:** Yes.[12]

So what Socrates has drawn at this point looks like:

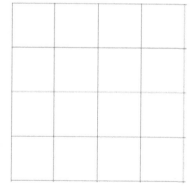

Suppose each square is a foot on a side. Socrates will now ask the boy how to make a square that is of eight square feet, or twice the size of their initial 2×2 square. Socrates has a goal and method in drawing the square four times the size of the original.

> Socrates: And how many times larger is this space than the other?
> Boy: Four times.
> Socrates: But it ought to have been twice only, as you will remember.
> Boy: True.
> Socrates: And does not this line, reaching from corner to corner, bisect each of these spaces?

By "spaces", Socrates means each of the 2×2 squares. Socrates has now drawn the following:

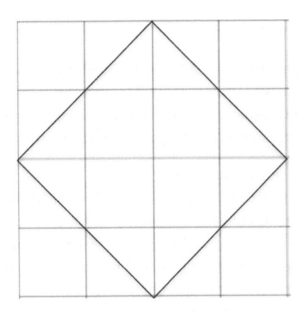

> Boy: Yes.
> Socrates: And are there not here four equal lines that contain this new square?
> Boy: There are.
> Socrates: Look and see how much this new square is.
> Boy: I do not understand.

After some discussion, Socrates gets the boy to see that where the new line cuts a small square, it cuts it in half. So, adding the whole small squares inside this new square, and adding the half small squares inside this new square, the boy is able to answer.

> **Socrates:** The new square is of how many feet?
> **Boy:** Of eight feet.
> **Socrates:** And from what line do you get this new square?
> **Boy:** From this. [The boy presumably points at the dark line in our diagram.]
> **Socrates:** That is, from the line which extends from corner to corner of the each of the spaces of four feet?
> **Boy:** Yes.
> **Socrates:** And that is the line that the educated call the "diagonal". And if this is the proper name, then you, Meno's slave, are prepared to affirm that the double space is the square of the diagonal?
> **Boy:** Certainly, Socrates.

For the original square that was 2×2 feet, by drawing a diagonal of the square we were able to draw one side of a square that is twice the area. Socrates has demonstrated how to make a square twice the area of any given square: make the new square's sides each as large as the diagonal of the given square.

It is curious that merely by questioning the slave (who would have been a child of a Greek family defeated in battle, and would have been deprived of any education), Socrates is able to get him to complete a proof. Plato takes this as a demonstration of a strange metaphysical doctrine that each of us once knew everything and have forgotten it, and now we just need to be helped to remember the truth. But we should note a different and interesting fact. Neither Socrates nor the slave boy ever doubts that Socrates's demonstration is true of all squares. That is, while Socrates draws squares in the dirt, the slave boy never says, "Well, Socrates, you've proved that to make a square twice as big as this square that you have drawn, I need to take the diagonal of this square as a side of my new square. But what about a square that's much smaller or larger than the one you drew here?"

That is in fact a very perplexing question. Why is Socrates's demonstration good for all, for any, squares?

14.2 A familiar strangeness

We have saved for last the most subtle issue about reasoning with quantifiers: how shall we prove something is universally true?

Consider the following argument. We will assume a first order logical language that talks about numbers, since it is sometimes easier to imagine something true of everything in our domain of discourse if we are talking about numbers.

> All numbers evenly divisible by eight are evenly divisible by four.
>
> All numbers evenly divisible by four are evenly divisible by two.
>
> ———
>
> All numbers evenly divisible by eight are evenly divisible by two.

Let us assume an implicit translation key, and then we can say that the following is a translation of this argument.

$\forall x(Fx \rightarrow Gx)$

$\forall x(Gx \rightarrow Hx)$

———

$\forall x(Fx \rightarrow Hx)$

This looks like a valid argument. Indeed, it may seem obvious that it is valid. But to prove it, we need some way to be able to prove a universal statement.

But how could we do such a thing? There are infinitely many numbers, so surely we cannot check them all. How do we prove that something is true of all numbers, without taking an infinite amount of time and creating an infinitely long proof?

The odds are that you already know how to do this, although you have never reflected on your ability. You most likely saw a proof of a universal claim far back in grade school, and without reflection concluded it was good and proper. For example, when you were first taught that the sum of the interior angles of a triangle is equivalent to two right angles, you might have seen a proof that used a single triangle as an illustration. It might have gone something like this: assume lines AB and CD are parallel, and that two other line segments EF and EG cross those parallel lines, and meet on AB at E. Assume also that the alternate angles for any line crossing parallel lines are equal. Assume that a line is equivalent to two right angles, or 180 degrees. Then, in the following picture, b'=b, c'=c, and b'+c'+a=180 degrees. Thus, a+b+c=180 degrees.

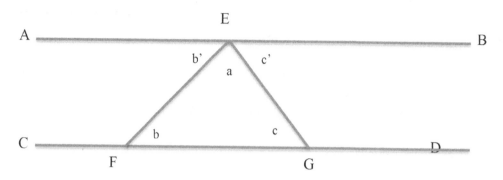

Most of us think about such a proof, see the reasoning, and agree with it. But if we reflect for a moment, we should see that it is quite mysterious why such a proof works. That's because, it aims to show us that the sum of the interior angles of any triangle is the same as two right angles. But there are infinitely many triangles (in fact, logicians have proved that there are more triangles than there are natural numbers!). So how can it be that this argument proves something about all of the triangles? Furthermore, in the diagram above, there are infinitely many different sets of two parallel lines we could have used. And so on.

This also touches on the case that we saw in the *Meno*. Socrates proves that the area of a square A twice as big as square B does not simply have sides twice as long as the sides of B; rather, each side of A must be the length of the diagonal of B. But he and the boy drew just one square in the dirt. And it won't even be properly square. How can they conclude something about every square based on their reasoning and a crude drawing?

In all such cases, there is an important feature of the relevant proof. Squares come in many sizes, triangles come in many sizes and shapes. But what interests us in such proofs is all and only the properties that all triangles have, or all and only properties that all squares have. We refer to a triangle, or a square, that is abstract in a strange way: we draw inferences about, and only refer to, its properties that are shared with all the things of its kind. We are really considering a special, generalized instance.

We can call this special instance the "arbitrary instance". If we prove something is true of the arbitrary triangle, then we conclude it is true of all triangles. If we prove something is true of the arbitrary square, then we conclude it is true of all squares. If we prove something is true of an arbitrary natural number, then we conclude it is true of all natural numbers. And so on.

14.3 Universal derivation

To use this insight, we will introduce not an inference rule, but rather a new proof method. We will call this proof method "universal derivation" or, synonymously, "universal proof". We need something to stand for the arbitrary instance. For a number of reasons, it is traditional to use unbound variables for this. However, to make it clear that the variable is being used in this special way, and that the well-formed formula so formed is a sentence, we will use a prime—that is, the small mark "'"—to mark the variable. Let α be any variable. Our proof method thus looks like this.

$$
\boxed{\alpha'}
$$
$$
\vdots
$$
$$
\phi(\alpha')
$$
$$
\forall \alpha \phi(\alpha)
$$

> *Where α' does not appear in any open proof above the beginning of the universal derivation.*

Remember that an open proof is a subproof that is not completed.

We will call any symbolic term of this form (x', y', z'...) an "arbitrary term", and it is often convenient to describe it as referring to the arbitrary object or arbitrary instance. But there is not any one object in our domain of discourse that such a term refers to. Rather, it stands in for an abstraction: what all the things in the domain of discourse have in common.

The semantics of an arbitrary instance is perhaps less mysterious when we consider the actual syntactic constraints on a universal derivation. One should not be able to say anything about an arbitrary instance α' unless one has done universal instantiation of a universal claim. No other sentence should allow claims about α'. For example, you cannot perform existential instantiation to an arbitrary instance, since we required that existential instantiation be done to special indefinite names that have not appeared yet in the proof. But if we can only makes claims about α' using universal instantiation, then we will be asserting something about α' that we could have asserted about anything in our domain of discourse. Seen in this way, from the perspective of the syntax of our proof, the universal derivation hopefully seems very intuitive.

This schematic proof has a line where we indicate that we are going to use α' as the arbitrary object, by putting α' in a box. This is not necessary, and is not part of our proof. Rather, like the explanations we write on the side, it is there to help someone understand our proof. It says, *this is the beginning of a universal derivation, and α' stands for the arbitrary object.* Since this is not actually a line in the proof, we need not number it.

We can now prove our example above is valid.

1. $\forall x(Fx \rightarrow Gx)$	premise
2. $\forall x(Gx \rightarrow Hx)$	premise
$\boxed{x'}$	
3. Fx'	assumption for conditional derivation
4. $(Fx' \rightarrow Gx')$	universal instantiation, 1
5. Gx'	modus ponens, 4, 3
6. $(Gx' \rightarrow Hx')$	universal instantiation, 2
7. Hx'	modus ponens, 6, 5
8. $(Fx' \rightarrow Hx')$	conditional derivation, 3-7
9. $\forall x(Fx \rightarrow Hx)$	universal derivation, 3-8

Remember that our specification of the proof method has a special condition, that α' must not appear earlier in an open proof (a proof that is still being completed). This helps us avoid confusing two or more arbitrary instances. Here, there is no x' appearing above our universal derivation in an open proof (in fact, there is no other arbitrary instance appearing in the proof above x'), so we have followed the rule.

14.4 Two useful theorems: quantifier equivalence

Our definition of "theorem" remains the same for the first order logic and for the propositional logic: a sentence that can be proved without premises. However, we now have a distinction when it comes to the semantics of sentences that must be true. Generally, we think of a tautology as a sentence that must be true as a function of the truth-functional connectives that constitute that sentence. That is, we identified that a tautology must be true by making a truth table for the tautology. There are, however, sentences of the first order logic that must be true, but we cannot demonstrate this with a truth table. Here is an example:

$$\forall x(Fx \vee \neg Fx)$$

This sentence must be true. But we cannot show this with a truth table. Instead, we need the concept of a model (introduced briefly in section 17.6) to describe this property precisely. But even with our intuitive semantics, we can see that this sentence must be true. For, we require (in our restriction on predicates) that everything in our domain of discourse either is, or is not, an F.

We call a sentence of the first order logic that must be true, "logically true". Just as it was a virtue of the propositional logic that all the theorems are tautologies, and all the tautologies are theorems; it is a virtue of our first order logic that all the theorems are logically true, and all the logically true sentences are theorems. Proving this is beyond the scope of this book, but is something done in most advanced logic courses and texts.

Here is a proof that $\forall x(Fx \vee \neg Fx)$.

```
┌
│  ┌──────┐
│  │  x′  │
│  └──────┘
│ │  1. ¬(Fx′ ∨ ¬Fx′)                      assumption for indirect derivation
│ │ │  2. ¬Fx′                             assumption for indirect derivation
│ │ │  3. (Fx′ ∨ ¬Fx′)                     addition, 2
│ │ │  4. ¬(Fx′ ∨ ¬Fx′)                    repeat, 1
│ │
│ │  5. Fx′                               indirect derivation, 2-4
│ │  6. (Fx′ ∨ ¬Fx′)                      addition, 5
│ │  7. ¬(Fx′ ∨ ¬Fx′)                     repeat, 1
│ │
│ │  8. (Fx′ ∨ ¬Fx′)                      indirect derivation, 1-7
│  9. ∀x(Fx ∨ ¬Fx)                        universal derivation, 1-8
```

Let us consider another example of a logically true sentence that we can prove, and thus, practice universal derivation. The following sentence is logically true.

$$((\forall x\,(Fx \to Gx) \land \forall x\,(Fx \to Hx)) \to \forall x\,(Fx \to (Gx \land Hx))$$

Here is a proof. The formula is a conditional, so we will use conditional derivation. However, the consequence is a universal sentence, so we will need a universal derivation as a subproof.

1. $(\forall x(Fx \to Gx) \wedge \forall x(Fx \to Hx))$ assumption for conditional derivation

$\boxed{x'}$

2. Fx' assumption for conditional derivation

3. $\forall x(Fx \to Gx)$ simplification, 1
4. $(Fx' \to Gx')$ universal instantiation, 3
5. Gx' modus ponens, 4, 2
6. $\forall x(Fx \to Hx)$ simplification, 1
7. $(Fx' \to Hx')$ universal instantiation, 6
8. Hx' modus ponens, 7, 2
9. $(Gx' \wedge Hx')$ adjunction, 5, 8

10. $(Fx' \to (Gx' \wedge Hx'))$ conditional derivation, 2-9

11. $\forall x(Fx \to (Gx \wedge Hx))$ universal derivation, 2-10

12. $((\forall x(Fx \to Gx) \wedge \forall x(Fx \to Hx)) \to \forall x(Fx \to (Gx \wedge Hx)))$ conditional derivation, 1-11

Just as there were useful theorems of the propositional logic, there are many useful theorems of the first order logic. Two very useful theorems concern the relation between existential and universal claims.

$(\exists xFx \leftrightarrow \neg\forall x\neg Fx)$

$(\forall xFx \leftrightarrow \neg\exists x\neg Fx)$

Something is F just in case not everything is not F. And, everything is F if and only if not even one thing is not F.

We can prove the second of these, and leave the first as an exercise.

```
 │   1. ∀xFx                              assumption for conditional derivation
 │  ┌─ 2. ∃x¬Fx                           assumption for indirect derivation
 │  │   3. ¬Fp                            existential instantiation, 2
 │  │   4. Fp                             universal instantiation, 1
 │   5. ¬∃x¬Fx                            indirect derivation, 2-4
 │
 │   6. (∀xFx → ¬∃x¬Fx)                   conditional derivation 1-5
 │  ┌─ 7. ¬∃x¬Fx                          assumption for conditional derivation
 │  │  ┌──────┐
 │  │  │  x'  │
 │  │  └──────┘
 │  │  ┌─ 8. ¬Fx'                         assumption for indirect derivation
 │  │  │   9. ∃x¬Fx                       existential generalization, 8
 │  │  │   10. ¬∃x¬Fx                     repeat, 7
 │  │   11. Fx'                           indirect derivation, 8-10
 │  │   12. ∀xFx                          universal derivation, 8-11
 │   13. (¬∃x¬Fx → ∀xFx)                  conditional derivation 7-12
 │   14. (∀xFx ↔ ¬∃x¬Fx))                 bicondition, 6, 13
```

14.5 Illustrating invalidity

Consider the following argument:

$$\forall x(Hx \to Gx)$$

$$\neg Hd$$

_____

$$\neg Gd$$

This is an invalid argument. It is possible that the conclusion is false but the premises are true.

Because we cannot use truth tables to describe the semantics of quantifiers, we have kept the semantics of the quantifiers intuitive. A complete semantics for first order logic is called a "model", and requires some set theory. This presents a difficulty: we cannot demonstrate that an argument using quantifiers is invalid without a semantics.

Fortunately, there is a heuristic method that we can use that does not require developing a full model. We will develop an intuitive and partial model. The idea is that we will come up with an interpretation of the argument, where we ascribe a meaning to each predicate, and a referent for each term, and where this interpretation makes the premises obviously true and the conclusion obviously false. This is not a perfect method, since it will depend upon our understanding of our interpretation, and because it requires us to demonstrate some creativity. But this method does illustrate important features of the semantics of the first order logic, and used carefully it can help us see why a particular argument is invalid.

It is often best to create an interpretation using numbers, since there is less vagueness of the meaning of the predicates. So suppose our domain of discourse is the natural numbers. Then, we need to find an interpretation of the predicates that makes the first two lines true and the conclusion false. Here is one:

Hx: x is evenly divisible by 2

Gx: x is evenly divisible by 1

d: 3

The argument would then have as premises: All numbers evenly divisible by 2 are evenly divisible by 1; and, 3 is not evenly divisible by 2. These are both true. But the conclusion would be: 3 is not evenly divisible by 1. This is false. This illustrates that the argument form is invalid.

Let us consider another example. Here is an invalid argument:

$\forall x(Fx \rightarrow Gx)$

Fa

———

Gb

We can illustrate that it is invalid by finding an interpretation that shows the premises true and the conclusion false. Our domain of discourse will be the natural numbers. We interpret the predicates and names in the following way:

Fx: x is greater than 10

Gx: x is greater than 5

a: 15

b: 2

Given this interpretation, the argument translates to: Any number greater than 10 is greater than 5; 15 is greater than 10; therefore, 2 is greater than 5. The conclusion is obviously false, whereas the premises are obviously true.

In this exercise, it may seem strange that we would just make up meanings for our predicates and names. However, as long as our interpretations of the predicates and names follow our rules, our interpretation will be acceptable. Recall the rules for predicates are that they have an arity, and that each predicate of arity n is true or false (never both, never neither) of each n things in the domain of discourse. The rule for names is that they refer to only one object.

This illustrates an important point. Consider a valid argument, and try to come up with some interpretation that makes it invalid. You will find that you cannot do it, if you respect the constraints on predicates and names. Make sure that you understand this. It will clarify much about the generality of the first order logic. Take a valid argument like:

$\forall x(Fx \rightarrow Gx)$

F*a*

G*a*

Come up with various interpretations for *a* and for F and G. You will find that you cannot make an invalid argument.

In summary, an informal model used to illustrate invalidity must have three things:

1. a domain of discourse;
2. an interpretation of the predicates; and
3. an interpretation of the names.

If you can find such an informal model that makes the premises obviously true and the conclusion obviously false, you have illustrated that the argument is invalid. This may take several tries: you can also sometimes come up with interpretations for invalid arguments that make all the premises and the conclusion true; this is not surprising, when you remember the definition of valid (that necessarily, if the premises are true then the conclusion is true—in other words, it is not enough that the conclusion just happens to be true).

14.6 Problems

1. Prove the following. These will require universal derivation. (For the third, remember that the variables used in quantifiers are merely used to indicate the place in the following expression that is being bound. So, if we change the variable nothing else changes in our proof or use of inference rules.) The last three are challenging. For these last three problems, do not use the quantifier negation rules.

   a. Premises: ∀xFx, ∀x (Fx ↔ Gx). Conclusion: ∀xGx.
   b. Premises: ∀x(Fx → Gx). Conclusion: ∀x(¬Gx → ¬Fx).
   c. Premises: ∀x(Fx ↔ Hx), ∀y(Hy ↔ Gy). Conclusion: ∀z(Fz ↔ Gz).
   d. Premises: ∀x(Fx ∧ Hx), ∀x(Gx ↔ Hx). Conclusion: ∀x(Fx → Hx).
   e. Premises: ∀x(Fx v Gx), ¬∃xGx. Conclusion: ∀xFx.
   f. Conclusion: (∀x(¬Fx v Gx) → ∀x(Fx → Gx)).
   g. Conclusion: (∀x(Fx ↔ Gx) → (∀xFx ↔ ∀xGx)).
   h. Conclusion: (¬∃xFx ↔ ∀x¬Fx).
   i. Conclusion: (¬∀xFx ↔ ∃x¬Fx).
   j. Conclusion: (∃xFx ↔ ¬∀x¬Fx).

2. Create a different informal model for each of the following arguments to illustrate that it is invalid.

   a. Premises: ∀x(Fx → Gx), ¬Ga. Conclusion: ¬Fb.
   b. Premises: ∀x(Fx v Gx), ¬Fa. Conclusion: Gb.
   c. Premises: ∀x(Fx → Gx), ∃xFx. Conclusion: Gc.

3. In normal colloquial English, write your own valid argument with at least two premises and with a conclusion that is a universal statement. Your argument should just be a paragraph (not an ordered list of sentences or anything else that looks like formal logic). Translate it into first order logic and prove it is valid.

4. Do we have free will? Much of the work that philosophers have done to answer this question focuses on trying to define or understand what free will would be, and understand the consequences if we do not have free will. Doubts about free will have often been raised by those who believe that physics will ultimately explain all events using deterministic laws, so that everything had to happen one way. Here is a simplified version of such an argument.

> Every event is caused by prior events by way of natural physical laws. Any event caused by prior events by way of natural physical laws could not have happened otherwise. But, if all events could not have happened otherwise, then there is no freely willed event. We conclude, therefore, that there are no freely willed events.

Symbolize this argument and prove it is valid. You might consider using the following predicates:

> Fx: x is an event.

> Gx: x is caused by prior events by way of natural physical laws.

> Hx: x could have happened otherwise.

> Ix: x is a freely willed event.

(Hint: this argument will require universal derivation. The conclusion can be had using modus ponens, if you can prove: all events could not have happened otherwise.) Do you believe that this argument is sound?

5. In chapter 13, problem 9, you translated an argument from Brown v. The Board of Education. Now prove that the argument is valid.

[12] These passages are adapted from the Benjamin Jowett translation of the *Meno*. Versions of this translation are available for free on the web. Students hoping to read other works by Plato should consider Cooper and Hutchinson (1997).

15. Relations, functions, identity, and multiple quantifiers

15.1 Relations

We have developed a first order logic that is sufficient to describe many things. The goal of this chapter is to discuss ways to extend and apply this logic. We will introduce relations and functions, make some interesting observations about identity, and discuss how to use multiple quantifiers.

Recall that if we have a predicate of arity greater than one, we sometimes call that a "relation". An arity one predicate like "... is tall" does not relate things in our domain of discourse. Rather, it tells us about a property of a thing in our domain of discourse. But an arity two predicate like "... is taller than ..." relates pairs of things in our domain of discourse.

More generally, we can think of a relation as a set of ordered things from our domain of discourse. An arity two relation is thus a collection of ordered pairs of things; the relation "...is taller than..." would be all the ordered pairs of things where the first is taller than the second. The predicate "... is taller than..." would be true of all these things. The relation "... sits between ... and ..." would be the collection of all the triples of things where the first sat between the second and third. The predicate "... sits between ... and ..." would be true of all of these things.

Logicians have developed a host of useful ways of talking about relations, especially relations between just two things. We can illustrate this with an example. Hospitals and other medical treatment facilities often need blood for transfusions. But not any kind of blood can do. One way to classify kinds of blood is using the ABO system. This divides kinds of blood into four groups: A, B, AB, and O. This classification describes antigens on the surface of the blood cells. It is a very useful classification, because some people have an immune system that will not tolerate the antigens on other kinds of blood. This tolerance is determined by one's blood group.

Those with type O blood can give blood to anyone, without causing an immune reaction. Those with type A can give blood to those with type A and type AB. Those with type B can give blood to those with type B and type AB. And those with type AB can only give to type AB. Let arrows mean, *can be given to people with this blood type without causing an allergic reaction* in the following diagram:

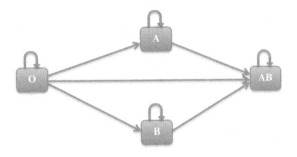

Notice a number of things. First, every blood type can share blood with people of that blood type. But it is not always the case that if I can share blood with you, you can share blood with me: it could be that I am type O and you are type B. Also, if I can share blood with you, and you can share blood with Tom, then I can share blood with Tom.

The first feature of relations is called "reflexive". For any relation Φ(*xy*), the relation is reflexive if and only if:

$\forall x\Phi(xx)$

Examples of reflexive relations in English include "...is as old as...". Each person is as old as herself. A relation that is not reflexive is, "...is older than ...". No person is older than herself.

For any relation Φ, the relation is symmetric if and only if:

$\forall x\forall y(\Phi(x\,y) \rightarrow \Phi(y\,x))$

Examples of symmetric relations in English include "...is married to...". In our legal system at least, if Pat is married to Chris, then Chris is married to Pat.

Finally, call a relation "transitive" if and only if

$$\forall x \forall y \forall z ((\Phi(x\,y) \wedge \Phi(y\,z)) \rightarrow \Phi(x\,z))$$

Examples of transitive relations in English include "...is older than...". If Tom is older than Steve, and Steve is older than Pat, then Tom is older than Pat.

Return now to our example of blood types. We introduce the following translation key:

Gxy: x can give blood to y without causing an immune reaction

It is the case that

$$\forall x Gxx$$

And so we know that the relation G is reflexive. A person with type O blood can give blood to himself, a person with type AB blood can give blood to herself, and so on. (People do this when they store blood before a surgery.) Is the relation symmetric? Consider whether the following is true:

$$\forall x \forall y (Gxy \rightarrow Gyx)$$

A moment's reflection reveals this isn't true. A person of type O can give blood to a person of type AB, but the person with type AB blood cannot give blood to the person with type O, without potentially causing a reaction. So G is not symmetric.

Finally, to determine if G is transitive, consider whether the following is true.

$$\forall x \forall y \forall z ((Gxy \wedge Gyz) \rightarrow Gxz)$$

A person with type O blood can give blood to a person with type A blood, and that person can give blood to someone of type AB. Does it follow that the person with type O can give blood to the person with AB? It does. And similarly this is so for all other possible cases. G is a transitive relation.

15.2 Functions

A function is a kind of relation between two or more things. What all functions have in common is that they relate some specific number of things to precisely one thing. A familiar example from mathematics might be the squaring function. We write for this, n^2. This takes one number, say 7, and then relates it to exactly one other number, 49. Or addition is a function that takes two numbers and relates them to exactly one other number, their sum.

The idea of a function is very general, and extends beyond mathematics. For example, each of the following could be a function (if certain things are assumed beforehand):

the mother of...

the father of...

Think of how you could use something like this in our logical language. You could say, "The father of Tom is Canadian". But now, who is Canadian? Not Tom. Tom's father is. In this sentence, "the father of..." acts as a function. It relates a person to another person. And, in our predicate, "the father of Tom" acts like a name, in that it refers to one thing.

Functions have an arity. Addition is an arity two function; it takes two objects in order to form a symbolic term. But in order to be a function, the resulting symbolic term must always refer to only one object. (This rule gets broken a lot in mathematics, where some relations are called "functions" but can have more than one output. This arises because in circumscribed domains of discourse, those operations are functions, and then they get applied in new domains but are still called "functions". Thus, the square root function is a function when we are studying the natural numbers, but once we introduce negative numbers it no longer is a function. But mathematicians call it a "function" because it is in limited domains a function, and because the diverse output is predictable in various ways. Logic is the only field where one earns the right to call mathematicians sloppy.)

Functions are surprisingly useful. Computers, for example, can be understood as function machines, and programming can be usefully described as the writing of functions for the computer. Much of mathematics is concerned with studying functions, and they often prove useful for studying other things in mathematics that are not themselves functions.

We can add functions to our logical language. We will let **f**, **g**, **h**, ... be functions. Each function, as noted, has an arity. A function of arity n combined with n symbolic terms is a symbolic term.

Thus, to make a key to translate the sentence above, we can have:

Kx: x is Canadian.

fx: the father of x.

a: Tom

b: Steve

(Obviously, we are assuming that each person has only one father. Arguably that is only one use of the word "father," but our goal here is to create a familiar example, not to take sides in any issue about family relations. So we will allow the assumption just to make our point.) Using that key, the following would mean "Tom is Canadian":

K*a*

And the following would mean "The father of Tom is Canadian":

Kf*a*

We can also say something like, "Tom's paternal grandfather is Canadian":

Kff*a*

Or even, "Tom's paternal great-grandfather is Canadian":

Kfff*a*

That works because the father of the father of Tom is the paternal grandfather of Tom, which then is a symbolic term, and we can apply the function to it. Recall that, when a rule can be applied repeatedly to its product, we call this "recursion".

15.3 Identity

There is one predicate that has always been enormously useful, and which in most logical systems is singled out for special attention. This is identity.

In English, the word "is" is multiply ambiguous, and we must sort out identity from predication and existence. For example, consider the following sentences:

Malcolm X is a great orator.

Malcolm X is Malcolm Little.

Malcolm X is.

The last example is not very common in English usage, but it is grammatical. Here we see the "is" of existence. The sentence asserts that Malcolm X exists. In the first sentence, we would treat "...is a great orator" as an arity one predicate. The "is" is part of the predicate, and in our logic, cannot be distinguished from the predicate. But the second case uses the "is" of identity. It asserts that Malcolm X and Malcolm Little are the same thing.

Because it is so common to use the symbol "=" for identity, we will use it, also. Strictly speaking, our syntax requires prefix notation. But for any language we create, we could introduce an arity two predicate

Ixy: x is identical to y

And then we could say, whenever we write "$\alpha = \beta$" we really mean "$I\alpha\beta$".

Note identity describes a relation that is reflexive, symmetric, and transitive. Everything is identical to itself. If $a=b$ then $b=a$. And if $a=b$ and $b=c$ then $a=c$.

One special feature of identity is that we know that if two things are identical, then anything true of one is true of the other. In fact, the philosopher Leibniz defined identity with a principle that we call Leibniz's Law: a and b are identical if and only if they have all and only the same properties. Our logic must take identity as a primitive, however, because we have no way in our logic of saying "all properties" (this is what "first order" in "first order logic" means: our quantifiers have only particular objects in their domain).

Leibniz's insight, however, suggests an inference rule. If α and β are symbolic terms, and Φ(α) means that Φ is a formula in which α appears, we can say

$$\Phi(\alpha)$$

$$\alpha = \beta$$

———

$$\Phi(\beta)$$

Where we replace one or more occurrences of α in Φ with β. We can call this rule, "indiscernibility of identicals". We sometimes also call this, "substitution of identicals".

This is an interesting kind of rule. Some logicians would call this a "non-logical rule". The reason is, we know it is proper because we know the meaning of "=". Unlike, for example, modus ponens, which identifies a logical relation between two kinds of sentences, this rule relies not on the semantics of a connective, but rather on the meaning of a predicate. This notion of "non-logical" is a term of art, but it does seem profound. Adding such rules to our language can strengthen it considerably.

Adding identity to our language will allow us to translate some expressions that we would be unable to translate otherwise. Consider our example above, for functions. How would we translate the expression, "Steve is the father of Tom"? We could add to our language a predicate, "… is the father of …". However, it is interesting that in this expression ("Steve is the father of Tom"), the "is" is identity. A better translation (using the key above) would be:

$$b = fa$$

We can also say things like, "The father of Steve is the paternal grandfather of Tom":

$$fb = ffa$$

Consider now a sentence like this: someone is the father of Tom. Again, if we had a predicate for "… is the father of …", we could just say, there is something that is the father of Tom. But given that we have a function for "the father of x" we could also translate this phrase as:

$\exists x\ x{=}fa$

We can see from these examples that there are interesting parallels between relations (including functions) and predicates. To represent some kind of function, we can introduce a function into our language, which acts as a special kind of symbolic term, but it is also possible to identify a predicate that is true of all and only those things that the function relates. Nonetheless, we must be careful to distinguish between predicates, which when combined with the appropriate number of names form a sentence; and functions, which when combined with the appropriate number of other terms are symbolic terms. In our logic, treating predicates like functions (that is, taking them as symbolic terms for other predicates) will create nonsense.

Finally, we had as an example above, the sentence "Malcolm X is". This is equivalent to "Malcolm X exists". Let c mean *Malcolm X*. Identity allows us to express this sentence. We say that there is at least one thing that is Malcolm X:

$\exists x\ x{=}c$

15.4 Examples using multiple quantifiers

We have only just begun to explore the power of quantifiers. Consider now the following sentences:

Every number is greater than or equal to some number.

Some number is greater than or equal to every number.

Every number is less than or equal to some number.

Some number is less than or equal to every number.

Depending upon our domain of discourse, some of these sentences are true, and some of them are false. Can we represent them in our logical language?

Suppose that we introduce an arity two predicate for "greater than or equal to":

Gxy: x is greater than or equal to y

We can follow tradition, and use "≥". Thus, when we write "α≥β" we understand that this is "Gαβ". Let us also assume that our domain of discourse is the natural numbers. That is, we are talking only about 1, 2, 3, 4....

We can see now how to take a first step toward expressing these sentences. If we write:

$x{\geq}y$

We have said that x is greater than or equal to y. We have used quantifiers to say "all", and we can write

$\forall x \; x{\geq}y$

Which says that every number is greater than or equal to y. But how will we capture the sentences above? We will need to use multiple quantifiers. To say that "every number is greater than some number", we will write

$\forall x \exists y \; x{\geq}y$

This raises important questions about how to interpret multiple quantifiers. Using multiple quantifiers expands the power of our language enormously. However, we must be very careful to understand their meaning.

Consider the following two sentences, which will use our key above.

$\forall x \exists y \; x{\geq}y$

$\exists y \forall x \; x{\geq}y$

Do they have the same meaning?

As we understand the semantics of quantifiers, we will say that they do not. The basic idea is that we read the quantifiers from left to right. Thus, the first sentence above should be translated to English as "Every number is greater than or equal to some number". The second sentence should be translated, "Some number is less than or equal to every number". They have very different meanings. Depending upon our domain of discourse, they could have different truth values. For example, if we use the natural numbers as our domain of discourse, the first sentence is true and the second sentence is true. However, if we used the integers for our domain of discourse, so that we included negative numbers, then the first sentence is true but the second sentence is false.

It may be helpful to think of multiple quantifiers in the following way. If we were to instantiate the quantifiers, then, we would work from left to right. Thus, the first sentence says something like, pick any number in our domain of discourse, then there will be at least one number in our domain of discourse that is less than or equal to that first number that you already picked. The second sentence says something quite different: there is at least one number in our domain of discourse such that, if you pick that number, then any number in our domain of discourse is greater than or equal to it.

With this in mind, we are now able to translate the four phrases above. We include the English with the translation to avoid any confusion.

Every number is greater than or equal to some number.

$\forall x \exists y \; x \geq y$

Some number is greater than or equal to every number.

$\exists x \forall y \; x \geq y$

Every number is less than or equal to some number.

$\forall x \exists y \; y \geq x$

Some number is less than or equal to every number.

$\exists x \forall y \; y \geq x$

As we noted above, the truth value of these sentences can change if we change our domain of discourse. If our domain of discourse is the natural numbers, then only the second sentence is false; this is because for the natural numbers there is a least number (1), but there is no greatest number. But if our domain of discourse is the integers, then the second and fourth sentences are false. This is because with the negative numbers, there is no least number: you can always find a lesser negative number.

Hopefully it becomes very clear now why we need the possibility of a number of variables for our quantifiers. We could not write the expressions above if we did not have discernibly distinct variables to allow different quantifiers to bind different locations in the predicate.

15.5 Capturing specific quantities

It can be interesting to see a powerful use of multiple quantifiers. In 1905, the British philosopher Bertrand Russell (1872-1970) published a very insightful and influential paper, "On Denoting". This paper, and additional work by Russell that followed it, made brilliant use of a series of problems in logic and language that perplexed Russell. Russell was concerned about a number of puzzles that arise around phrases like, "The current President of the United States...". Such a phrase seems to act like a name, and yet a number of strange outcomes arise if we treat it as a name.

First, suppose we say

It is not the case that Sam is bald.

Now suppose that anyone who is not bald has hair. Then, we could reason that:

Sam has hair.

That seems correct, if we grant the premise that all those who are not bald have hair. But now consider the following sentence.

It is not the case that the present King of France is bald.

By the same reasoning, this would seem to entail that:

The present King of France has hair.

But that's not right. There is no present King of France!

It gets worse. Let us assert that

The present King of France does not exist.

This seems to pick out a thing, the present King of France, and ascribe to it a property, not existing. After all, in our logical language, each name must refer to something. But if we can pick out that thing in order to describe it as not existing, does it not exist? That is, is there not a thing to which the term refers?

Some philosophers indeed argued that every term, even in a natural language, must have a thing that it refers to. The philosopher Alexius Meinong (1853-1920), for example, proposed that every name has a referent that has being, but that existence was reserved for particular actual objects. This is very strange, when you consider it: it means that "the round square" refers to something, a something that has being, but that lacks existence. Russell thought this a terrible solution, and wanted to find another.

Russell uses a different example to illustrate a third problem. Suppose that

> George IV wished to know whether Scott was the author of *Waverley*.

Here Russell raises a problem related to one that the mathematician Gottlob Frege had already observed. Namely, if Scott=the author of *Waverley*, then one might suppose that we could substitute "Scott" where we see "the author of *Waverley*" and get a sentence that has the same truth value. That is, we introduced above a rule—indiscernibility of identicals—that, if applied here, should allow us to replace "the author of *Waverley*" with "Scott" if Scott=the author of *Waverley*. But that fails: it is not the case that

> George IV wished to know whether Scott was Scott.

George IV already knows that Scott is Scott.

Russell put forward a brilliant solution to these puzzles. He developed an analysis of some English phrases into a logical form that is rather different than we might expect. For example, he argues the proper form to translate "It is not the case that the present King of France is bald" is something like this. Let "Gx" mean "x is the present king of France" and "Hx" mean "x is bald", then this sentence is translated:

$$\exists x((Gx \wedge Hx) \wedge \forall y(Gy \to x=y))$$

This says there is something—call it x for now—that is the present king of France, and that thing is bald, and if anything is the present king of France it is identical to x. This second clause is a way of saying that there is only one king of France, which is how Russell captures the meaning of "the" in "the present king of France".

This sentence is false, because there is no present king of France. But to deny that the present king of France is bald is to assert rather that

$$\exists x((Gx \wedge \neg Hx) \wedge \forall y(Gy \rightarrow x=y))$$

This sentence is false also. It cannot be used to conclude that there is a present king of France who is hirsute.

Similar quick work can be done with the puzzle about existence. "The present king of France does not exist" is equivalent to "It is not the case that the present king of France exists" and this we translate as:

$$\neg \exists x(Gx \wedge \forall y(Gy \rightarrow x=y))$$

Note that there is no need in this formula for a name that refers to nothing. There is no name in this formula.

Finally, when George IV wished to know whether Scott was the author of *Waverley*, we can let "*a*" stand for "Scott", and "Wx" mean "x authored *Waverley*", and now assert that what the king wanted to know was whether the following is true:

$$\exists x((Wx \wedge \forall y(Wy \rightarrow x=y)) \wedge x=a)$$

In this, the part of the formula that captures the meaning of "the author of *Waverley*" requires no name, and so there is no issue of applying the indiscernibility of identicals rule. (Remember that the indiscernibility of identicals rule allows the replacement of a symbolic term with an identical symbolic term. In this formula, there is no symbolic term for "the author of *Waverley*", and so even if Scott is the author of *Waverley*, the indiscernibility of identicals rule cannot be applied here.)

Russell has done something very clever. He found a way to interpret a phrase like "the present king of France" as a complex logical formula; such a formula can be constructed so that it uses no names to capture the meaning of the phrase. It is an interesting question whether Russell's analysis should be interpreted as describing, in some sense, what is really inside our minds when we use a phrase like "The present king of France." That's perhaps an issue for cognitive scientists to settle. Our interest is that Russell inspires a new and flexible way to use first order logic to understand possible interpretations of these kinds of utterances.

Russell's translations also suggest a surprising possibility: perhaps many names, or even all names, are actually phrases like these that are uniquely true of one and only one thing. That was of interest to philosophers who wanted to explain the nature of reference; it suggests that reference could be explained using the notion of a complex predicate expression being true of one thing. That is a radical suggestion, and one that Russell developed and defended. He proposed that the only names were the very basic primitive "this" and "that". All other natural language names could then be analyzed into complex phrases like those above. This is an issue for the philosophy of language, and we will not consider it further here.

Another benefit of Russell's translation is that it illustrates how to count with the quantifier. This is of great interest to our logic. Any sentence of the form "there is only one thing that is Φ" can be translated:

$$\exists x (\Phi(x) \wedge \forall y (\Phi(y) \rightarrow x=y))$$

Russell's insight is that if only one thing is Φ, then anything that turns out to be Φ must be the same one thing.

A little ingenuity shows that we can use his insight to say, there are exactly two things that are Φ. It might be helpful at first to separate out "there are at least two" and "there are at most two". These are:

$$\exists x \exists y ((\Phi(x) \wedge \Phi(y)) \wedge \neg x = y)$$

$$\forall x \forall y \forall z (((\Phi(x) \wedge \Phi(y)) \wedge \Phi(z)) \rightarrow ((x=y \vee x=z) \vee y=z))$$

The first sentence says, there exists a thing x and a thing y such that x has property Φ and y has property Φ and x and y are not the same thing. This asserts there are at least two things that have property Φ. The second sentence says for any x, y, z, if each has the property Φ, that at least one of them is the same as the other. This asserts that there are at most two things that have property Φ.

Combine those with a conjunction, and you have the assertion at least two things are Φ, and at most two things are Φ. That is, there are exactly two things that are Φ.

$$(\exists x \exists y ((\Phi(x) \wedge \Phi(y)) \wedge \neg x = y) \wedge \forall x \forall y \forall z (((\Phi(x) \wedge \Phi(y)) \wedge \Phi(z)) \rightarrow ((x=y \vee x=z) \vee$$
$$y=z)))$$

That's awkward, but it shows that we can express any particular quantity using our existing logical language. We will be able to say, for example, that there are exactly 17 things that are Φ. It is quite surprising to think that we do not need numbers to be able to express particular finite quantities, and that our logic is strong enough to do this.

15.6 Problems

1. For each of the following, describe whether the relation is reflexive, symmetric, or transitive. If it lacks any of these properties, give an example of where the property would fail for the relation. (That is, if you say a relation is not symmetric, for example, then give an example of an exception.) Assume a domain of discourse of humans.

   a. ... is the sibling of ...
   b. ... is the mother of ...
   c. ... is the same nationality as ...
   d. ... is older than ...
   e. ... is in love with ...

2. Make your own key and then translate the following into our logical language. You should use a function in your translation of each sentence that has an implicit function.

   a. The mother of Ludwig is musical.
   b. Ludwig is not musical.
   c. Ludwig's paternal grandmother is musical, but his maternal grandmother is not.
   d. Ludwig's father is taller than his mother.
   e. Ludwig's mother is not taller than Ludwig, or his father.
   f. Ludwig's mother is not Ludwig's father.
   g. Someone is Ludwig's mother.
   h. Someone is someone's mother.
   i. Everyone has a mother.
   j. No one is the mother of everyone.

3. Provide your own key and translate the following into our logic. This will require multiple quantifiers.

    a. Everyone is friends with someone.
    b. Someone is friends with someone.
    c. Someone is friends with everyone.
    d. Everyone is friends with everyone.
    e. No one is friends with everyone.

4. Use Russell's interpretation to translate the following expressions. Make your own key.

    a. The Emperor of New York is rotund.
    b. The Emperor of New Jersey is not rotund.
    c. The Emperor of New York is not the Emperor of New Jersey.
    d. There is no Emperor of New York but there is an Emperor of New Jersey.
    e. There are two and only two Emperors of New York.

5. Use our logic to express the claim: exactly three things have property F.

6. Consider this sentence from *The Phaedo* by Plato, in which Phaedo praises Socrates: "Such was the end, Echecrates, of our friend; concerning whom I may truly say, that of all the men of his time whom I have known, he was the wisest and most just." Can you capture the comparison "he was the wisest and most just"? What is of interest here is that we have seen how to use quantifiers and identity to say something like, "other than". This will be needed for a more accurate translation. Let the domain of discourse be, people whom Phaedo knew. You might want to translate this with a predicates to express "x is at least as wise as y" and "x is at least as just as y" before attempting the more difficult but more accurate translation with predicates "x is wiser than y" and "x is more just than y".

16. Summary of first order logic

16.1 Elements of the language

- Symbolic terms are either names, indefinite names, variables, or arbitrary terms.
    - Names: a, b, c, d, e....
    - Indefinite names: p, q, r....
    - Variables: x, y, z....
    - Arbitrary terms: x', y', z'....
- Each predicate has an arity, which is the number of symbolic terms required by that predicate to form a well-formed formula. The predicates of our language are: F, G, H, I....
- Each function has an arity, which is the number of symbolic terms required by the function in order for it to form a symbolic term. The functions of our language are: f, g, h, i....
- There are two quantifiers.
    - ∀, the universal quantifier.
    - ∃, the existential quantifier.
- The connectives are the same as those of the propositional logic.

16.2 Syntax of the language

- An arity n function combined with n symbolic terms is a symbolic term.
- An arity n predicate combined with n symbolic terms is a well-formed formula.
- If Φ and Ψ are well-formed formulas, then the following are also well-formed formulas. (And if Φ and Ψ are sentences, then the following are also sentences.)

- ○ ¬Φ
- ○ (Φ → Ψ)
- ○ (Φ ∧ Ψ)
- ○ (Φ ∨ Ψ)
- ○ (Φ ↔ Ψ)
- We write Φ(α) to mean Φ is a well-formed formula in which the symbolic term α appears.
- If there are no quantifiers in Φ(x) then x is a free variable in Φ. (Names are never described as being free.) If for that formula Φ we write ∀xΦ(x) or ∃xΦ(x), we say that x is now bound in Φ. A variable that is bound is not free.
- A well-formed formula with no free variables is a sentence.

16.3 Semantics of the language

- The semantics of names, predicates, and the quantifiers will remain intuitive for us. Advanced logic (with set theory) is required to make these more precise. We say:
  - ○ The domain of discourse is the collection of objects that our language is about.
  - ○ A name refers to exactly one object from our domain of discourse.
  - ○ A predicate of arity n describes a property or relation of n objects.
  - ○ ∀xΦ(x) means that any object in our domain of discourse has property Φ.
  - ○ ∃xΦ(x) means that at least one object in our domain of discourse has property Φ.
- If Φ and Ψ are sentences, then the meanings of the connectives are fully given by their truth tables. These semantics-defining truth tables are:

Φ	¬Φ
T	F
F	T

Φ	Ψ	(Φ → Ψ)
T	T	T
T	F	F
F	T	T
F	F	T

Φ	Ψ	(Φ ∧ Ψ)
T	T	T
T	F	F
F	T	F
F	F	F

Φ	Ψ	(Φ ∨ Ψ)
T	T	T
T	F	T
F	T	T
F	F	F

Φ	Ψ	(Φ ↔ Ψ)
T	T	T
T	F	F
F	T	F
F	F	T

- Each sentence must be true or false, never both, never neither.
- A sentence that must be true is logically true. (Sentences of our logic that have the same form as tautologies of the propositional logic we can still call

"tautologies". However, there are some sentences of the first order logic that must be true but that do not have the form of tautologies of the propositional logic. Examples would include ∀x(Fx → Fx) and ∀x(Fx v ¬Fx).)

- A sentence that must be false is a contradictory sentence.
- A sentence that could be true or could be false is a contingent sentence.
- Two sentences Φ and Ψ are "equivalent" or "logically equivalent" when (Φ↔Ψ) is a theorem.

16.4 Reasoning with the Language

- An argument is an ordered list of sentences, one sentence of which we call the "conclusion" and the others of which we call the "premises".
- A valid argument is an argument in which: necessarily, if the premises are true, then the conclusion is true.
- A sound argument is a valid argument with true premises.
- Inference rules allow us to write down a sentence that must be true, assuming that certain other sentences must be true. We say that the sentence is derived from those other sentences using the inference rule.
- Schematically, we can write out the inference rules in the following way (think of these as saying, if you have written down the sentence(s) above the line, then you can write down the sentence below the line; also, the order of the sentences above the line, if there are several, does not matter):

Modus ponens	Modus tollens	Double negation	Double negation
$(\Phi \rightarrow \Psi)$ Φ ___ Ψ	$(\Phi \rightarrow \Psi)$ $\neg\Psi$ ___ $\neg\Phi$	Φ ___ $\neg\neg\Phi$	$\neg\neg\Phi$ ___ Φ
Addition	**Addition**	**Modus tollendo ponens**	**Modus tollendo ponens**
Φ ___ $(\Phi \vee \Psi)$	Ψ ___ $(\Phi \vee \Psi)$	$(\Phi \vee \Psi)$ $\neg\Phi$ ___ Ψ	$(\Phi \vee \Psi)$ $\neg\Psi$ ___ Φ
Adjunction	**Simplification**	**Simplification**	**Bicondition**
Φ Ψ ___ $(\Phi \wedge \Psi)$	$(\Phi \wedge \Psi)$ ___ Φ	$(\Phi \wedge \Psi)$ ___ Ψ	$(\Phi \rightarrow \Psi)$ $(\Psi \rightarrow \Phi)$ ___ $(\Phi \leftrightarrow \Psi)$
Equivalence	**Equivalence**	**Equivalence**	**Equivalence**
$(\Phi \leftrightarrow \Psi)$ Φ ___ Ψ	$(\Phi \leftrightarrow \Psi)$ Ψ ___ Φ	$(\Phi \leftrightarrow \Psi)$ $\neg\Phi$ ___ $\neg\Psi$	$(\Phi \leftrightarrow \Psi)\neg\Psi$ ___ $\neg\Phi$
Repeat	**Universal instantiation**	**Existential generalization**	**Existential instantiation**
Φ ___ Φ	$\forall\alpha\Phi(\alpha)$ ___ $\Phi(\beta)$ where β is any symbolic term	$\Phi(\beta)$ ___ $\exists\alpha\Phi(\alpha)$ where β is any symbolic term	$\exists\alpha\Phi(\alpha)$ ___ $\Phi(\chi)$ where χ is an indefinite name that does not appear above in any open proof

- A proof (or derivation) is a syntactic method for showing an argument is valid. Our system has four kinds of proof (or derivation): direct, conditional, indirect, and universal.

- A direct proof (or direct derivation) is an ordered list of sentences in which every sentence is either a premise or is derived from earlier lines using an inference rule. The last line of the proof is the conclusion.
- A conditional proof (or conditional derivation) is an ordered list of sentences in which every sentence is either a premise, is the special assumption for conditional derivation, or is derived from earlier lines using an inference rule. If the assumption for conditional derivation is Φ, and we derive as some step in the proof Ψ, then we can write after this (Φ→Ψ) as our conclusion.
- An indirect proof (or indirect derivation, and also known as a *reductio ad absurdum*) is: an ordered list of sentences in which every sentence is either 1) a premise, 2) the special assumption for indirect derivation (also sometimes called the "assumption for reductio"), or 3) derived from earlier lines using an inference rule. If our assumption for indirect derivation is ¬Φ, and we derive as some step in the proof Ψ and also as some step of our proof ¬Ψ, then we conclude that Φ.
- A universal proof (or universal derivation) is an ordered list of sentences in which every sentence is either a premise or is derived from earlier lines (not within a completed subproof) using an inference rule. If we are able to prove Φ(x') where x' does not appear free in any line above the universal derivation, then we conclude that ∀xΦ(x).

- The schematic form of the direct, conditional, and indirect proof methods remain the same as they were for the propositional logic. We can use Fitch bars to write out this fourth proof schema in the following way:

$$\boxed{\alpha'}$$

$$\vdots$$

$$\phi(\alpha')$$
$$\forall\alpha\phi(\alpha)$$

- A sentence that we can prove without premises is a theorem.

16.5 Some advice on translations using quantifiers

Most phrases in English that we want to translate into our first order logic are of the following forms.

Everything is Φ	Something is Φ
$\forall x \Phi(x)$	$\exists x \Phi(x)$
Nothing is Φ	Something is not Φ
$\neg \exists x \Phi(x)$	$\exists x \neg \Phi(x)$
All Φ are Ψ	Some Φ are Ψ
$\forall x(\Phi(x) \to \Psi(x))$	$\exists x(\Phi(x) \wedge \Psi(x))$
No Φ are Ψ	Some Φ are not Ψ
$\neg \exists x(\Phi(x) \wedge \Psi(x))$	$\exists x(\Phi(x) \wedge \neg \Psi(x))$
Only Φ are Ψ	All and only Φ are Ψ
$\forall x(\Psi(x) \to \Phi(x))$	$\forall x(\Phi(x) \leftrightarrow \Psi(x))$

PART III: A LOOK FORWARD

17. Some advanced topics in logic

17.1 What do we study in advanced logic?

Students may imagine that in more advanced logic we continue with first order logic, translating more complex sentences and using them in proofs. But, in advanced logic, we often turn toward quite different, and more significant, issues. This chapter is meant as a brief look forward. It will give you a sense of what various topics in advanced logic are like. This will hopefully encourage you to continue to study logic, and also, perhaps, this chapter can act as a bridge from what you have learned to what can come next.

This chapter will provide brief illustrations of the following topics:

> 17.2 Axiomatic propositional logic
>
> 17.3 Mathematical induction
>
> 17.4 The deduction theorem for propositional logic
>
> 17.5 Set theory
>
> 17.6 Axiomatic first order logic
>
> 17.7 Modal logic
>
> 17.8 Peano arithmetic

17.2 Axiomatic propositional logic

The kinds of logical systems we have been studying up to now are called "natural deduction systems". In a natural deduction system, we add rules as we need them, and we make no attempt to specify the language in a compact form. As logic became much more sophisticated in the twentieth century, logicians and mathematicians began to study what logic could do. For example, are all logical truths provable? To answer a question like this, we must be much more precise about the nature of our logic. In particular, we need to boil it down to its essential elements. Then we can study what those essential elements are capable of doing.

We call this "the axiomatic approach". It is ancient, and familiar to all of us who have studied some geometry and seen Euclid's methods. But, in the last century, mathematicians developed a much more rigorous understanding of the axiomatic approach than is present in Euclid's work. In this section, we will describe an axiom system for the propositional logic. I hope that you are pleasantly shocked to find how compact we can make the propositional logic.

We will use what are actually called "axiom schemas". These are sentences in our metalanguage that describe the form of any number of other sentences. Any sentence that has the form of the axiom schema is an instance of the axiom. Our first three axiom schemas are:

(L1): $(\Phi \rightarrow (\Psi \rightarrow \Phi))$

(L2): $((\Phi \rightarrow (\Psi \rightarrow \chi)) \rightarrow ((\Phi \rightarrow \Psi) \rightarrow (\Phi \rightarrow \chi)))$

(L3): $((\neg\Phi \rightarrow \neg\Psi) \rightarrow ((\neg\Phi \rightarrow \Psi) \rightarrow \Phi))$

We suppose that we have some number of atomic sentences, P_1, P_2, P_3 and so on (it is useful, at this point, to use a single letter, with subscripts, so we do not find ourselves running out of letters). We have one rule: modus ponens. We have one proof method: direct derivation. However, we have now a new principle in doing proofs: we can at any time assert any instance of an axiom. Thus, each line of our direct derivation will be either a premise, an instance of an axiom, or derived from earlier lines using modus ponens.

Later, we will loosen these restrictions on direct derivations in two ways. First, we will allow ourselves to assert theorems, just as we have done in the natural deduction system. Second, we will allow ourselves to apply principles that we have proven and that are general. These are metatheorems: theorems proved about our logic.

The semantics for this system are like those for the propositional logic: we assign to every atomic formula a truth value, and then the truth value of the sentences built using conditionals and negation are determined by the truth tables for those connectives.

Amazingly, this system can do everything that our propositional logic can do. Furthermore, because it is so small, we can prove things about this logic much more easily.

What about conjunction, disjunction, and the biconditional? We introduce these using definitions. Namely, we say, whenever we write "$(\Phi \wedge \Psi)$" we mean "$\neg(\Phi \rightarrow \neg \Psi)$". Whenever we write "$(\Phi \vee \Psi)$" we mean "$(\neg \Phi \rightarrow \Psi)$". Whenever we write "$(\Phi \leftrightarrow \Psi)$" we mean "$((\Phi \rightarrow \Psi) \wedge (\Psi \rightarrow \Phi))$"; or, in full, we mean "$\neg((\Phi \rightarrow \Psi) \rightarrow \neg(\Psi \rightarrow \Phi))$".

We will introduce a useful bit of metalanguage at this point, called the "turnstile" and written "$\vdash$". We will write "$\{\Psi_i, \Psi_j, \ldots\} \vdash \Phi$" as a way of saying that Φ is provable given the assumptions or premises $\{\Psi_i, \Psi_j, \ldots\}$. (Here the lower case letter i and j are variables or indefinite names, depending on context—so "Ψ_i" means, depending on the context, either any sentence or some specific but unidentified sentence. This is handy in our metalanguage so that we do not have to keep introducing new Greek letters for metalanguage variables; it is useful in our object language if we want to specify arbitrary or unknown atomic sentences, P_i, P_j....) The brackets "{" and "}" are used to indicate a set; we will discuss sets in section 17.5, but for now just think of this is a collection of things (in this case, sentences). If there is nothing on the left of the turnstile—which we can write like this, "$\{\} \vdash \Phi$"—then we know that Φ is a theorem.

Proving theorems using an axiomatic system is often more challenging than proving the same theorem in the natural deduction system. This is because you have fewer resources, and so it often seems to require some cleverness to prove a theorem. For this reason, we tend to continue to use the methods and rules of a natural deduction system when we aim to apply our logic; the primary benefit of an axiom system is to allow us to study our logic. This logical study of logic is sometimes called "metalogic".

An example can be illustrative. It would be trivial in our natural deduction system to prove $(P \rightarrow P)$. One proof would be:

```
  ┌
  │ ┌ 1. P                    assumption for conditional derivation
  │ └ 2. p                    repeat, 1
  │   3. (P → P)              conditional derivation, 1-2
```

To prove the equivalent in the axiom system is more difficult. We will prove $(P_1 \to P_1)$. That is, we will prove $\{\} \vdash (P_1 \to P_1)$. What we must do in this system is find instances of our axioms that we can use to show, via modus ponens, our conclusion. We will not be using the Fitch bars. The proof will begin with:

    1. $((P_1 \to ((P_1 \to P_1) \to P_1)) \to ((P_1 \to (P_1 \to P_1)) \to (P_1 \to P_1)))$ instance of (L2)

To see how why we are permitted to assert this sentence, remember that we are allowed in this system to assert at any time either a premise or an axiom. We are trying to prove a theorem, and so we have no premises. Thus, each line will be either an instance of an axiom, or will be derived from earlier lines using modus ponens. How then is line 1 an instance of an axiom?

Recall that axiom (L2) is: $((\Phi \to (\Psi \to \chi)) \to ((\Phi \to \Psi) \to (\Phi \to \chi)))$. We replace Φ with P_1, and we get $((P_1 \to (\Psi \to \chi)) \to ((P_1 \to \Psi) \to (P_1 \to \chi)))$. We replace Ψ with $(P_1 \to P_1)$ and we have $((P_1 \to ((P_1 \to P_1) \to \chi)) \to ((P_1 \to (P_1 \to P_1)) \to (P_1 \to \chi)))$. Finally, we replace χ with P_1, and we end up with the instance that is line 1.

Continuing the proof, we have:

1.	$((P_1 \to ((P_1 \to P_1) \to P_1)) \to ((P_1 \to (P_1 \to P_1)) \to (P_1 \to P_1)))$	instance of (L2)
2.	$(P_1 \to ((P_1 \to P_1) \to P_1))$	instance of (L1)
3.	$((P_1 \to (P_1 \to P_1)) \to (P_1 \to P_1))$	modus ponens 1, 2
4.	$(P_1 \to (P_1 \to P_1))$	instance of (L1)
5.	$(P_1 \to P_1)$	modus ponens 3, 4

That proof is a bit longer, and less intuitive, than our natural deduction proof. Nonetheless, it does illustrate that we can prove $(P_1 \to P_1)$ in this system.

We can recreate this proof at the level of our metalanguage, and show that $(\Phi \to \Phi)$. That would simply mean doing the same proof, where every P_1 is replaced by Φ.

With the axiomatic propositional logic, it is not difficult to prove two important results about the logic. First, others have proven that this propositional logic is complete. Intuitively, a logical system is complete when all of the truths of that system are provable. In practice, we must carefully define for each particular logical system what completeness will mean. For the propositional logic, "completeness" means that all the tautologies are theorems. That is, every sentence that must be true is provable. This is in fact the case. Intuitively, a logical system is consistent if it is not possible to prove some sentence and also prove its denial. The propositional logic is also consistent.

Unfortunately, these proofs of completeness and consistency are a bit longer than we want to include in this chapter's brief overview.[13] However, to give a sense of how one goes about proving things about the axiomatic propositional logic, we can prove another result, the deduction theorem. It is helpful to quickly add to the axiomatic system additional results that simplify proofs. The most useful of these is the deduction theorem; but before we can prove the deduction theorem, we need to introduce a new proof method. We do this in the next section; and prove the deduction theorem in the section after that.

17.3 Mathematical induction

In mathematics, and in advanced logic, we often make use of a special form of reasoning called "mathematical induction". (This name is unfortunate, since "induction" is also the name of a reasoning method that is not a deductive method. However, mathematical induction is a deductive method.) The idea of mathematical induction is very powerful, and proves to be one of the most useful methods for proving things about our logic. It can be used whenever the collection of things that we aim to prove something about is ordered in the right way. An example of a set that is ordered the right way is the natural numbers, where there is a least number (1), and each number after 1 has a unique predecessor.

Here is the method. Suppose we want to prove that a property Φ is had by every member of some collection of objects that can be ordered in the right way.

First, we prove the base case. This means that we find the least element(s) and prove that it has (or they have) the property in question.

Second, we make the induction hypothesis. We assume that some arbitrary object in our collection—the nth objection in our ordered collection—has the property Φ.

Third, we prove the induction step. We show that if the arbitrary n^{th} object in our ordering of the objects in our domain has property Φ, then the next object (the $n+1^{th}$ object) in our ordering of the objects in our domain has property Φ.

We are then done: we conclude that every object in our domain has the property Φ.

An alternative way of formatting a proof using mathematical induction uses a different formulation of the induction hypothesis. We pick an arbitrary object in our ordering, the nth item. Then, we assume that every object in our ordering before the nth item has the property Φ. For the induction step, we prove that if each object in the ordering before the nth object has the property Φ, then the nth item has the property Φ. (This is sometimes called "strong mathematical induction", and then the method above is called "weak mathematical induction". Some logicians insist that the two methods are identical and so they do not appreciate the difference in terms.)

The reasoning here is hopefully intuitive. We show the first item has the property, and that if any object has the property then the next object does. In that case, every object must have the property, because, like falling dominoes, we know the first element has the property, but then the second element does, but then the third element does, and so on.

It will be helpful to give an example of mathematical induction that backs away from our logic and assumes some very basic mathematics, since many people are familiar with arithmetic from years of schooling. Legend has it that as a young child the mathematician Carl Friedrich Gauss (1777-1855) was instructed by a teacher—seeking to occupy the boy in order to shut him up for a while—to add up all the numbers to 100. Gauss very quickly gave the teacher the answer. The legend is that he promptly saw a pattern in adding a sequence of numbers, and derived the following result: $1 + 2 + 3 + \ldots + n = (n^2+n)/2$. Let's prove this using mathematical induction.

First, we prove the base case. The sum of 1 is 1. This we see from our own reasoning. The equation is $(n^2+n)/2$, and so we have $(1^2+1)/2 = (1+1)/2$, and $(1+1)/2 =$

2/2, and 2/2 = **1**. Thus, the equation works for the base case: it matches our independent reasoning about the base case.

Second, we make the induction hypothesis. We assume for some arbitrary n that the sum of numbers up to the nth number is $(n^2+n)/2$.

Third, we prove the induction step. The next step after n is n+1. Since we assume in the induction hypothesis that the sum of numbers up to n[th] number is $(n^2+n)/2$, the sum up to the n+1th number is: $((n^2+n)/2) + (n+1)$.

So our task is to show that this is equivalent to the proposed theorem, for the n+1th case. Substitute in **(n+1)** for n in the equation **$(n^2+n)/2$**. That gives us: **$((n+1)^2+ n+1)/2$**.

If we can show that $((n^2+n)/2) + (n+1) = ((n+1)^2+ n+1)/2$, we will have proven the induction step. Note that the left hand side we got from our induction step plus a simple observation. The right hand side we got from applying the equation. Our question then is, are the results the same? That is, does the equation match what we showed to be true?

Consider the left side. We see:

$$((n^2+n)/2) + (n+1) = ((n^2+n)/2) + (2n+2)/2)$$

and

$$((n^2+n)/2) + (2n+2)/2) = ((n^2+n) + (2n+2))/2$$

and

$$((n^2+n) + (2n+2))/2 = (n^2 + 3n + 2)/2$$

Consider now the right side. Here, we are applying the equation. We are hoping it will come out the same as our independent reasoning above. We see:

$$((n+1)^2+ n+1)/2 = ((n^2 + 2n + 1) + n + 1)/2$$

and

$$((n^2 + 2n + 1) + n + 1)/2 = (n^2 + 3n + 2)/2$$

So, since the two are identical (that is, our reasoning based on induction and basic observations matched what the equation provides), we have proven the equation applies in the n+1th case, and so we have proven the induction step.

Using mathematical induction we now conclude that the sum of numbers up to the nth number, for any n, is always $(n^2+n)/2$.

17.4 The deduction theorem

How can mathematical induction be useful for something like studying our logic? Here is a practical case. In chapter 6, we introduced conditional derivations. We reasoned that the proof method looked obviously correct, and then we continued using it from that point on. Instead, using mathematical induction, we will now prove that conditional derivation works. We will do this by proving a theorem about our logic: the deduction theorem.

The deduction theorem states that, in our propositional logic, if with some premises, including Φ, we can prove Ψ, then $(\Phi \rightarrow \Psi)$. This is precisely what we want from conditional derivation. We are saying that if we have Φ as a premise, and we are then able to prove Ψ, then we can assert the conditional $(\Phi \rightarrow \Psi)$.

To prove this, we will use mathematical induction. At this point, students will no doubt notice a significant change in our approach to logic. As logic becomes more advanced, we tend to more frequently perform proofs that are stated partly in English, and that are given in what seems a more informal manner. The proofs are in fact not less formal, but they are being done in the metalanguage, supplemented with our natural language. This may at first seem strange, because by working in an axiom system we are also making some aspects of our system more formal. But the axiomatic approach is there to demonstrate certain features of our language. Having convinced ourselves of the basics, we will allow ourselves to leap ahead often now in our explanation of proofs.

Let S be a set of sentences of our logical language. S can be the empty set. These are (all but one of) our premises. We want to single out a particular premise, call it Φ. The deduction theorem says that if $S \cup \{\Phi\} \vdash \Psi$ then $S \vdash (\Phi \rightarrow \Psi)$. The expression "$S \cup \{\Phi\}$" just means the set that collects together both all the things in S and also all the things in {Φ}. Or, put informally: it means take the set S and add to it also the sentence Φ.

What will be our ordered list of things upon which we perform mathematical induction? A proof, recall, is an ordered list of sentences, the last of which is our conclusion. So we can do induction upon a proof. We let $\Phi_1, \Phi_2, \Phi_3...\Phi_n$ be the list of sentences in our proof. Since this is a proof of Ψ and Φ_n is our last step in the proof, Φ_n is our conclusion Ψ. We prove the theorem by considering an arbitrary proof of Ψ that assumes $S \cup \{\Phi\}$.

First, we consider the first line of our proof. Φ_1 must be either (a) an axiom, (b) one of the sentences in the set of premises S, (c) or it must be Φ. Axiom (L1) tells us that $(\Phi \rightarrow (\Psi \rightarrow \Phi))$, and an instance of this is $(\Phi_1 \rightarrow (\Phi \rightarrow \Phi_1))$. Thus, with this instance of (L1), and modus ponens, we could derive $(\Phi \rightarrow \Phi_1)$. This tells us that if either (a) Φ_1 is an axiom or (b) it is a premise, we can prove $(\Phi \rightarrow \Phi_1)$. In case (c), where the first line of the proof is Φ, we can provide a proof like the one above (in section 17.2) to show that $(\Phi \rightarrow \Phi)$. Thus, in each case, if we can have Φ_1 as a first step of our proof, we know that we could also prove that $(\Phi \rightarrow \Phi_1)$. The deduction theorem is true of our base case (the first step of the proof).

Now we make the inductive assumption. Let j be any step in our proof. We assume that for any sentence in our ordering before step j, the deduction theorem applies. That is, for any i<j, $S \vdash (\Phi \rightarrow \Phi_i)$.

We now prove that for the jth step of our proof, the deduction theorem applies. The next step in the proof is line Φ_j. This step j is either (a) an axiom, (b) one of the sentences in the set of premises S, (c) it is Φ, or (d) it follows from earlier steps in the proof Φ_g and Φ_h with modus ponens. In handling the base case, we have already shown how cases (a), (b), and (c) can be used to show that the deduction theorem is true of these cases. The same arguments would apply for step j of the proof. We need only consider the additional case of (d).

We consider then the case where Φ_j follows from earlier steps in the proof Φ_g and Φ_h. That means that one of these (either Φ_g or Φ_h) is a conditional, and the other is the antecedent to the conditional. Our induction hypothesis says that for any Φ_i, where i<j, $S \vdash (\Phi \rightarrow \Phi_i)$. So, that means for g and h, because g<j and h<j,

$(\Phi \rightarrow \Phi_g)$ and also $(\Phi \rightarrow \Phi_h)$. We have noted that one of these formulas must be a conditional; suppose the conditional is Φ_h. Thus, Φ_h has the form $(\Phi_g \rightarrow \Phi_j)$. So we have by the induction hypothesis that $(\Phi \rightarrow \Phi_g)$ and also $(\Phi \rightarrow (\Phi_g \rightarrow \Phi_j))$. But we have as an instance of axiom (L2) that $((\Phi \rightarrow (\Phi_g \rightarrow \Phi_j)) \rightarrow ((\Phi \rightarrow \Phi_g) \rightarrow (\Phi \rightarrow \Phi_j)))$. Repeated applications of modus ponens would give us $(\Phi \rightarrow \Phi_j)$.

This applies to any arbitrary step of our proof, and so it applies when j=n. That is, it applies to the last step of the proof. We have shown that $(\Phi \rightarrow \Phi_n)$. Since this was a proof of Ψ, Φ_n is Ψ. We have thus shown that if $S \cup \{\Phi\} \vdash \Psi$ then $S \vdash (\Phi \rightarrow \Psi)$.

This proof was made simple by the fact that we had very few cases to consider: each line of the proof is either a premise, an axiom, or derived from earlier lines using a single rule, modus ponens. By reducing our system to its minimal elements, an axiom system allows us to prove results like these much more briefly than would be possible if we had many more cases to consider.

Although it adds no power to the system (anything that can be proved using the deduction theorem can be proved in the system without it), the deduction theorem makes many proofs smaller. For example, we can quickly prove other principles, such as the kind of inference traditionally called the "chain rule". We can call this the "chain rule theorem".

1. $(P_1 \rightarrow P_2)$ assumption

2. $(P_2 \rightarrow P_3)$ assumption

3. P_1 assumption

4. P_2 modus ponens 1, 3

5. P_3 modus ponens 2, 4

Which is sufficient to show that $\{(P_1 \rightarrow P_2), (P_2 \rightarrow P_3), P_1\} \vdash P_3$, and, therefore, by the deduction theorem $\{(P_1 \rightarrow P_2), (P_2 \rightarrow P_3)\} \vdash (P_1 \rightarrow P_3)$. Using the axioms alone, this proof would require many steps.

17.5 Set theory

One of the most useful tools of logic and mathematics is set theory. Using very simple principles, set theory allows us to construct some of the most complex elements of logic and mathematics. This allows for a pleasing elegance: it seems we can understand and construct many phenomena from very intuitive and basic assumptions.

Set theory was first developed by the mathematician Georg Cantor (1845-1918). The fundamental idea is that of a set. A set is a collection of things, and the identity of a set is determined by its elements. A set is not identical to its elements, however. There is, for example, an empty set: a set that contains nothing. It is however something: it is the set with no members.

With the notion of a set, some basic ideas about set formation, and our first order logic, we have a powerful theory that is useful throughout logic, and allows us to do additional things such as construct the numbers and study infinity. In this section, we can review some concepts of basic intuitive set theory, which we will call "natural set theory".

The idea of a set is that it is a collection of things. Once we pick our domain of discourse, we can describe collections of things from that domain of discourse as sets. We write these sets using braces. So, if our domain of discourse were the natural numbers, the following would be a set:

{1, 2, 3}

A set is determined by its members (also sometimes called "elements"), but it is not the same thing as its members: 1 is not the same thing as {1}. And, we assume there is an empty set, the set of nothing. We can write this as {} or as ø. Sets can contain other sets: the following is a set containing three different members.

{{}, {{}}, {{{}}}}

This is also an example of a pure set: it contains nothing but sets. If we develop our set theory with sets alone (if our domain of discourse is only sets) and without any other kinds of elements, we call it "pure set theory".

The members of sets are not ordered. Thus

$$\{1, 2, 3\} = \{3, 2, 1\}$$

But an ordered set is a set in which the order does matter. We can indicate an ordered set using angle brackets, instead of curly brackets. Thus:

$$<1, 2, 3> = <1, 2, 3>$$

but

$$<1, 2, 3> \neq <3, 2, 1>$$

We will write $\{...\}$ for a set when we want to show its contents, and A, B, ... for sets when we are dealing with them more generally. We write $x \in A$ to mean that x is a member of the set A. As noted, sets can be members of sets.

Sets are defined by their contents, so two sets are the same set if they have the same contents.

$$A = B \text{ if and only if } \forall x(x \in A \leftrightarrow x \in B)$$

This is interesting because it can be a definition of identity in set theory. In the natural deduction system first order logic, we needed to take identity as a primitive. Here, we have instead defined it using membership and our first order logic.

If all the contents of a set A are in another set B, we say A is a subset of B.

$$A \subseteq B \text{ if and only if } \forall x(x \in A \rightarrow x \in B)$$

A proper subset is a subset that is not identical (that means B has something not in A, in the following case):

$$A \subset B \text{ if and only if } (A \subseteq B \wedge A \neq B)$$

The empty set is a subset of every set.

The power set operation gives us the set of all subsets of a set.

$$\wp(A) = B \text{ if and only if } \forall x(x \subseteq A \rightarrow x \in B)$$

There are always 2^n members in the power set of a set with n members. That is, if A has n members, then $\wp(A)$ has 2^n members.

The cardinal size of a set is determined by finding a one-to-one correspondence with the members of the set. Two sets have the same cardinal size (we say, they have the same cardinality) if there is some way to show there exists a one-to-one correspondence between all the members of one set and all the members of the other. For the cardinality of some set A, we can write

$$|A|$$

There is a one-to-one correspondence to be found between all the members of A and all the members of B, if and only if

$$|A| = |B|$$

If $A \subseteq B$ then $|A| \leq |B|$.

The union of two sets is a set that contains every member of either set.

$A \cup B$ is defined as satisfying $\forall x((x \in A \lor x \in B) \rightarrow x \in A \cup B)$

The intersection of two sets is a set that contains every member that is in both the sets.

$A \cap B$ is defined as satisfying $\forall x((x \in A \land x \in B) \rightarrow x \in A \cap B)$

A shorthand way to describe a set is to write the following:

$$\{ x \mid \Phi(x) \}$$

This is the set of all those things x such that x has property Φ. So for example if our domain of discourse were natural numbers, then the set of all numbers greater than 100 could be written: $\{ x \mid x > 100 \}$.

A relation is a set of ordered sets of more than one element. For example, a binary relation meant to represent squaring might include {... <9, 81>, <10, 100> ...}; a trinary relation meant to represent factors might include {... <9, 3, 3>, <10, 2, 5> ...}; and so on.

One useful kind of relation is a product. The product of two sets is a set of all the ordered pairs taking a member from the first set and a member from the second.

$A \times B$ is defined as satisfying $\forall x \forall y((x \in A \land y \in B) \leftrightarrow <x, y> \in A \times B)$

Many of us are familiar with the either of the Cartesian product, which forms the Cartesian plane. The x axis is the set of real numbers R, and the y axis is the set of real numbers R. The Cartesian product is the set of ordered pairs R × R. Each such pair we write in the form <*x*, *y*>. These form a plane, and we can identify any point in this plane using these "Cartesian coordinates".

Another useful kind of relation is a function. A function **f** is a set that is a relation between the members of two sets. One set is called the "domain", and the other is called the "range". Suppose A is the domain and B is the range of a function, then (if we let **a** be a member of A and **b** and **c** be members of B, so by writing **fab** I mean that function **f** relates **a** from its domain to **b** in its range):

If **f** is a function from A into B, then if **fab** and **fac** then b=c

This captures the idea that for each "input" (item in its domain) the function has one "output" (a single corresponding item in its range). We also say a function **f** is

- *from* a set A if its domain is a subset of A
- *on* a set A if its domain is A
- *into* a set B if its range is a subset of B
- *onto* a set B if its range is B

If a function **f** is from A and into B, and also **f** is such that

If **fab** and **fcb** then a=c

then **f** is a 1-to-1 function from A and into B. The idea of being 1-to-1 is that **f** is a function that if reversed would be a function also. As we noted above, if there is a 1-to-1 function that is on A and onto B, then |A| = |B|.

If a function **f** is 1-to-1 on A and is into B, then we know that |B| ≥ |A|. (Such a function has every member of A in its domain, and for each such member picks out exactly one member of B; but because we only know that the function is into B, we do not know whether there are members of B that are not in the range of the function, and we cannot be sure that there is some other 1-to-1 function on A and onto B.)

A common notation also is to write **f(a)** for the function **f** with **a** from its domain. So, when we write this, we identify the expression with the element from the range that the function relates to **a**. That is, **f(a) = b**.

We can prove many interesting things using this natural set theory. For example, Cantor was able to offer us the following proof that for any set S, $|\wp(S)| > |S|$. That is, the cardinality of the power set of a set is always greater than the cardinality of that set.

We prove the claim by indirect proof. We aim to show that $|\wp(S)| > |S|$, so we assume for reductio that $|\wp(S)| \leq |S|$. We note that there is a function on S and into $\wp(S)$; this is the function that takes each member of S as its domain, and assigns to that member the set of just that element in $\wp(S)$. So, for example, if $a \in S$ then $\{a\} \in \wp(S)$; and there is function on S and into $\wp(S)$ that assigns a to $\{a\}$, b to $\{b\}$, and so on.

Since there is such a function, $|\wp(S)| \geq |S|$. But if $|\wp(S)| \leq |S|$ and $|\wp(S)| \geq |S|$, then $|\wp(S)| = |S|$. Therefore, there is a one-to-one function on S and onto $\wp(S)$. Let f be one such function.

Consider that each object in S will be in the domain of f, and be related by f to a set in $\wp(S)$. It follows that each element of S must be related to a set that either does, or does not, contain that element. In other words, for each $s \in S$, f(s) is some set $A \in \wp(S)$, and either $s \in A$ or $\neg s \in A$. Consider now the set of all the objects in the domain of f (that is, all those objects in S) that f relates to a set in $\wp(S)$ that does not contain that element. More formally, this means: consider the set C (for crazy) where C={ s | $s \in S \land \neg s \in f(s)$}. This set must be in $\wp(S)$, because every possible combination of the elements of S is in $\wp(S)$—including the empty set and including S. But now, what object in the domain of f is related to this set? We suppose that f is a 1-to-1 function on S and onto $\wp(S)$, so some element of S must be related by f to C, if f exists. Call this element c; that is, suppose f(c)=C.

Is $c \in C$? If the answer is yes, then it cannot be that f(c)=C, since by definition C is all those elements of S that f relates to sets not containing those elements. So $\neg c \in C$. But then, C should contain c, because C contains all those elements of S that are related by f to sets that do not contain that element. So $c \in C$ and $\neg c \in C$. We have a contradiction. We conclude that the source of the contradiction was the assumption for reductio, $|\wp(S)| \leq |S|$. Thus, for any set S, $|\wp(S)| > |S|$.

This result is sometimes called "Cantor's theorem". It has interesting consequences, including that there cannot be a largest set: every set has a powerset that is larger than it. This includes even infinite sets; Cantor's theorem shows us that there are different sized infinities, some larger than others; and, there is no largest infinity.

17.6 Axiomatic first order logic

In this section we briefly describe how the axiomatic approach can be taken toward the first order logic, and how a semantics can be constructed. For simplicity, we shall assume our example language does not include functions.

The basic elements of our language are connectives " $\rightarrow$ ", " $\neg$ "; predicates $F_i(...)$, each with a specific arity; the quantifier $\forall$; and two kinds of symbolic terms: variables $x_1...x_i...$ and names $a_1...a_i...$.

Our syntax is similar to the syntax described in 13.2. Each predicate of arity n followed by n symbolic terms is well formed. If Φ and Ψ are well formed, then $\neg\Phi$ and $(\Phi \rightarrow \Psi)$ are well formed. Every well-formed formula preceded by $\forall x_i$ is well formed.

A typical axiom system for first order logic takes the axioms of propositional logic and strengthens them with two additional axioms and an additional rule.

> (L4) $(\forall x_i \Phi(x_i) \rightarrow \Phi(a))$

> (L5) $(\forall x_i(\Phi \rightarrow \Psi) \rightarrow (\Phi \rightarrow \forall x_i \Psi))$ if x_i is not free in Φ.

Where a is any symbolic term.

The additional rule is generalization. From $|\!\!-\, \Phi$ we can conclude $|\!\!-\, \forall x_i \Phi(x_i)$. This plays the role of universal derivation in our natural deduction system for the first order logic.

This compact system, only slightly larger than the axiomatic propositional logic, is as powerful as our natural deduction system first order logic.

This is a convenient place to describe, in a preliminary and general way, how we can conceive of a formal semantics for the first order logic. When we introduced the first order logic, we kept the semantics intuitive. We can now describe how we could start to develop a formal semantics for the language. The approach here is one first developed by Alfred Tarski (1901-1981).[14] Tarski introduces a separate concept of satisfaction, which he then uses to define truth, but we will cover over those details just to illustrate the concept underlying a model.

The approach is to assign elements of our language to particular kinds of formal objects. We group these all together into a model. Thus, a model $\mathbf{M}$ is an ordered set that contains a number of things. First, it contains a set $\mathbf{D}$ of the things that our language is about—our domain of discourse. Second, the model includes our interpretation, I, which contains functions for the elements of our language. For each name, there is a function that relates the name to one object in our domain of discourse. For example, suppose our domain of discourse is natural numbers. Then a name a_1 in our language might refer to 1. We say then that the "interpretation" of a_1 is 1. The object in our interpretation that captures this idea is a function that includes $< a_1, 1>$.

The interpretation of each predicate relates each predicate to a set of ordered sets of objects from our domain. Each predicate of arity n is related to a set of ordered sets of n things. We can write $\mathbf{D}^n$ for all the ordered sets of n elements from our domain. Then, each predicate of arity n has as an interpretation some (not necessarily all) of the relations in $\mathbf{D}^n$. For example, an arity two predicate F_1 might be meant to capture the sense of "... is less than or equal to...". Then the interpretation of F_1 is a function from F_1 to a set of ordered pairs from our domain of discourse, including such examples as $\{... <1, 2>, <1, 1000>, <8, 10>, ...\}$ and so on.

We then say that a sentence like $F_1 a_2 a_3$ is true if the interpretation for a_2 and the interpretation for a_3 are in the interpretation for F_1. So, if a_2 is 2, and a_3 is 3, then $F_1 a_2 a_3$ would be true because $<2, 3>$ will be in the interpretation for F_1.

We will need an interpretation for the quantifiers. Without going into the details of how we can describe this rigorously (Tarski uses a set of objects called "sequences"), the idea will be that if we could put any name into the bound variable's position, and get a sentence that is true, the universally quantified statement is true. To return to our example: assuming again that our domain of discourse is natural numbers, so there is a least number 1, then the sentence $\forall x_j F a_1 x_j$ would be true if $F_1 a_1 x_j$ would be true for any number we put in for x_j.

Suppose that the interpretation of a_1 is **1**. Then $F_1a_1x_j$ would be true no matter what element from our domain of discourse we took x_j to be referring to, because **1** is less than or equal to every number is our domain of discourse. Therefore, $\forall x_j F a_1 x_j$ would be true.

We need only add the usual interpretation for negation and the conditional and we have a semantics for the first order logic.

This is all very brief, but it explains the spirit of the semantics that is standard for contemporary logic. Much more can be said about formal semantics, and hopefully you will feel encouraged to study further.

17.7 Modal logic

Philosophers have always been interested in questions of time and possibility, and have often thought that these were intimately related. In his book, *De Interpretatione* (titles were given to Aristotle's books by later editors—he wrote in Greek, and did not name his book with Latin titles), Aristotle wonders about the following. Consider a sentence like "There will be a sea battle tomorrow". Suppose our prediction turns out true; is it necessarily true when it is made as a prediction? This seems absurd. That is, there might be a sea battle tomorrow, but it does not seem that there must be a sea battle tomorrow.

> For there is nothing to prevent someone's having said ten thousand years beforehand that this would be the case, and another's having denied it; so that whichever the two was true to say then, will be the case of necessity. (18b35)[15]

Here is Aristotle's worry. Suppose tomorrow is June 16, 2014. Necessarily there either will or will not be a sea battle tomorrow (let us assume that we can define "sea battle" and "tomorrow" well enough that they are without vagueness or ambiguity). If there is a sea battle tomorrow, is the person who said today, or even ten thousand years ago, "There will be a sea battle on June 16, 2014" necessarily right? That is, if there is a sea battle tomorrow, is it necessary that there is a sea battle tomorrow?

Aristotle concludes that, if there is a sea battle tomorrow, it is not necessary now.

What is, necessarily is, when it is; and what is not, necessarily is not, when it is not. But not everything that is, necessarily is; and not everything that is not, necessarily is not.... It is necessary for there to be or not to be a sea-battle tomorrow; but it is not necessary for a sea-battle to take place tomorrow, nor for one not to take place—though it is necessary for one to take place or not to take place. (19b30)

Aristotle's reasoning seems to be, from "necessarily (P v ¬P)", we should not conclude: "necessarily P or necessarily ¬P".

Philosophers would like to be able to get clear about these matters, so that we can study and ultimately understand necessity, possibility, and time. For this purpose, philosophers and logicians have developed modal logic. In this logic, we have most often distinguished possibility from time, and treated them as—at least potentially—independent. But that does not mean that we might not ultimately discover that they are essentially related.

In this section, we will describe propositional modal logic; it is also possible to combine modal logic with first order logic, to create what is sometimes called "quantified modal logic". Our goal however is to reveal the highlights and basic ideas of modal logic, and that is easiest with the propositional logic as our starting point.

Thus, we assume our axiomatic propositional logic—so we have axioms (L1), (L2), (L3); modus ponens; and direct derivation. We also introduce a new element to the language, alone with atomic sentences, the conditional, and negation: "necessary", which we write as "□". The syntax of this operator is much like the syntax of negation: if Φ is a sentence, then

     □Φ

is a sentence. We read this as saying, "necessarily Φ" or "it is necessary that Φ". The semantics for necessity are a bit too complex to be treated fairly in this overview. However, one intuitive way to read "necessarily Φ" is to understand it as saying, *in every possible world Φ is true*. Or: *in every possible way the world could be, Φ is true.*

It is useful to introduce the concept of possibility. Fortunately, it appears reasonable to define possibility using necessity. We define "possible" to mean, *not necessarily not.* We use the symbol "◊" for *possible.*

Thus, if Φ is a sentence, we understand

◊Φ

to be a sentence. Namely, this is the sentence,

¬□¬Φ

We read "◊Φ" as saying, *it is possible that Φ*. One intuitive semantics is that it means *in at least one possible world, Φ is true*; or: *in at least one possible way the world could be, Φ is true*.

The difficult and interesting task before us is to ask, what axioms best capture the nature of necessity and possibility? This may seem an odd way to begin, but in fact the benefit to us will come from seeing the consequence of various assumptions that we can embody in different axioms. That is, our choice of axioms results in a commitment to understand necessity in a particular way, and we can discover then the consequences of those commitments. Hopefully, as we learn more about the nature of necessity and possibility, we will be able to commit to one of these axiomatizations; or we will be able to improve upon them.

All the standard axiomatizations of modal logic include the following additional rule, which we will call "necessitation".

ø |— Φ

_____

ø |— □Φ

This adds an element of our metalanguage to our rule, so let's be clear about what it is saying. Remember that "ø |— Φ" says that one can prove Φ in this system, without premises (there is only an empty set of premises listed to the left of the turnstile). In other words, "ø |— Φ" asserts that Φ is a theorem. The necessitation rule thus says, if Φ is a theorem, then □Φ. The motivation for the rule is hopefully obvious: the theorems of our propositional logic are tautologies. Tautologies are sentences that must be true. And "must" in this description hopefully means at least as much as does "necessarily". So, for our propositional logic, the theorems are all necessarily true.

Different axiomatizations of modal propositional logic have been proposed. We will review four here, and discuss the ideas that underlie them.

The most basic is known variously as "M" or "T". It includes the following additional axioms:

(M1) $(\Box\Phi \rightarrow \Phi)$

(M2) $(\Box(\Phi \rightarrow \Psi) \rightarrow (\Box\Phi \rightarrow \Box\Psi))$

Both are intuitive. Axiom (M1) says that if Φ is necessary, then Φ. From a necessary claim we can derive that the claim is true. Consider an example: if necessarily 5 > 2, then 5 > 2.

Axiom (M2) says that if it is necessary that Φ implies Ψ, then if Φ is necessary, Ψ is necessary.

An extension of this system is to retain its two axioms, and add the following axiom:

(M3) $(\Phi \rightarrow \Box\Diamond\Phi)$

The resulting system is often called "Brouwer," after the mathematician Luitzen Brouwer (1881-1966).

Axiom (M3) is more interesting, and perhaps you will find it controversial. It says that if Φ is true, then it is necessary that Φ is possible. What people often find peculiar is the idea that a possibility could be necessary. On the other hand, consider Aristotle's example. Suppose that there is a sea battle today. Given that it actually is happening, it is possible that it is happening. And, furthermore, given that it is happening, is it not the case that it must be possible that it is happening? Such, at least, is one possible motive for axiom (M3).

More commonly adopted by philosophers are modal systems S4 or S5. These systems assume (M1) and (M2) (but not (M3)), and add one additional axiom. S4 adds the following axiom:

(M4) $(\Box\Phi \rightarrow \Box\Box\Phi)$

This tells us that if Φ is necessary, then it is necessary that Φ is necessary.

In S4, it is possible to prove the following theorems (that is, these are consequences of (M1), (M2), and (M4)):

$$(\Box \Phi \leftrightarrow \Box\Box \Phi)$$

$$(\Diamond \Phi \leftrightarrow \Diamond\Diamond \Phi)$$

The modal system S5 instead adds to M the following axiom:

(M5) $(\Diamond \Phi \rightarrow \Box\Diamond \Phi)$

This axiom states that if something is possible, then it is necessary that it is possible. This is often referred to as the "S5 axiom". It is perhaps the most controversial axiom of the standard modal logic systems. Note these interesting corollary theorems of S5:

$$(\Box \Phi \leftrightarrow \Diamond\Box \Phi)$$

$$(\Diamond \Phi \leftrightarrow \Box\Diamond \Phi)$$

These modal logics are helpful in clarifying a number of matters. Let's consider several examples, starting with questions about meaning in a natural language.

Many philosophers pursued modal logic in the hopes that it would help us understand and represent some features of meaning in a natural language. These include attempting to better capture the meaning of some forms of "if...then..." expressions in a natural language, and also the meaning of predicates and other elements of a natural language.

A problem with some "if...then..." expressions concerns that sometimes what appears to be a conditional is not well captured by the conditional in our propositional logic. In chapter 3, we had an example that included the sentence "If Miami is the capital of Kansas, then Miami is in Canada". This sentence is troubling. Interpreting the conditional as we have done, this sentence is true. It is false that Miami is the capital of Kansas, and it is false that Miami is in Canada. A conditional with a false antecedent and a false consequent is true.

However, some of us find that unsatisfactory. We have recognized from the beginning of our study of logic that we were losing some, if not much, of the meaning of a natural language sentence in our translations. But we might want to capture the meaning that is being lost here, especially if it affects the truth value of the sentence. Some people want to say something like this: Kansas is in the United States, so if it were true that Miami were the capital of Kansas, then Miami would be in the United States, not in Canada. By this reasoning, this sentence should be false.

It seems that what we need is a modal notion to capture what is missing here. We want to say, if Miami were in Kansas, then it would be in the United States. Some philosophers thought we could do this by reading such sentences as implicitly including a claim about necessity. Let us fix the claim that Kansas is in the United States, and fix the claim that anything in the United States is not in Canada, but allow that Miami could be the capital of other states. In other words, let us suppose that it is necessary that Kansas is in the United States, and it is necessary that anything in the United States is not in Canada, but possible that Miami is the capital of Kansas. Then it appears we could understand the troubling sentence as saying,

Necessarily, if Miami is the capital of Kansas, then Miami is in Canada.

Assuming an implicit key, we will say,

$\Box(P_1 \rightarrow P_2)$

This seems to make some progress toward what we were after. We take the sentence "if Miami is the capital of Kansas, then Miami is in Canada" to mean: *in any world where Miami is in Kansas, then in that world Miami is in Canada.* But, given the assumptions we have made above, this sentence would be false. There would be worlds where Miami is the capital of Kansas, and Miami is not in Canada. This at least seems to capture our intuition that the sentence is (on one reading) false. There are further subtleties concerning some uses of "if... then...." in English, and it is not clear that the analysis we just gave is sufficient, but one can see how we appear to need modal operators to better capture the meaning of some utterances of natural languages, even for some utterances that do not appear (at first reading) to include modal notions.

Another problem concerning meaning has to do with attempts to better capture the meaning of more fundamental elements of our language, such as our predicates. Our first order logics have what philosophers call an "extensional semantics". This means that the meaning of terms is merely their referent, and the meaning of predicates is the sum of things that they are true of (see section

17.6). However, upon reflection, this seems inadequate to describe the meaning of terms and predicates in a natural language.

Consider predicates. The philosopher Rudolf Carnap (1891-1970) used the following example; suppose that human beings are the only rational animals ("rational" is rather hard to define, but if we have a strong enough definition—language using, capable of some mathematics, can reason about the future—this seems that it could be true, assuming by "animal" we mean Terrestrial metazoans).[16] Then the following predicates would be true of all and only the same objects:

> ... is a rational animal.

> ... is a human.

That means the extension of these predicates would be the same. That is, if we corralled all and only the rational animals, we would find that we had corralled all and only the humans. If the meaning of these predicates were determined by their extensions, then they would have the same meaning. So the sentence:

> All and only humans are rational animals.

would be sufficient, in an extensional semantics, to show that these predicates mean the same thing.

But obviously these predicates do not mean the same thing. How can we improve our logic to better capture the meaning of such natural language phrases? The philosopher Rudolf Carnap proposed that we use modal logic for this purpose. The idea is that we capture the difference using the necessity operator. Two sentences have the same meaning, for example, if necessarily they have the same truth value. That is, "... is a human" and "... is a rational animal" would have the same meaning if and only if they necessarily were true of all and only the same things.

We have not introduced a semantics for modal logic combined with our first order logic. However, the semantics we have discussed are sufficient to make sense of these ideas. Let us use the following key:

> F_1x: x is a rational animal.

> F_2x: x is a human.

Then we can translate "All and only rational animals are human" as:

$$\forall x(F_1 x \leftrightarrow F_2 x)$$

And if the meaning of a predicate were merely its extension (or were fully determined by its extension) then these two predicates F_1 and F_2 would mean the same thing. The proposal is that in order to describe the meanings of predicates in a natural language, we must look at possible extensions. We could then say that F_1 and F_2 have the same meaning if and only if the following is true:

$$\Box\forall x(F_1 x \leftrightarrow F_2 x)$$

Much is going to turn on our semantics for these predicates and for the necessity operator, but the idea is clear. We see the difference in the meaning between "... is a human" and "... is a rational animal" by identifying possible differences in extensions. It is possible, for example, that some other kind of animal could be rational also. But then it would not be the case that necessarily these two predicates are true of the same things. In a world where, say, descendants of chimpanzees were also rational, there would be rational things that are not human.

The meaning of a predicate that is distinct from its extension is called its "intension". We have just described one possible "intensional semantics" for predicates: the intension of the two predicates would be the same if and only if the predicates have the same extension in every world (or: in every way the world could be). This seems to get us much closer to the natural language meaning. It also seems to get to something deep about the nature of meaning: to understand a meaning, one must be able to apply it correctly in new and different kinds of situations. One does not know beforehand the extension of a predicate, we might argue; rather, one knows how to recognize things that satisfy that predicate—including things we may not know exist, or may even believe do not exist.

Many philosophers and others who are studying semantics now use modal logic as a standard tool to try to model linguistic meanings.

Modal logics have important uses outside of semantics. Here are two problems in metaphysics that it can help clarify. Metaphysics is that branch of philosophy that studies fundamental problems about the nature of reality, such as the nature of time, mind, or existence.

Consider Aristotle's problem: is it the case that if there necessarily is or is not a sea battle tomorrow, then it is the case that necessarily there is, or necessarily there is not, a sea battle tomorrow? In each of the systems that we have described, the answer is no. No sentence of the following form is a theorem of any of the systems we have described:

$$(\Box(\Phi \lor \neg\Phi) \to (\Box\Phi \lor \Box\neg\Phi))$$

It would be a problem if we could derive instances of this claim. To see this, suppose there were a sea battle. Call this claim S. In each of our systems we can prove as a theorem that $(S \to \Diamond S)$, which by definition means that $(S \to \neg\Box\neg S)$. (Surely it is a good thing that we can derive this; it would be absurd to say that what is, is not possible.) It is a theorem of propositional logic that $(S \lor \neg S)$, and so by necessitation we would have $\Box(S \lor \neg S)$. Then, with few applications of modus ponens and modal logic, we would have $\Box S$.

1. $(\Box(S\lor\neg S) \to (\Box S\lor\Box\neg S))$	the problematic premise	
2. S	premise	
3. $(S \lor \neg S)$	theorem	
4. $\Box(S \lor \neg S)$	necessitation, 3	
5. $(\Box S \lor \Box\neg S)$	modus ponens, 1, 4	
6. $(S \to \neg\Box\neg S)$	theorem	
7. $\neg\Box\neg S$	modus ponens 6, 2	
8. $\Box S$	modus tollendo ponens, 5, 7	

But that seems wrong. It was possible, after all, that there would not be a sea battle. Worse, this reason could be applied to any claim. If some claim is true, then it will be necessary. So Aristotle was right to deny the claim that $(\Box(\Phi \lor \neg\Phi) \to (\Box\Phi \lor \Box\neg\Phi))$, and fortunately this is not a theorem of any of our standard modal logic systems.

Although we agree with Aristotle here, we may disagree with him on another point. Aristotle says that what is, is necessary. That is not a claim in any of our logical systems, and it seems right to keep it out. Most likely, Aristotle mixed notions of time and modality together, in a way that, at least from our perspective, seems confusing and perhaps likely to lead to errors. That is, he seems to have thought that once something is true now, that makes it necessary; as if some feature of time determined necessity.

Here is an interesting case from contemporary metaphysics where the axiom (M5) plays an important role. The philosopher David Chalmers (1966-) has argued that contemporary science will not be able to explain the character of consciousness—that is, nothing like contemporary science will explain what it is like to taste a strawberry or listen to Beethoven.[17] This is not an anti-science argument; rather, his point is that contemporary science does not have the tools required, and will ultimately require radical new additional theory and methods. That has happened before: for example, at one time many philosophers hoped to explain all of nature in terms of the motion and impact of small, rigid particles. This theory, called "atomism", had great trouble accounting for gravity and magnetism. Ultimately, we added fields to our physical theories. From the perspective of an atomist, this would have meant the overthrow of their view: one needed radical new additions to atomism to explain these phenomena.

Chalmers predicts a similar kind of revolution is required for progress in the study of consciousness. However, one of his primary arguments is very controversial. It goes like this (I revise the argument slightly, to avoid some technical terminology):

1. We can conceive of beings that are physically identical to us but that lack conscious experiences.

2. If we can conceive of beings that are physically identical to us and that lack conscious experiences, then it is possible that there are beings that are physically identical to us but that lack conscious experiences.

3. If it is possible that there are beings that are physically identical to us and that lack conscious experiences, then physical sciences alone cannot explain conscious experience.

4. The physical sciences alone cannot explain conscious experience.

This argument is obviously valid; it requires only two applications of modus ponens to show line 4.

But is the argument sound? This is very important. Many people study the human mind, and many more people would benefit if we better understood the mind. Understanding consciousness would seem to be an important part of that. So, psychologists, psychiatrists, philosophers, artificial intelligence researchers, and many others should care. But, if this argument is sound, we should start spending grant money and time and other resources on radical new methods and approaches, if we want to understand consciousness.

Many philosophers have denied premise 1 of this argument. Those philosophers argue that, although it is easy to just say, "I can conceive of beings that are physically identical to us but that lack conscious experiences", if I really thought hard about what this means, I would find it absurd and no longer consider it conceivable. After all, imagine that the people weeping next to you at a funeral feel nothing, or that a person who has a severe wound and screams in pain feels nothing. This is what this argument claims is possible: people could exist who act at all times, without exception, as if they feel pain and sadness and joy and so on, but who never do. Perhaps, if we think that through, we'll say it is not really conceivable.

Premise 2 is very controversial, since it seems that we might fool ourselves into thinking we can conceive of something that is not possible. It seems to mix human capabilities, and thus subjective judgments, with claims about what is objectively possible.

Premise 3 turns on technical notions about what it means for a physical science to explain a phenomenon; suffice it to say most philosophers agree with premise 3.

But what is interesting is that something appears to be wrong with the argument if we adopt the S5 axiom, (M5). In particular, it is a theorem of modal logic system S5 that ($\Box\Phi \leftrightarrow \Diamond\Box\Phi$). With this in mind, consider the following argument, which makes use of key claims in Chalmers's argument.

> 1. We can conceive of it being true that necessarily a being physically identical to us will have the same conscious experience as us.

> 2. If we can conceive of it being true that necessarily a being physically identical to us will have the same conscious experience as us, then it is possible that necessarily a being physically identical to us will have the same conscious experience as us.

3. It is possible that necessarily a being physically identical to us will have the same conscious experience as us.

4. If it is possible that necessarily a being physically identical to us will have the same conscious experience as us, then necessarily a being physically identical to us will have the same conscious experience as us.

5. Necessarily a being physically identical to us will have the same conscious experience as us.

Premise 1 of this argument seems plausible; surely it is at least as plausible as the claim that we can conceive of a being physically identical to us that does not have phenomenal experience. If we can imagine those weird people who act like they feel, but do not feel, then we can also imagine that whenever people act and operate like us, they feel as we do.

Premise 2 uses the same reasoning as premise 2 of Chalmers' argument: what is conceivable is possible.

Line 3 is introduced just to clarify the argument; it follows from modus ponens of premises 2 and 1.

Line 4 uses ($\Diamond\Box\Phi \rightarrow \Box\Phi$), which we can derive in S5.

The conclusion, line 5, follows by modus ponens from 4 and 3. The conclusion is what those in this debate agree would be sufficient to show that the physical sciences can explain the phenomenon (via the same reasoning that went into line 3 of Chalmers's argument).

If we accept modal system S5, then it seems that there is something wrong with Chalmers's argument, since the kind of reasoning used by the argument can lead us to contradictory conclusions. Defenders of Chalmers's argument must either reject axiom (M5), or deny line 1 of this new argument. As I noted above, this matters because we would like to know how best to proceed in understanding the mind; whether either of these arguments is sound would help determine how best we can proceed.

17.8 An example of another axiom system: Peano arithmetic

We close this brief introduction to the axiomatic approach with a look at how we can extend the first order logic to enable us to study a familiar specific task: arithmetic.

We have mentioned Gottlob Frege several times in this text. This mathematician and philosopher made essential contributions to first order logic, the philosophy of mathematics, and the philosophy of language. His primary goal in all his work, however, was to prove that mathematics was an extension of logic. This view was called "logicism".

Why would anyone be interested in such a project? When Frege was writing, there were many disagreements about some fundamental issues in mathematics. These included the status of set theory, which many found very useful, but others disliked. Frege's proposed solution was very elegant. If we could derive arithmetic from a handful of logical axioms that everyone would find unobjectionable, then we would have a way to settle all disputes about arithmetic. To put a controversial claim beyond criticism, we would have to show that we could derive it directly from our unobjectionable axioms.

Unfortunately, Frege's project failed. His ultimate axiomatization of arithmetic proved to have a fatal flaw. While Frege had the final volume of this project at the press, he received a postcard from a young philosopher, Bertrand Russell. Russell was attempting the same project as Frege, but he had noticed a problem. In Frege's system, Russell was able to derive a contradiction. This was devastating: just as in our logic, in Frege's logic you could derive anything from a contradiction. And so this meant Frege's system was inconsistent: it could prove falsehoods.

What Russell proved is now called "Russell's Paradox". It would be better called "Russell's Contradiction", since it is explicitly a contradiction. The logical systems that Russell and Frege used had special entities called "classes", but given that most people today are more familiar with sets, we can restate Russell's Contradiction with sets. Russell showed that in Frege's system he could derive a sentence that meant something like: there is a set of all sets that do not belong to themselves.

Think about this for a moment. Does this set belong to itself? If it does, it should not, because it is supposedly the set of all and only those things that do not belong to themselves. Thus, it should not belong to itself. But then, it would be one of those sets that do not belong to themselves, and so it should belong to itself. We have a contradiction.

Frege was devastated. From our perspective, this is unfortunate, because his accomplishments were already so great that he need not have felt this error was a refutation of all his work.

Logicism did not die. Russell found a way to avoid the contradiction using a kind of logical system called "type theory", and he pursued the construction of arithmetic in his huge book, written with Alfred Whitehead, *Principia Mathematica*. This book's system is, unfortunately, much more cumbersome than Frege's system, and earned few converts to logicism. Today, however, there are still mathematicians who believe that type theory may be the best way to understand mathematics.

More often, however, treatments of the foundations of arithmetic turn directly to an axiomatization that includes explicitly mathematical elements. The most familiar of these is typically called "the Peano axioms", although these are significantly modified from the version of Giuseppe Peano (1858-1932) after whom they are named. Peano himself cites Richard Dedekind (1831-1916) as his source. A standard version of Peano's axioms is surprisingly compact, and proves sufficient to do all the things we want arithmetic to do. The axioms, however, clearly assume and specify things about numbers and operations on numbers. We sometimes call such axioms "non-logical axioms" or "proper axioms", not because there is something irrational about them, but because they clearly aim to capture some rich notion that may appear to be more specific than a highly general logical notion.

Here is one possible set of axioms for arithmetic, restricted to addition and multiplication.

We assume all the axioms of the first order logic described in section 17.6 (that is, we have (L1) through (L5)). We have a single special term, 0. We have three special function letters in our language, f_1 and f_2, which are arity two, and f_3, which is arity one. f_1 and f_2 are to be given an interpretation consistent with addition and multiplication. f_3 is the successor function; think of it as adding one to any number. We have an arity-two predicate P_1, which we interpret as we would "=".

However, for reasons of familiarity, we will write "+" and "·" and "=". For the successor function we will use "'". Thus we write the successor of 0 by writing 0'. The successor of 0 is of course 1. The successor of 1 is 2, expressed 0", and so on.

With all that in mind, one such axiom system is:

(A1) $(x_1 = x_2 \rightarrow x_1' = x_2')$

(A2) $(x_1' = x_2' \rightarrow x_1 = x_2)$

(A3) $(x_1 = x_2 \rightarrow (x_1 = x_3 \rightarrow x_2 = x_3))$

(A4) $\neg x_1' = 0$

(A5) $x_1 + 0 = x_1$

(A6) $x_1 + x_2' = (x_1 + x_2)'$

(A7) $x_1 \cdot 0 = 0$

(A8) $x_1 \cdot x_2' = (x_1 \cdot x_2) + x_1$

(Remember that "+" and "·" are used here only as shorthand for our functions; in our object language we do not have infix notation and we do not need the disambiguating parentheses shown here for axioms (A6) and (A8). That is, axiom (A6), for example, is actually $P_1 f_1 x_1 f_3 x_2 f_3 f_1 x_1 x_2$. Looking at that sentence, you will no doubt realize why it is very helpful to switch over to our usual way of writing these things.)

We can also make mathematical induction an explicit part of this system (instead of a principle of our metalogical reasoning alone), and include it as an axiom:

(A9) $(\Phi(0) \rightarrow (\forall x_i(\Phi(x_i) \rightarrow \Phi(x_i')) \rightarrow \forall x_i \Phi(x_i)))$

These axioms are sufficient to do everything that we expect of arithmetic. This is quite remarkable, because arithmetic is very powerful and flexible, and these axioms are few and seemingly simple and obvious. Since these explicitly formulate our notions of addition, multiplication, and numbers, they do not achieve what Frege dreamed; he hoped that the axioms would be more general, and from them one would derive things like addition and multiplication. But this is still a powerful demonstration of how we can reduce great disciplines of reasoning to compact fundamental principles.

Axiomatizations like this one have allowed us to study and discover shocking things about arithmetic, the most notable being the discovery by the logician Kurt Godel (1906-1978) that arithmetic is either incomplete or inconsistent.

In closing our discussion of axiomatic systems, we can use this system to prove that 1+1=2. We will use the indiscernibility of identicals rule introduced in 15.3. We start by letting x_1 be $0'$ and x_2 be 0 to get the instance of axiom (A6) on line 1, and the instance of (A5) on line 2.

1.	$0' + 0' = (0' + 0)'$	axiom (A6)
2.	$0' + 0 = 0'$	axiom (A5)
3.	$0' + 0' = 0''$	indiscernibility of indenticals, 1, 2

Because line 2 tells us that $0' + 0$ and $0'$ are the same, using indiscernibility of identicals we can substitute $0'$ for $0' + 0$ in the right hand side of the identity in line 1. Remember that the parentheses are there only to disambiguate our shorthand; this means $(0')'$ and $0''$ are actually the same.

17.9 Problems

1. Use a truth table to show that the following sentences are equivalent (using your natural deduction system definitions of the connectives, as given in part I of the book).

    a. $(\Phi \wedge \Psi)$ and $\neg(\Phi \rightarrow \neg\Psi)$.
    b. $(\Phi \vee \Psi)$ and $(\neg\Phi \rightarrow \Psi)$.
    c. $(\Phi \leftrightarrow \Psi)$ and $\neg((\Phi \rightarrow \Psi) \rightarrow \neg(\Psi \rightarrow \Phi))$.

2. Prove the following arguments are valid, using only our axioms of the axiomatic propositional logic, modus ponens, and the deduction theorem. For some of these problems, you will need to translate some of the sentences as required into the corresponding formula with only negation and conditional as our connectives (follow the interpretation you studied in problem 1).

a. $|— (\neg\neg P_1 \to P_1)$

b. $\{(P_1 \wedge P_2)\} \mid — P_1$

c. $\{(\neg P_2, (P_1 \to P_2)\} \mid — \neg P_1$

d. $\{(P_1 \vee P_2), \neg P_2\} \mid — P_1$

e. $\{(P_1 \to (P_2 \to P_3))\} \mid — (P_2 \to (P_1 \to P_3))$

3. Describe a function that is on A and onto B and also 1-to-1, so that we know that $|A| = |B|$, for each of the following. Your function can be stated in informal mathematical notation. Remember that the natural numbers are $\{1, 2, 3...\}$ and the integers are all the whole numbers, both negative and positive, and including 0.

   a. A is the even natural numbers, B is the odd natural numbers.
   b. A is the natural numbers, and B is the numbers $\{10, 11, 12...\}$.
   c. A is the natural numbers, B is the negative integers.

4. Prove the following claims. Your proof can use the definitions given in 17.5 and any theorems of our first order logic, and can be stated in English.

   a. For any sets A and B, $(\{A\}=\{B\} \leftrightarrow A=B)$.
   b. For any sets A and B, $(A \subseteq B \leftrightarrow A \cap B = A)$.
   c. For any sets A and B, $(A \subseteq B \leftrightarrow A \cup B = B)$.
   d. For any set A, $(A \cap \varnothing = \varnothing)$.

5. Prove the following, keeping as resources the propositional logic and the specified modal system.

   a. In M: $(\Phi \to \Diamond\Phi)$
   b. In S4: $(\Box\Phi \leftrightarrow \Box\Box\Phi)$.
   c. In S4: $(\Diamond\Phi \leftrightarrow \Diamond\Diamond\Phi)$
   d. In S5: $(\Box\Phi \leftrightarrow \Diamond\Box\Phi)$.

For these problems and the next, you will find they are much easier if you allow yourself two rules sometimes added to natural deduction systems. These are: (1) Contraposition, which allows one to assert that $(\neg\Psi \to \neg\Phi)$ given $(\Phi \to \Psi)$; and (2) a relaxing of double negation that allows one to remove any double negation from anywhere in a formula, or insert any double negation anywhere in a formula as long as the result is well formed.

6. Show that S5 is equivalent to the combination of Brouwer and S4. You can do this by showing that from the axioms of Brouwer ((M1), (M2), and (M3)) and S4 (axiom (M4)) you can derive the additional axioms of S5 (in this case, just (M5)). Then show that from the axioms of S5 ((M1), (M2), and (M5)) you can derive the additional axioms of Brouwer and S4 (that is, (M3) and (M4)).

7. Prove the following theorems, using only our axioms of the axiomatic first order logic, modus ponens, and the deduction theorem.

    a. $\forall x_1(P_1(x_1) \rightarrow P_2(x_1)) \rightarrow (\forall x_1 P_1(x_1) \rightarrow \forall x_1 P_2(x_1))$

    b. $\forall x_1(\neg P_2(x_1) \rightarrow \neg P_1(x_1)) \rightarrow \forall x_1(P_1(x_1) \rightarrow P_2(x_1))$

    c. $\forall x_1(P_1(x_1) \rightarrow \neg P_2(x_1)) \rightarrow \forall x(P_2(x_1) \rightarrow \neg P_1(x_1))$

    d. $\forall x_1 \neg(P_1(x_1) \rightarrow \neg P_2(x_1)) \rightarrow \forall x_1 P_1(x_1)$

8. Using only first order logic, the Peano axioms, and indiscernibility of identicals, prove that

    a. $1+0 = 0+1$
    b. $2+2 = 4$
    c. $2{\cdot}2 = 4$
    d. $2{\cdot}2 = 2+2$

---

[13] A good source is (Mendelson 2010: 32-34).

[14] See Tarski (1956).

[15] This translation is based on that in (Barnes 1984: 29).

[16] See Carnap (1956).

[17] See Chalmers (1996).

Bibliography

Barnes, J. (1984) (ed.), *The Complete Works of Aristotle* (Princeton: Princeton University Press).

Blassingame, J. W. (1985) (ed.), *The Frederick Douglass Papers*. Series One: Speeches, Debates, and Interviews. Volume 3: 1855-63 (New Haven: Yale University Press).

Carnap, R. (1956), *Meaning and Necessity: A Study in Semantics and Modal Logic* (Chicago: University of Chicago, Phoenix Books).

Carter, K. C. (ed., tr.) (1983), *The Etiology, Concept, and Prophylaxis of Childbed Fever*, by Ignaz Semmelweis (Madison: University of Wisconsin Press).

—— and Carter, B. R. (2008), *Childbed Fever: A Scientific Biography of Ignaz Semmelweis* (New Brunswick, NJ: Transaction Publishers).

Chalmers, D. (1996), *The Conscious Mind* (New York: Oxford University Press).

Cooper, J. M. and Hutchinson. D. S. (1997) (eds.), *Plato: Complete Works* (Indianapolis: Hackett Publishing).

Drake, S. (1974) (ed. and translator) *Galileo: The Two New Sciences* (Madison: University of Wisconsin Press).

Duhem, P. (1991), *The Aim and Structure of Physical Theory* (Princeton: Princeton University Press).

Grice, P. (1975), "Logic and conversation" in P. Cole and J. Morgan (eds.), *Syntax and Semantics, 3: Speech Acts.* (New York: Academic Press), 41–58.

Hobbes, T. (1886), *Leviathan,* with an introduction by Henry Morley (London: Routledge and Sons).

Mendelson, E. (2010), *Introduction to Mathematical Logic.* (5th edn., New York: Taylor & Francis Group, CRC Press).

Russell, B. (1905), "On Denoting." *Mind*, 14: 479-493.

Selby-Bigge, L. A. and Nidditch, P. H. (1995) (eds.), *An Enquiry Concerning Human Understanding and Concerning the Principles of Morals,* by David Hume (Oxford: Oxford University Press).

Tarski, A. (1956), *Logic, Semantics, Metamathematics* (Oxford: Oxford University Press).

Wason, P. C. (1966), "Reasoning," In Foss, B. M. *New Horizons in Psychology 1.* (Harmondsworth, England: Penguin).

About the Author

Craig DeLancey is Professor of Philosophy and Chair of the Department of Philosophy at SUNY Oswego. He received his Ph.D. from Indiana University. His publications include *Passionate Engines: What Emotions Reveal about the Mind and Artificial Intelligence*, with Oxford University Press. He has been a fellow of the Center for the Philosophy of Science at the University of Pittsburgh, a fellow of the National Endowment of the Humanities, and has received research funding from the Army Institute of Basic Research. When not teaching philosophy or doing research, he writes science fiction.

About Open SUNY Textbooks

Open SUNY Textbooks is an open access textbook publishing initiative established by State University of New York libraries and supported by SUNY Innovative Instruction Technology Grants. This pilot initiative publishes high-quality, cost-effective course resources by engaging faculty as authors and peer-reviewers, and libraries as publishing service and infrastructure.

The pilot launched in 2012, providing an editorial framework and service to authors, students and faculty, and establishing a community of practice among libraries.

Participating libraries in the 2012-2013 and 2013-2014 pilots include SUNY Geneseo, College at Brockport, College of Environmental Science and Forestry, SUNY Fredonia, Upstate Medical University, and University at Buffalo, with support from other SUNY libraries and SUNY Press.

Changelog

CRAIG DELANCEY

2021 July 21:
— Corrected typo (substituting P for R) in line 10 of the first proof in section 9.6.
— Corrected typo (substituting G for H) in line 11 of the last proof in section 13.3.
— Corrected several typos in the last proof in section 4.2.
— Corrected typo (substituting negation for strike through) in line 24 of the second proof of section 9.6.
— Changed title of section 3.6 (substituting "Statistical reasoning" for "Probability".
— Added problem 6 to chapter 1 section 1.5.
— Added additional questions to problem 3 of chapter 2 section 2.7.
— Added additional questions to problem 4 of chapter 2 section 2.7.
— Added additional questions to problem 7 of chapter 2 section 2.7.
— Added additional questions to problem 1 of chapter 3 section 3.7.
— Added additional questions to problem 2 of chapter 3 section 3.7.
— Added additional questions to problem 1 of chapter 4 section 4.5.
— Added additional questions to problem 1 of chapter 5 section 5.6.
— Added additional questions to problem 2 of chapter 5 section 5.6.
— Added additional questions to problem 3 of chapter 5 section 5.6.
— Added additional questions to problem 4 of chapter 5 section 5.6.
— Added additional questions to problem 1 of chapter 6 section 6.5.
— Added additional questions to problem 3 of chapter 6 section 6.5.
— Added additional problem (5) to chapter 6 section 6.5.
— Re-ordered problems in chapter 7 section 7.6.
— Added additional questions to problem 1 of chapter 7 section 7.6.
— Added additional questions to problem 1 of chapter 8 section 8.4.
— Added additional questions to problem 2 of chapter 8 section 8.4.
— Added additional problem (4) to chapter 8 section 8.4.
— Added additional questions to problem 1 of chapter 9 section 9.8.
— Changed two questions of problem 2 of chapter 9 section 9.8.
— Added additional problem (3) to chapter 9 section 9.8.
— Added additional problem (6) to chapter 9 section 9.8.

2021 July 22:

— Added additional problem (7) to chapter 5 section 5.6.

— Added additional problem (3) to chapter 12 section 12.4.

— Added additional questions to problem 2 of chapter 13 section 13.4.

— Added additional questions to problem 3 of chapter 13 section 13.4.

— Added additional problem (8) to chapter 13 section 13.4.

— Added additional problem (9) to chapter 13 section 13.4.

— Added additional questions to problem 1 of chapter 14 section 14.6.

— Added additional problem (5) to chapter 14 section 14.6.

— Added additional problem (6) to chapter 15 section 15.6.

2021 July 31:

— Added additional problem (5) to chapter 3 section 3.7.

— Slight revision to question L of problem 1 of chapter 4 section 4.5.

2021 August 1:

— Added additional question to problem 2 of chapter 17 section 17.9.

2021 August 3:

— Added missing endnote #4 in chapter 2.